Creating Efficient
Industrial Administrations

Creating Efficient Industrial Administrations

ARTHUR L. STINCHCOMBE

Department of Sociology
University of California, Berkeley
Berkeley, California

With the assistance of
Zahava Blum and Rene Marder

ACADEMIC PRESS   *New York and London*

A Subsidiary of Harcourt Brace Jovanovich, Publishers

ACADEMIC PRESS, INC.
111 Fifth Avenue, New York, New York 10003

United Kingdom Edition published by
ACADEMIC PRESS, INC. (LONDON) LTD.
24/28 Oval Road, London NW1

Library of Congress Cataloging in Publication Data

Stinchcombe, Arthur L
  Creating efficient industrial administrations.

  Includes bibliographical references.
  1. Industry—Social aspects—South America.
2. Industrial management—South America. 3. Steel
industry and trade—South America—Management.
4. Bureaucracy—Case studies. I. Title.
HD60.5.S75S77   301.5′5′098   73-7447
ISBN 0–12–785805–9

The light dove, cleaving the air in its free flight, and feeling its resistance, might imagine that its flight would be still easier in empty space.

Immanuel Kant, *Critique of Pure Reason*

Contents

PART II.   COGNITION AND BUREAUCRATIC
STRUCTURE

PART III.   THE MOTIVATION OF ECONOMIC ACTIVITY

PART IV.   THE POLITICS OF ECONOMIC
DEVELOPMENT

Preface

This study was supported by a grant from the Olivetti Foundation to the Joint Center for Urban Studies of Harvard and MIT, which hired me to do the work. This is an academically unusual procedure, since any reputational points that the study earns will not accrue to those universities. Only great universities can conceive of their research budgets as something more than a set of opportunities to be monopolized by their own faculties. I suppose that the people who approved such a breaking of the monopoly were somewhat culpable, and in their defense I should say that I promised more to the universities than I am delivering with this report, and I still feel the debt.

Three people invested substantial efforts in getting me access to the research sites. Since I often sit for half an hour staring at the telephone and sweating when I have to call a stranger, I owe them a deep debt. They are Sra. Isolde de Villagrán, at that time Director of the Centro de Sociología at the Universidad de Concepción in Chile, James Q. Wilson of the Joint Center who arranged access for me in Venezuela, and my research associate Rene Marder, who negotiated the shoals of a hostile management and a suspicious union in Argentina to gain access, though the interviewing was finally done outside the plant. Some of the hostility of the Argentine management is returned in this report, though that is my doing rather than Mr. Marder's. Mrs. Katharine Bauer handled my access to the mysteries of MIT accounting with such finesse that I could only imagine what she meant by "bureaucracy" from my experience at other universities.

I loved Chilean society, Chilean food and wine, Chilean politics, Chilean university life, Chilean mountains, lakes, and forests. In many ways I prefer Chile to the United States. Often I find that the affection and respect we social scientists owe our subjects comes hard, comes as a matter of professional duty. When love and duty came so nicely together, it made me sad that I had arranged for my relationship to Chile to be an affair rather than a marriage. Of course the ancient wisdom is that a marriage is not like an affair.

Rene Marder did much of the work of perfecting the questionnaire, did much of the interviewing in Chile and all of it in Argentina (I did it in Venezuela), did most of the dirty work of analysis, discussed tentative interpretations with me, and wrote first drafts for Chapters 6 and 7. There seem to be no very clear norms about apportioning the credit under such circumstances. He spent more hours on the study than I did. He started out fairly unskilled at this kind of social research but more knowledgeable about Latin American society and the Spanish language. Now he is probably somewhat more sophisticated about the study than I am. Since I do not know what to do about it, and since my power is greater than his, I have claimed credit for all but Chapters 6 and 7, and I have rewritten those in the first person style that I find comfortable. May God have mercy on my soul.

Like most of my work, this one has been rejected for publication by my colleagues. Somehow my work makes my fellow sociologists unhappy. But it has never got the sustained critique necessary for me to figure out what is the matter. In this case, however, its rejection by the Joint Center for Urban Studies resulted in its getting paragraph by paragraph suggestions from Zahava Blum. The amount of change resulting from her comments is reflected in her appearance on the title page. It also got a detailed reading from Robert K. Merton, which resulted in many more changes.

My own belief is that this is the best empirical work I can do, using the best detailed criticism I ever received. A criticism of this book is more likely than anything I can think of to result in my intellectual self reconstruction. That reconstruction might seem a small accomplishment to a critic, but it is important to me.

When I went to Johns Hopkins from Berkeley after graduate school, I did so because I wanted to learn to study the problems of systems of action that Max Weber addressed—my fare at Berkeley—by quantitative research techniques. This then is a methodological companion piece to my *Constructing Social Theories*, in the sense that both might have the subtitle: *What I Learned at Johns Hopkins*.

The quotation from Kant about doves and air resistance is not meant to imply that I have read the *Critique of Pure Reason*. I found it in Ernest Gellner's *Thought and Change* and I thought it was beautiful. I might elaborate on Kant's image of a gentle resistance that allows one to fly higher, but my wife has already suffered two prefaces.

PART I

Introduction: The Sociology of Administrative Rationality in Industry

CHAPTER **1**

Introduction

The general purpose of this book is to explore the social sources of administrative rationality in underdeveloped countries. I have chosen to compare steel plant administrative behavior in three South American countries, Chile, Argentina, and Venezuela, with the behavior of other middle-class people in those same countries. Producing steel products is a type of administrative problem that is crucial for modernization of the economy. Steel products cannot be efficiently produced on a small scale; the technical system involves a high degree of interdependence of different stages of production, from the reduction of ore to iron, the processing of iron to steel of specified characteristics, the rolling of steel into basic shapes, and the finishing of steel products. The production of different steel products must be adjusted to a highly variable market for capital goods and durable consumer goods.

Advanced countries can do this job, and other jobs like it, with a high degree of labor productivity, high capital productivity, technical excellence of the product, and profitable operation in a market. Underdeveloped countries have had great difficulty managing such technical systems so as to be competitive with advanced countries. Thus, steel production is a strategic case for studying the problem of constructing social organizations in underdeveloped countries that can manage advanced technologies with efficiency equal to that of advanced countries.

The strategy of explanation will be indirect. Although I want to explain the social conditions of industrial efficiency in organizations, I have no data on industrial efficiency. Instead, I have data on how people behave in, and how people are oriented to, their roles in economic organizations. The basic reason for the indirect approach explaining individual role behavior rather than the true variable of interest is that in order to map social influences bearing on individuals onto their behavior in organizations, and *then* to map role behavior onto organizational performance, I would have had to conduct a much larger two-stage research project with many more organizations, and to solve the almost intractable problem of constructing comparable measures of performance for a large number of organizations. I have only three organizations whose internal structure of behavior in administrative roles I have tried to describe, and these three have forces bearing on organizational performance other than the ones I will analyze.

To deal with the fact that I have not studied the variable I will try to explain, I will follow a strategy introduced into the study of economic development by Max Weber, especially in *Economy and Society*. Briefly, this strategy is to argue on theoretical grounds that a certain set of structural and behavioral variables in organizations are required for rational decision making. Then, these structural and behavioral variables are taken as dependent variables to be explained by empirical investigation. For example, Weber argued that various structural characteristics of bureaucracy increased the degree of *discipline* in organizations. By discipline he meant that the actions of lower officials and workers were determined by the decisions of the owners of an enterprise or the legislative authorities in a state (for further elaboration, see Chapter 5). Then these structural variables of bureaucracy (files, career officials, differentiation of work status from kinship status, etc.) could be taken as the dependent variables in historical research. The object of defining the ideal type of bureaucracy, therefore, is to render the degree of discipline, a very hard variable to measure, into an investigable subject.

This monograph therefore has the following structure. In the remainder of this introduction I will describe two patterns of bureaucratic behavior, one from the Venezuelan traffic control bureaucracy, and one from the pipe or tube rolling mill of the Venezuelan steel plant. The purpose of these examples is to give a picture of the extreme values of the dependent variable, administrative efficiency. I will try to show that the degree of rationality characteristic of the traffic bureaucracy could not possibly solve the problems of keeping a steel plant's interdependent technical system going. Then I will briefly anticipate the theoretical connections of organizational role behavior to this dependent variable of rational industrial administration. This theoretical argument will connect the variables actually studied with the problem of this book. I will also briefly describe the general structure of the study from which the data came.

The second part of this book is devoted to the social sources of cognitively efficient problem solving. That is, the first problem of an administrative structure is to have the right answer (or *a* right answer) to the technical and economic problems confronting the organization. After exploring the sources of right answers, we can ask for the conditions under which this right answer is carried into action.

The structure of the argument of this section on organizational cognition comes closest to the structure that each section ought to have, and so can serve as an introduction to the research strategy I have outlined. Chapter 2 is devoted to the theoretical argument that certain characteristics of social interaction to solve a problem (characteristics such as written interaction, cosmopolitan sources of information and ideas, committee decision-making) increase the quality of the analysis of a cognitive problem in a bureaucracy. The purpose of Chapter 2 is to connect the behavioral and attitudinal variables actually studied to the problem of administrative rationality, and hence to economic development.

Chapter 3 is devoted to the role behavior of people in different kinds of economic administrative structures. The causes of this role behavior that form the core of the argument of Chapter 3 are variables describing the administrative structures themselves. In Chapter 4 we turn to the biographies of the individuals who people these structures to study the social sources of the attitudes and behavioral predispositions which facilitate the administrative behavior outlined in Chapter 2, and described in Chapter 3. That is, we use the men's biographies to explore the sources of a rational attitude toward administrative roles.

The data were collected with the assumption that the role requirements for solving complex problems in interdependent technical systems would be very different from those required for solving problems that come up in more traditional administrative and entrepreneurial roles. This assumption turned out to be well supported in the data of Chapter 3 on cognitive behavior and attitudes. Consequently, the data contrasting bureaucratic cognitive behavior in steel plants with the behavior of people in more traditional middle-class roles speaks directly to the theoretical problems raised in Chapter 2.

The third part of this book addresses the problem of the social sources of discipline in administrative structures. The problem here is how administrative structures can be set up so that rational decisions are actually enforced in the day-to-day actions in the plants, given that the people who do them are paid a salary rather than directly collecting the benefits of rationality. Chapter 5 is devoted to the theoretical argument, outlined briefly above from Weber, connecting the variables of bureaucratic discipline to administrative and economic rationality.

Unfortunately, the middle part of the argument of this section on discipline, the description of the role behavior implied in Chapter 5, is defective. The direct measures of the degree of discipline in role performances did not successfully contrast the administration of interdependent systems from traditional middle-class role behavior. Consequently, the data structure of this third section has a hole in the middle, and the chapter that should occupy the comparable place in this section to Chapter 3 in the cognitive section, does not appear. The hole is filled in Chapter 6 by some rather unsatisfactory ad hoc explanations of why the crucial behavioral links cannot be constructed with the materials at hand.

The main brunt of Chapter 6 is comparable to Chapter 4 of Part II. The theoretical argument of Chapter 5 concludes that career orientations are a crucial variable which determine different degrees of discipline, and that the structure of industrial bureaucracy must produce or recruit those orientations in order to produce sufficient discipline. The organizational and biographical sources of appropriate bureaucratic career orientations is the subject of Chapter 6.

The fourth part of this book is about the general political conditions under which structural requirements of rational administration are possible. That is, we hope that we have shown in the description of the dependent variable in this introduction, in the arguments about social requirements of cognitively adequate administrative behavior in the second part, and about the social requirements of bureaucratic discipline in the third part, that administrative rationality in industrial administration has structural requirements. Introducing these structural requirements into a society rearranges people's lives and affects the fates and power of social groups. Instituting these structural requirements, therefore, has political prerequisites.

In Chapter 7, theoretical arguments about what these political prerequisites are, and how they relate to South American political conditions are presented.

A few of the data are peripherally relevant to these arguments. Since, however, the study was designed basically to contrast the roles of industrial bureaucrats and more traditional middle-class roles, and since the political roles of most of these people are peripheral to their own lives and not crucial in the political system, the data do not fit the theoretical requirements. I cannot describe the role behavior of crucial participants in the political system because we did not interview many of them. I cannot describe the structural determinants of that role behavior because we did not interview their role partners, as we did in the steel plant. I cannot locate the biographical sources of the appropriate role dispositions of political actors, because I do not have a good sample of political biographies. Thus the two chapters that should follow Chapter 7 cannot be written in a telling fashion with the present data.

So the overall structure of this book begins with an attempt to induce in the reader by illustration a sense of what the dependent variable of administrative capacity to manage industrialization is. The following three parts analyze the social and organizational conditions of three components of that administrative capacity: cognitive adequacy of the solutions to industrial administrative problems, motivational adequacy of bureaucratic structures to produce disciplined performance of roles executing these solutions, and adequacy in the political creation and maintenance of the social relations required by these structures.

Within each of these three parts we ought to do three intellectual tasks. First, we should show by theoretical argument the characteristics of cognitive, motivational, and political role performances that ought to produce efficiency in industrial administration. Second, we should describe the actual role performances of our three case studies in terms of these variables, and explore their structural location in social life. Third, we should describe the social and biographical causes that explain variations in these variables. In this particular study, the three intellectual tasks can be done reasonably effectively for cognitive behavior, in the second section of the book. The third part on motivation is markedly defective in the achievement of the second of these tasks—that of describing variations in role performance. The fourth part on politics is markedly defective in achieving the second and third of these tasks—failing to describe variations in crucial political behavior, and to explore its structural sources.

An Introduction to the Dependent Variable

I will present two case studies of administrative behavior in San Felix—Puerto Ordaz in Eastern Venezuela. One is a typical case of traditional governmental behavior, the Traffic Inspector of San Felix issuing drivers licenses. The other is a typical problem of administration of interdependent technical systems, the problem of delays or downtime on the pipe or tube rolling mill in the steel plant at Matanzas, just outside Puerto Ordaz. The main point of this comparison is that the tube mill would not run at all if it were administered in the same way as the issuance of drivers licenses.

But the description has an additional purpose. The role behavior that we will analyze in other sections of this book will be meaningfully related to economic development only if it, in fact, solves the problems of industrial administration. We need a touchstone of actual administrative systems to give a criterion against which to judge the good sense of the theoretical arguments I will give for the importance of that role behavior.

In particular, people who do not deal with industrial administration have a tendency to think it is routine, and therefore easy. One of the points I want these examples to make is that keeping a production line operating routinely requires a great deal of creative problem solving. The notion that most of us have of physical systems is shaped by our learning about the Newtonian model of the solar system, which goes its way with no error in a perfectly regular fashion. An industrial system is more like the physics laboratories of ordinary people's high school experience, in which in spite of physical laws nothing ever comes out right. The problem of industrial administration is more like the problem of getting every student in a physics laboratory to get the right answer, than it is like making the solar system behave.

In particular, the easy theoretical distinction between innovation and routine administration breaks up when one looks closely at what has to be done to keep an interdependent technical system running. Troubles and chance variation in one component of a technical system ramify throughout the system. This ramified uncertainty has to be dealt with by intelligent, disciplined, coordinated, problem-solving behavior. The conditions for such behavior being intelligent are explored in Part II; the conditions for it being disciplined in Part III; and the conditions for it being coordinated, for the system of authority being legitimate and effective, in Part IV. The purpose of this introduction to the dependent variable, then, is to show that industrial administration creates enough problem-solving requirements so that the conditions for its effectiveness discussed in the rest of this book really matter.

An Incident of Venezuelan Bureaucracy

I asked one of the group of policemen sitting around with rifles on one side of the plaza in San Felix where to get a driver's license. He did not know but told me to ask in the *Municipalidad* on the other side. I went over there and asked someone behind a desk. He said he thought you had to go to the *Inspectoría* in Calle _____ . A grizzled old man from among the group of clients told me in a definite tone of voice that I *did* have to go to the *Inspectoría de Transito* and told me where the street was. I knew by that time that the signs on the streets did not agree with the names of the streets the people used, so I never thought of using the map. I walked a couple of blocks in the direction indicated and asked a shoeshine boy where the *Inspectoría* was. He offered to take me, so I took him to the car and we drove to the *Inspectoría*. I gave him a *bolívar* and went in to the main door and asked where to get licenses.

They directed me next door. I went next door and asked how to start the process to get a driver's license. The plump lady sitting next to the window told me that the Inspector was in Caracas, so I could not get one now.

"You mean he didn't leave anyone in charge?"

She said, "No. He has to sign them, and he's in Caracas."

"When will he be back?"

"I don't know. Maybe tomorrow."

I read in the newspaper that night that the Inspector had gone to Caracas to try to get more traffic police assigned to his office, and would be back the following Tuesday. But I went over anyway, out of curiosity, to see what the lady would say. "Is the Inspector in today?" I asked.

"No. He hasn't got back yet. I think he'll be back this afternoon."

"I read in the paper that he would be gone until next Tuesday."

"No. He'll be back today or tomorrow, I think. Stop in tomorrow at 8:30 or so."

I came back the next morning, allowing an extra hour and a half for the Inspector to get there, but he was not there. I tried to use this as evidence to the lady that the paper was right, but she insisted he would be back the next day. I waited until the following Tuesday anyway.

When I came back the following Tuesday, there was a very fat man at the window, instead of the lady. He told me that the Inspector had decided that they were not beginning the procedures to issue new licenses that week because Easter vacations were coming up, but only doing renewals. I hung around for awhile trying to pressure him into letting me start the process, picking up something about a *planilla* that had to be filled out first. This later turned out to be an application form.

He said, "You can go into the Inspector's office and see if you can fill out the *planilla*." I went around through the other entrance to a waiting room where several people were sitting outside the Inspector's office. The door to his office was closed, and there seemed to be no legitimate way to communicate with anyone inside without opening the door oneself, which I did not feel I dared do. I sat down in the waiting room to see whether I could talk to someone going in or out of the office, and to figure out what was going on, but shortly gave it up.

When I came back the following week, after Easter vacations (three office days not open), I got the *planilla* filled out, and was given a form for a medical inspection. It turned out that only one physician in town was considered competent to evaluate one's fitness to drive, so I went across town to his office, waited about an hour and a half, got an examination much less complete than is given by clerks in any driver's license inspection in the U.S., and paid the usual fee for seeing a physician (20 *bolívares*, about $4.50). I was strongly tempted to start walking out of the office, as if I assumed this was a free service of the government in the interests of public safety, so that the physician would be forced into the humiliating situation of having to request his payment.

I went back to the *Inspectoría de Transito* expecting to finish the application. I got back about 3:00 in the afternoon, and the office did not close until 5:00, so I assumed that I would have plenty of time. But the fat man said, "Of course, it's too late now. Come back tomorrow."

"About what time should I come?"

"From 8:30 on we're here."

I came back the next day at 10:00, and was told it was too late to start the process then. A couple of days later, I came at 8:30 and turned in my pictures (which had cost me another 6 *bolívares*, or a dollar), the physician's record, and the application form; after about an hour and a half these were processed so that I could go uptown to the *Banco de Venezuela* to pay the fee for the examination. When I got back, of course, it was too late to have the examination that day, so I was told I would have to come back tomorrow. This was after waiting 2 hours, and was at 3 :00 in the afternoon. I came back the next day, took the examination (which was to drive around the block, and answer some simple questions on traffic regulations), and got my temporary license, valid for 60 days. So far I had spent a total of 3 weeks and 2 days in trying to get the license.

After 60 days, I came back to claim my driver's license (for not even the Venezuelan government would trust anything of value to their mails). The fat man glanced at it, saw that it had been issued only 60 days previously, and stamped it valid again for another 60 days, apparently knowing perfectly well that the process of issuing driver's licenses was never really finished in the 60 days provided.

The whole reason that I had decided to get a Venezuelan driver's license in the first place, even though according to the law (as told to me in the *Inspectoría*) my Maryland driver's license was valid for a year as long as I carried my passport with me, was that several different policemen at traffic check points had told me that my license was valid for only 2 months, or 3 months, or 4 months.

The striking thing about all this is the idiocy of the process. It has apparently never occurred to any high police officer that it would be convenient for the policemen who are to inspect licenses to know the relevant laws. It has never occurred to the Inspector, nor to the fat man, that the forms could be freely available at the window as soon as people came in to inquire, that a list of steps to follow to get the license would save people from having to hang around bothering the clerks with questions, that much time would be saved for the applicant if the physician could have hours in the *Inspectoría* (or that such a simple examination could be carried out by anyone, though this would probably create problems with the physicians' professional association), or that it would also save time if they collected the fees in the *Inspectoría*.

Aside from this failure of analysis of the process, the bureaucrats feel perfectly free to decide whether they are going to work at all. I detected no embarrassment the various times they told me that they were not going to do any more that day, or that the Inspector had left his job and they did not know when he would be back.

Such lack of intelligence and irresponsibility are probably related to the generally political basis for appointments in the police and the *Inspectoría*. The disadvantage of this is *not* that it recruits mediocrites to public posts, though it may do that. Instead, it has its effect indirectly. The crucial thing is that the police Captain would never be fired because his officers inspect drivers licenses without knowing the laws, nor would he be promoted faster if they did know them. The Inspector may very well be fired when political combinations change, but he will never be fired for gross incompetence in running his office, so that it takes several days waiting in the office, and several months waiting at home to get a license.

This is what most Latin Americans mean by "bureaucracy." Their repeated experience is that all branches of the government, characterized by long hierarchies and rule-bound behavior, do not give a damn whether they do their jobs or not. The Inspector of Terrestrial Transport taking off from his job, without leaving a substitute, to request more men (while most of the ones he has enforce the law without knowing it and refuse to take on any more work after 10:00), is the picture of bureaucracy and public administration to the average Latin American. Max Weber's analysis of bureaucracy as the most efficient, disciplined type of administration of affairs on a large scale does not ring true.

But with this kind of administrative tradition, these countries are embarking on semisocialistic schemes of producing steel or petroleum or railroad service on a large scale. With the prestige and taxation power of the government behind these enterprises, with hundreds or thousands of workers who depend for their living on them and who wield political power, these enterprises will not be allowed to disappear. One of the principal questions of economic development is, then, whether, and how, the idiocy and irresponsibility of the traffic inspector of San Felix can be kept from invading these enterprises. In the following sections, I am going to describe a typical administrative problem that is presented by industrial production in the steel industry. Problems of similar complexity would be found in electric power production and distribution, railroad administration, the running of an airline, or any number of economic enterprises crucial to economic development, and generally carried out by governments rather than private enterprises in the modern underdeveloped world.[1] The reader can try to imagine the Traffic Inspector of San Felix being in charge of solving the following problem.

Conceptual Aspects of Industrial Administration

Administration may be defined as an attempt to manipulate possible causes in attaining goal or end-product through the human beings who are effecting that goal. Thus, in order to understand industrial administration, we must understand something of the causes of the phenomenon it wants to produce,

---

1. I do not want to imply that one could not find private enterprises, run with a degree of efficiency comparable to the *Inspectoría de Transito* of San Felix, protected by customs barriers or by lush government contracts from the failure that would accompany such inefficiency in a competitive system. And some oil fields or mining concessions are so rich that they yield profits no matter how they are run. But for various reasons to be developed in the argument further on, government bureaucracies are subject to inefficiency to a considerably greater extent than private enterprises.

for instance, the causes of high productivity in producing steel pipes of a certain quality.

By "cause" I mean *any* variable which, if changed, will in the given environment produce a change in the goal or end-product. For example, if a production line for pipe is stopped because of a difficulty in getting a bent unfinished pipe out of a furnace, all of the following may be considered "causes" of the delay:

(1) the imperfection of the operation that produced the bent pipe or put the bent pipe in the furnace
(2) the small size of the openings of the furnace which make it difficult to get the pipe out
(3) the lack of an alternative, stocked furnace which could be used while this one is cleared
(4) The decision to produce seamless rather than welded pipe, if welded pipe would not be subject either to the operation that bent the pipe or to the reheating

The analysis of industrial administration has been organized typically around one or the other of three basic conceptual foundations: (1) the superior—subordinate relation, (2) the decision, or (3) the flow of information.

Examples of (1), analyses based on the superior—subordinate relation, include discussions of the span of control, of centralization versus decentralization in administration, of statistical measures of performance versus orders as techniques of control of subordinates, of frequency of initiation of interaction by superiors or by subordinates, of democratic versus authoritarian administration, etc. But such aspects of the superior—subordinate relation affect the degree of success of an administrative system by affecting the *likelihood that the causes of low productivity will be found and acted upon*. Thus, a production executive should have such a span of control as will make it most likely that the causes of his subordinates' low (or high) productivity will be discovered and acted upon. What the production executive's span should be depends on the concrete nature of the causal system in question.

Largely inspired by developments in economic and statistical decision theory, the recent tendency has been to substitute for the superior—subordinate conceptual base that of (2) *analysis of decision making*. For all the advantages of this approach in introducing some of the substantive reality of the enterprise into the abstract organization chart, it has the disadvantage of missing what seems to me to be the fundamental reality of the chart. One can hardly walk through an industrial plant without noting that the responsibilities specified on the organization chart are very often responsibilities for integrated technical systems, that is to say, unified systems of causes. In a steel plant, these are generally such systems as the coke plant, if there is one, reduction furnaces, steel-making furnaces, production lines of different intermediate and final products, and technically distinct transportation systems. *What decisions have to be made* depend on the system of causes that one is trying to manipulate, and responsibilities are divided so that decisions about integrated technical systems will be made as part of a single process under a single authority. Thus, the decision-making approach requires an analysis of the causal system about which decisions have to be made.

The practical problems of redesigning administrative systems to make full use of computers has focused attention on (3) *the information-processing aspect* of administration. But what makes information worth processing is its relation to high or low productivity of the enterprise, and this is determined by the nature of the causal system about which information is sought.

In the illustrations given about the causes of a delay occasioned by a bent pipe in a furnace, the causes range from the specific activities of stocking the furnace to the basic technology of pipe making. Of course, no one expects industrial managers to switch basic processes with every small delay. The trick of industrial management is to choose that cause of high productivity which will result in an increase of production at the least cost—and obviously to change factories for each bent pipe would be costly. But the identification of such causes and the selection of which ones to work on provide the guts of industrial management.

I will describe the administrative system related to manipulating causes of interruptions of production in the hot rolling of seamless pipe from billets of steel in the government steel plant at Matanzas near Puerto Ordaz—San Felix, Venezuela. The hot rolling operations of the plant included the pipe or tube mill, another rolling mill that produced construction shapes, and a heavy rolling mill that produced the billets that were input for these two finished-product mills from the huge chunks of steel produced by the steel-making furnaces. About 2000 workers (of about 5000 in the plant) were involved in these rolling operations, all of which have similar technical characteristics.

First, I will consider the main types of causes of stoppages of the production line, as obtained from interviews and observation of the administration of production. I will describe the different patterns of routine coding of these causes to provide the relevant information for taking different sorts of administrative action. Then, I will outline the main alternative strategies for concentrating administrative attention on the causes of high and low productivity, taking examples from administrative activity related to interruptions. This will be followed by an evaluation of the advantages and disadvantages of each strategy.

The Problem of Interruptions

The process of rolling seamless tubes in the Venezuelan steel plant at Matanzas begins with cutting the long pieces of steel produced in a separate rolling mill to appropriate lengths for making pipes. This cutting is done to create an inventory of cut pieces ready to be loaded into the first reheating furnace; delays of reasonable length in the cutting operations do not, therefore, cause the whole line to be shut down.

From this point, there are a series of closely technically interdependent operations, of reheating the cut steel piece, pressing the corners down while it is still hot, and then immediately putting it into a "perforating press" which punches a hole in the middle of the softened steel. Then, it is loaded into another reheating furnace for a short period of time, a furnace designed not to have much more capacity than other machines in the line. After this second reheating, while still hot, it passes to an elongator, and then immediately to a rolling mill consisting of rotary hammers shaped so as to preserve the cylindrical character of the pipe. There it is pounded out into something that is recognizably a pipe. From this mill it goes to a saw which removes the jagged ends, and then to a third reheating furnace of relatively small capacity. After coming out of this furnace, it goes to a rectifying or calibrating machine to give it the appropriate final measurements and straighten it. After this it goes into an inventory for various operations on the cold pipe, to finish it.

From a technical point of view, these hot rolling machines are very highly interdependent because the permissible time lags between operations are quite small. This means, roughly, that if *any one* of the machines or human operations on the line is stopped or slowed down, the whole line is stopped or slowed. That is, the probability that the line will be functioning at any given time is *the product of the probabilities* that each machine will function. Since the machines and furnaces themselves function under relatively great temperature and pressure, the probability that any particular machine will function properly is not terribly high. Therefore, even under the best of conditions, the percentage of time that the whole line is running normally will inevitably be considerably short of 100%. In the tube factory attached to the steel plant in Venezuela, the percentage of time the various lines were running averaged about 35% of the time they were programmed to run.

The way delays are created by the technical interdependence of the rolling process was shown by a number of indicators:

(1) In a study carried out by the budget department of the company, over 80% of the losses occasioned by measured "delays" in production were in the hot rolling sections of the plant which employed less than half of the workers of the plant.

(2) This figure was *over*estimated for a very interesting reason—delays were not even measured, at least within the tube factory, in the cold part of the process, nor in the preparatory cutting of steel for rolling. That is, delays in the

hot rolling process were significant as an administrative problem, and consequently were measured, whereas delays in systems with less technical interdependence were not measured.

(3) Maintenance people asserted that they paid more attention, and put better men, into maintenance of these highly interdependent hot rolling processes. This was obvious if one walked through the tube factory on a Sunday or holiday, when they were not rolling and only maintenance men were working. The men were always heavily concentrated on the hot rolling section of the mill. Furthermore when the maintenance department started a preventive maintenance program, they started it in the hot section of the line. The basic purpose of "maintenance" as defined in the plant was to increase the probability that a given machine would function. Concentration of maintenance on the highly interdependent hot rolling sections shows that reduction of probability of failures was most salient to the management on those lines.

If we consider this *interdependence* as such to be a principal variable or "cause" of production delays, then any means of reducing that interdependence will be a cause of high productivity. There are two basic devices for reducing the interdependence of such a production process:

(1) The most common is to detach two operations from each other by having the first operation produce for an "inventory" of goods in process. Then the second operation works from that inventory. If appropriately designed, the stock in the inventory can allow the second operation to go on when the first is delayed, and the possibility of building up the inventory allows the first to proceed even when the second is not using up its production. The problem of applying this technique in hot rolling of steel, is, of course, that maintaining steel near 1300°C is quite expensive in gas or other fuel, furnace construction and maintenance, space, etc. Thus, the high cost of maintaining inventories of goods in process, given the technical fact that they have to be hot for the next operation, is the fundamental explanation of the interdependence of the operations in hot rolling.

(2) When maintaining inventories of goods in process is either technically impossible or too costly, another basic device is to *duplicate machinery*. That is, if the capacity of one machine is needed for the line to run, and each such machine breaks down 10% of the time, then a duplicate machine which can be used when the first is down reduces the probability that the line will be stopped for lack of that machine from 10 to 1%. In the Venezuelan plant, such a technique was often used with factory-wide services (for instance, they had reserve thermoelectric generating capacity in case of power failure in their hydro-

electric supply), and for relatively inexpensive parts of different technical systems (valves, switches, and the like). But maintaining a reserve furnace or rolling mill ready to function would be very expensive.

The Causes of Interruptions

If we assume that there are practically irreducible amounts of technical interdependence in hot rolling, we can proceed to outline the types of causes of interruptions. In classifying causes from the point of view of an administrative system, we are classifying variables that can be changed by manipulating human beings, which in turn will presumably help to produce the effect we are interested in—namely, the continuous running of the production line. Consequently, we want to classify such causes according to the general type of corrective action necessary. We will first classify such causes according to broad types of decisions that have to be made, and then, according to the main types of information-processing activities involved to show the relation of the system of causes to be controlled to the more traditional approaches to production management.

The types of decisions can be grouped into (1) problems of *design* of the production line, (2) problems of *maintenance* of the machinery, (3) problems of *scheduling*, and (4) problems of *personnel*.

(1) *Problems of Design.*   This group falls naturally into three main categories: (*a*) basic decisions about which products to produce by which basic processes, the capacity that production lines ought to have, which country's rolling mills the lines were going to imitate, and so forth; (*b*) decisions about large modifications, either in the production line or in particular machines or furnaces, and (*c*) small modifications, which would use only resources already under the control of the management of the tube mill or of its maintenance division.

Examples of basic decisions in the first category include whether or not to produce a seamless tube (e.g., rather than the relatively simpler welded tube, which is not generally as strong) and consequently whether to get into the difficulties of hot rolling of tubes at all; whether to design extra capacity (and how much) into the basic production process; whether to use the basic designs of Italian or American mills when setting up the production line (and consequently from whom to buy the heavy pieces of capital equipment); and whether to buy new equipment or equipment from an archaic plant (in order to get experience cheaper). If some of these decisions had been made differently, some of the difficulties that presently exist with the plant would not have existed.

The thing that distinguishes such basic design decisions is that they are decisions about the fundamental question: What business are we in? Consequently, they always involve the top levels of the company and the investing public. Since steel plants, in underdeveloped countries always and in developed countries usually, involve considerable investments of public powers (tax and tariff privileges, often government money, government provision of all sorts of auxiliary services to the enterprise, government intervention in labor relations), such considerations often involve the highest officials of the government itself. From the point of view of *nearly* everyone involved in production management, such decisions (and any troubles they cause) are taken as given. The main exceptions are foreign advisors, who may come from places where such basic decisions are taken differently, and who may therefore have far more tendency to criticize basic management policy than is characteristic of production managers in general.

In the second category, large modifications, either of the arrangement of the line or in particular machines or furnaces, are defined by the administrative process as those originated by the management of the production line, and designed and approved by the industrial engineering or plant engineering departments or both, and usually put into effect on the basis of such approval. Such improvements are generally approved on the basis of special studies of costs and returns (taking as given the rest of the production line, the types of products produced, and their prices). The decision process uses a rough "return of principal" criterion which decides whether the investments are worth the effort if they will pay for themselves in 1, 2, 3, or 10 years. This criterion seemed to be determined in the steel plant at Matanzas not according to the interest rate, as it should in economic theory, but according to the crucially scarce resource of administrative attention. During the early stages of getting a production line running efficiently, administrative attention will only stretch far enough to cover the decision-making work for investments that will pay for themselves within a year or two. Presumably, when more administrative talent has been trained by experience, and when the easy improvements have been introduced, investments would be determined as if the scarce resource were money, as is always presumed by the economic theory of the firm.

Examples of such large modifications would be substitution of mechanical or electrical materials handling at a certain place for hydraulic handling, expansion of the pumping capacity of the production line hydraulic pressure plant, increasing the size of the openings in a furnace so that bent tubes can be extracted more easily, major reorganization (with new manning requirements) of the cutting and warehousing of the steel which is the raw material, etc. Many such modifications are explicitly designed to reduce production delays.

Small modifications in the last category are defined by the administrative criterion that they can be carried out with resources already under the control of the production management itself. A recurrent machine malfunction may quite often be relieved greatly by welding on a guide or a support, or putting in an extra valve, or substituting hose for pipe (or vice versa) in a cooling system for a machine, or putting hooks on welding machines so that they can be moved by cranes instead of over the floor. Such modifications, often invented by workers or foremen, have far greater importance for industrial efficiency than is generally realized. In general, it would be too much work to compute costs and returns for such modifications; and all such modifications can be causes of less downtime on the production line.

(2) *Problems of Maintenance.* If one main way of reducing the probability of the whole line shutting down is by redesigning the line or the machines, another is by maintaining the machines in the state that they were designed to be in. From a practical point of view, there are two great classes of maintenance problems: anticipated breakdowns, and unanticipated breakdowns; and two great classes of corresponding actions: preventive maintenance, and "fire fighting."

The principal advantages of anticipating "repairs" (i.e., the putting of the machine into the state it was originally designed to be in, in order to function with as high a probability as possible) are: (1) repairs can be planned to take place along with other necessary stoppages of the line, for example, for modifications, retooling, or holidays; (2) the tools, parts, and men can be programmed ahead so that the work can be done as well and as efficiently as possible; (3) certain variable costs of production (such as waiting production workers) can be minimized if maintenance stoppages are known in advance; (4) the maintenance men work under less pressure, which may or may not dispose them to do a better job, but at any rate makes both them and production management more comfortable and less irritable. In general, in the plant studied, such programmed stoppages were not measured as stoppages.

Conversely, an unanticipated malfunction of a machine often must be acted on in the absence of appropriate parts (especially until historical experience can provide a basis of a parts inventory policy), with whomever happens to be working, under angry pressure from production management. In the plant studied, the causes of these unanticipated interruptions were extensively recorded and analyzed from several points of view, and their costs at the end of an accounting period were computed. No such analysis of the causes or costs of *programmed* delays was carried out. However, in the tube factory, when they changed from three shifts to two shifts for each production line, production *increased* rather than decreased—one of the reasons being superior anticipation of maintenance problems and their remedy during the night shift.

(3) *Scheduling Problems.* This cause of delays (and consequently solutions causing high productivity) seems to be of two main types in an operation of this kind: *daily* scheduling and *long-term* scheduling.

One *daily* scheduling problem is that it takes some time to heat up the metal before working it, and then some more time to reheat the processed materials for further working, and so forth. Thus, the last part of the production line cannot start producing after any extended stoppage (say over a weekend or overnight) until some considerable time after the first operations are started. This shows up in reports of the causes of delays as "cold materials in furnaces _____" appearing during the first hours of a shift. Sometimes such a problem is left by one shift which has been rolling, for the next shift.

An example of a *long-term* scheduling problem may be that usually in order to change the size of a pipe produced on a production line, all the machines have to be retooled at once, new sizes of steel pieces loaded, etc. This means that the whole line has to be stopped until all the machines are retooled, so that retooling of each machine cannot be planned when it is convenient or while the others are working. In view of the fact that a certain product-mix of tube sizes needs to be produced to satisfy the market, and in view of the inventory capacity and costs of inventory necessary to make long runs of the same tube size before changing to another size, fairly frequent retooling is necessary. The basic determinant of retooling frequency is the relation between the *size of the market* (the smaller, the more retooling), and the *capacity of the production line* (the larger, the more retooling).

Scheduling such retooling when the line is stopped anyway (holidays, off-shifts, stoppages for repairs, etc.) reduces the costs of retooling; but retooling can cause delays during programmed production time if not appropriately planned or if it takes longer than planned. Again, there are two principal remedies—decreasing the interdependence of tooling on the different machines (e.g., by redesigning the last process of hot rolling to produce more different final tube size for each unfinished size the enters it from the rest of the production line), and by appropriate scheduling so as to minimize the costs of such stoppages as are necessary.

(4) *Personnel Problems.* Finally, production managers mentioned two types of *personnel* causes of delays.

First, problems of incompetence and inexperience of many of the personnel they had to use, variously explained by the lack of industrial tradition in Venezuela, by low wages and high cost of living in the interior of the country, by the youth of the factory, and by having let crucial foreign technical help go back home too soon. Second, problems of not having enough personnel to do any more than treat the most urgent cases of delays, without sufficient attention to the detailed studies on a large scale which would be involved, for example, in setting up a complete program of preventive maintenance or studying materials flows throughout the whole line of a factory.

Naturally, the incompetence or small number of planning personnel in its turn creates difficulties with *each* of the other types of causes. Scheduling difficulties, lack of anticipation of maintenance problems, or designing to solve minor problems when major ones go unattended, all could result either from administrative incompetence, *or* from lack of time to think among those who are competent.

Roughly speaking, this division of types of causes of delays corresponds to divisions of administrative responsibility in the plant. For modifications, the great ones of new products and large investments are the responsibility of top management, the middle-sized ones are the province of the higher levels of operating management and the engineering departments, and the small ones are done by operating management within the production line itself. Maintenance departments usually divide responsibility for preventive and emergency maintenance between different offices, often roughly divided so that preventive maintenance is planned by engineers and clerks, and emergency maintenance by foremen of skilled workers. Manning so as to begin production at the beginning of a shift and doing reheating ahead of time is planned by the supervision of each production line, perhaps based on studies by industrial engineers. Planning of production so as to minimize retooling delays is negotiated between the production and maintenance personnel on the one side (led by the superintendent), with a production planning department on the other. The latter department is presumably sensitive to market and inventory problems and supply of materials, as well as to production delays.

This, then, is an outline of the set of causes of a particular aspect of productivity of a pipe rolling mill. The task of industrial administration is to manipulate this set of causes (and, of course, a number of others). An efficient administration will be one that manipulates these causes well. In general, the causes can be better manipulated than they are, and they can be better manipulated this year than last. Consequently, much of the key to efficient administration is a constant stream of innovations.

In order to affect this set of causes, a crucial requirement is information about them. There are a variety of ways of getting that information and relating it to decisions about the action to be taken. The information flowing through the administrative apparatus is, in part at least, given its meaning by its relation to these causes. The process of coding information about the causes, transmitting the information to relevant decision points, and turning the decision made on the basis of that information into a cause of lower delay time, is the central task of administration. Only a relatively small part of that information flow goes to the hierarchical superior responsible for the productivity of the mill; the organization chart is a poor guide to the information-processing system.

Administrative Coding of Causes and Information Flows

The distinctive characteristic of "bureaucratic" production management is the regularization and routinization of written communication channels. Since in different parts of the enterprise a cause of a production delay has to be acted on from different points of view, there are a variety of written information coding schemes relevant to the delays.

An observation about a particular production delay is coded in different ways, depending on the various kinds of action to be taken. Each "fact" of production delay is viewed in terms of different conceptual schemes. One uses a different coding system to determine when to buy a part than one does to determine how many men to schedule for the line, or to determine whether to invest in a new hydraulic system. The causes of a particular delay may be the lack of all of these, and the remedy may be to take action along all these lines. The actions are responsibilities of different authorities—the purchasing manager, the industrial engineering department, or top management. Information about when to buy a repair part, given in a proposal to install a new hydraulic system, would be worse than useless. The separate coding systems for information thus also correspond to the division of authority for taking different kinds of action. Some of these coding schemes are as follows.

(1) *The Delay as a Cost.*   Daily reports of the causes of delays in production are turned in by the shift foreman of each production line in the tube factory. These are summed up and organized by a clerk who works for the tube factory, and then one of the copies, on which the detailed causes of each delay are eliminated, is passed to a detached member of the department of costs. He sends it to the costs department, where the first simplification involves eliminating all references to the *technical systems* causing the delays, but retaining the division according to the "unit responsible" for the delay. Then in a continuing study of the costs of production delays by the budget department, reference to the unit responsible disappears and the costs are attributed to broad classes of products (e.g., small, middle-sized, and large pipes). Arithmetic operations are performed to obtain the total losses from production delays (by comparing actual delays with an estimate of technically necessary delays). From this, the cost per ton of delays for different finished products is determined.

In general, such "cost" coding according to final product seems to be the central type of data collection and coding used by top management. It is used to analyze such problems as pricing, evaluating the general efficiency of the plant (and consequently for such decisions as whether to contract technical assistance, whether to promote superintendents, whether to enter or leave various broad product lines, what will be capital requirements for the future, and so forth), and for formulating economic criteria by which technical decisions in the plant should be guided (e.g., how much investment is justified for saving an hour per month of delay). The common term used by operating units for such criteria of decisions, when stated in the form of numbers, is "data"— the central management sends data to production management and engineering, for example, on how much an investment should pay.

(2) *The Delay as a Responsibility.* A number of times after I started study-ing production delays, people I interviewed assumed that I was trying to find out whose fault it is. And when I heard people talking about which department a delay would be "charged" to, I supposed that the "cost" would be coded primarily by the department responsible for the delay, and that one main purpose of such records would be the evaluation of executives of all kinds. However, as already noted, the principal coding relevant to the general manage-ment was according to the final product.

But within the tube factory, there was a system for dividing the causes of delays according to whose "fault" it was, with three main divisions: plant operation, maintenance, and outside department. For the maintenance unit assigned to the tube factory, the proportion of delays attributable to machinery in substandard or improper condition was a principal measure of performance, both in their own minds and in the minds of the operating production manage-ment. There were graphs and charts all over the administrative offices of main-tenance on the proportions of programmed production time in which there was stoppage because of imperfections in the equipment.

It is interesting to note that the dependence of top management on coding according to final product tended to make the operating management of the tube mill "responsible," in their own eyes and presumably, in the eyes of top management, for all types of delays, and therefore interested in seeking out the causes of such delays, no matter whose formal responsibility they were. This turns the superintendency of the tube factory into a central focus of the com-munications system about the causes of production delays.

(3) *The Cause as a Difficulty with a Specified Technical System.* In order to focus administrative attention (for modifications, maintenance, training of personnel, scheduling) on a technical cause of delays, the first coding within the tube factory of the causes of delays as recorded by the shift foreman includes a cross classification according to the *machine affected* and the *motive system* in which there was a difficulty (hydraulic, electrical, or mechanical). Thus, for example, a record would be kept of the number of hours lost because of imperfec-tions in the hydraulic motive system of the rotary hammers (called Pilsen mills in English). The detailed reports of the foremen are used directly by both opera-tional and maintenance management for locating the specific sources of difficul-ties. Furthermore, various automatic recording equipment locates problems with the furnaces' different technical subsystems.

(4) *Causes Classified According to the Ordering Unit.* Many of the causes of production failure involve buying something to fix them. Since buying of capital equipment generally is a complex operation, much of the information processing takes place according to the units to be bought.

There are two broad classes of units to be bought (which might be called "parts" and "capital"), which receive different administrative treatment. Decisions to buy parts generally do not require studies of cost versus return, since such studies were made when it was decided to buy the machine originally. Consequently, the decision process is much more routine, and reaches lower levels in the plant hierarchy. In contrast, decisions to buy capital equipment usually do involve studies of costs and returns, and involves higher levels of the hierarchy.

The classification of causes of failure of parts in the modern maintenance system takes the form of an estimate of the reliable life of the part, so that it can be replaced or inspected before it is very likely to fail.

(5) *The Cause as a* Manning Requirement. The manning requirements of the production line and maintenance are worked out by a cooperative arrangement between the operating management, the industrial engineering department, and the personnel office. Of course, the central purpose of scheduling workers and providing enough workers of appropriate competence is to make the production line run. Delays are either caused or avoided by scheduling or failing to schedule enough workers to cover the work to be done, and the cost of avoiding delays may depend on whether scheduling involves overtime or not. Organization charts and various approximations and modifications of them are ways of coding manning requirements. Manning requirements, if they are not filled, may obviously be causes of delays, and, in fact, sometimes are. Such manning requirements may not be filled because of lack of prepared personnel, bad scheduling, strikes, an epidemic, difficulties getting to work with a hangover on Monday morning, and so forth.

Strategies for Focusing Administrative Attention

Before causes of production delays can be studied and acted upon, someone with sufficient power or influence has to notice the problem and decide that it is worth doing something about.

In the particular case of seamless pipe production in the Venezuelan plant, given the basic technical capacities of the production lines, economic output was mainly determined by the behavior of four output indexes: (1) the proportion of time worked; (2) the quality of the finished product, determined by a combination of the chemical and physical properties of the steel used and mechanical and crystalline changes during the rolling process; (3) the proportion of the steel supply which goes into scrap versus the proportion that is sold as pipe; and (4) the adjustment of the product mix to market demand, of production to schedules of clients, and minimization of the retooling costs implied by these considerations.[2] The first problem of the focusing of attention, then, is the distribution of attention to these different aspects of productivity. I could not determine how this division was affected, but I suppose it was in the relations of the superintendent with higher management, and it depended on what higher management noticed.

In view of this general determination of which broad sets of causes are operated on by the administrative system, we can set down a number of strategies for concentrating administrative attention on the causes of changes in these productivity measures.

(1) *Problems Brought to Administrative Attention by Routine Data Collection Procedures.* In the plant, the costs of "delays" were considered a problem, but not nearly so much as the costs of "hours not programmed," because there was no system for routinely requiring people to explain why they had not programmed a certain hour.

Likewise, the maintenance department was extremely sensitive to its implications for production delays since delays because of maintenance difficulties were used as a principal measure of performance. But the production programming department was not measured by the costs of time devoted to retooling, and I was told by production managers that the programming department "has nothing to do with delays." My impression was that no one was very sensitive to the costs of not programming time of the line. That is, the structure of routine data collection determined *which* causes of delays had most administrative attention paid to them.

(2) *Problems Brought to Superiors' Attention Because They Constitute Problems to Subordinates.* One typical situation in which subordinates need the help of their superiors to solve one of their problems is when remedial action is required of someone outside their own chain of command. Two principal outside departments on which production was technically dependent were inplant transportation (which was centralized for technical reasons) and certain parts of the central maintenance workshop (which was centralized for reasons I was

2. There are many other problems which, under different circumstances, might be basic indexes of differences in productivity. In multiplant operations, scheduling production so as to minimize transportation costs of both raw materials and finished products might be crucial. Without a protected market, developing new products might be crucial. Under conditions of rapid improvement of capital equipment, getting rid of surplus workers in the face of trade union opposition might be critical. In sum, technical and economic considerations will determine which are the "bottleneck factors," in terms of which rational planning will proceed. The above seemed to be the bottleneck factors in the plant studied.

not able to determine).[3] A large part of the day of a production superintendent is, then, devoted to trying to get the transportation system and tool maintenance shops to do something that will allow production to continue. I once saw a division head, who supervised thousands of men, spending hours, day after day, trying to influence the order of priorities with which a half dozen lathe opetors in the maintenance shop would work.

(3) *Problems Brought to Administrative Attention and Action by Studies Which have a General Mandate to find the Causes of a General Class of Difficulties.* These studies may be conducted, from an administrative point of view, by a staff department (e.g., I saw one study of delays on another rolling mill done by the industrial engineering department in the plant), by a consultant study group, by a group of subordinates of a production manager, or by a combination (e.g., a study group composed of subordinates of maintenance and outside consultants were developing a preventive maintenance program when I was in the plant).

What is distinctive of such bodies is that they do not need to respond to immediate problems of subordinates nor to data routinely collected, but are free to follow the causes where they lead, and determine for themselves what data are relevant.

(4) *Problems Brought to Administrative Attention by People Who Compare the Production Process with Standards Derived from Outside the Plant.* For instance, in the Venezuelan plant an estimate of losses from delays was made by comparing performance with a standard for each line. This standard was estimated by a member of a contracted consulting firm from the United States. For another example, an accountant I talked to calculated for me comparisons of the sales prices of Venezuelan steel products inside the country with sales prices of steel produced in a number of other South American countries. I heard a discussion of centralized versus decentralized maintenance in which practices in Germany, Italy, and Argentina were mentioned. I saw people with German, American, French, and Italian technical journals and books, from which they presumably got ideas and standards with which to compare processes in the plant.

(5) *Periodic Decision Requirements of Higher Administration Focus Attention of Subordinates on Means for Improving Performance.* For example, in working out the budget and the capital budget for the enterprise for the coming year, the

---

3. The existence in all major industrial countries of job shops doing work similar to the central maintenance workshop of all different sizes indicates that the economies of scale are not very great in this kind of work. Consequently, the savings by centralization are probably not very great.

accountants demand predictions from the various departments of their expenditures. This forces production managers to think about what they would need, if they could have it. Weekly meetings with production programming likewise focused attention on retooling as a source of delays.

(6) *Attention Focused by Administrative Initiative*. Sometimes without stimulation, production managers, maintenance personnel, or engineering departments would work out ways in which things could be done better. These innovations were often not answers to specific current problems. This occurred quite often when an unusual opportunity presented itself. For instance, if a furnace had to be shut off for certain repairs, initiatives would be taken to see whether anything else useful could be done at the same time. Modifications of the furnace were more likely to be thought of at that time. Detailed acquaintance with the problem and with administrative practice, a general preoccupation with that problem in one's daily work, and the general encouragement of initiative by the way rewards and responsibilities were distributed in the plant, are likely the central determinants of such initiative.

Operating Characteristics of the Strategies for Focusing Attention

What are the consequences of using these different strategies for success in manipulating the causes of high productivity?

(1) *Advantages and Limitations of Routine Data Collection*. Attention focused by routine data collection procedures tends to be much more inflexible than attention focused by problems of subordinates. It only adjusts when the routines of data collection are changed. Consequently, it makes most sense when applied to the main indexes of success, as in this case: quality of product, percentage of scrap, percentage of time the line is operated, or the satisfactoriness of delivery times and inventories of finished products. An overall index is the cost of production. (The indexes of inventory and delivery time are not actually used. Instead, performance is considered satisfactory when the programming department is satisfied.) When these indexes go awry, it indicates something is wrong, though it does not indicate what.

The other techniques are more flexible in finding out the what. For example, the concentration of administrative attention on the hot rolling part of the mill was probably never deliberately planned, and routine data collection for top management makes no separation of problems there from problems elsewhere in the tube factory. Broadly speaking, top management could tell, in this plant, when there were problems in *producing a specific product* from their cost data, but not when there were problems with a *specific type of operation* common to several products.[4]

(2) *Advantages and Disadvantages of Problems of Subordinates.* If the maximum responsiveness to changes in the nature of the production problem comes from administrative attention focused by problems of subordinates, this technique has the disadvantage of tending to focus attention on causes which can be influenced in a short period of time. Staff departments quite generally complain that their recommendations for long term improvements do not get much *administrative energy* from production managers. Each of these departments tends to see this as distinctively their problem, but it is in fact general. Among things that did not get sufficient energy according to various staff departments I talked to were better data collection (two departments), reorganization of materials flow (two departments), training programs that will take people away from production (two departments), and general studies of the whole line resulting in a number of recommendations (one department among my interviews, but there must be more). Conversely, managers talk about how projects are buried by sending them to a staff department. A recurrent problem caused by such differences in the time span of planning is the project originated by production management, studied for some time in a staff department, and then met with lack of enthusiasm by production management because by the time it comes back they are worried about a different (and urgent) problem.

I heard a number of administrative arrangements proposed to handle this problem, from insisting that no study should be started without prior approval by the superintendent of production, to proposals to give a staff department executive responsibility with the plant for such long-term functions. (This latter type of proposal came from two different staff departments.) It seems doubtful that any of these devices can resolve the fundamental conflict between *responsiveness* to changes in problems of production, and *profundity* in the analysis of all possible remedies of a particular problem.

4. This is an exaggeration for the sake of emphasis. The chemical composition of steels is a common factor in several production lines on which good routine data collection exists. What I mean is that this orientation to similar operations in several units is relatively rare. Even chemical composition is not, from the evidence of what goes into general published reports, considered a matter for top management attention. But the point here is that top management would have difficulty finding out at all from routine data collection procedures that almost all of the maintenance cost is on the hot rolling part of each line, which is obvious from walking through the plant or listening to problems brought in by subordinates. I am not saying this as a criticism. If all the data necessary for all conceivable types of analysis were collected routinely, we would have a plant of data collectors with no steel coming out.

(3) *Advantages and Disadvantages of Outside Comparisons.* The principal advantage of outside comparisons as a method of focusing attention on causes of low productivity is that it can locate problems in productivity that are not problems in any particular person's performance of his job. That is, in the performance of any job, a person tends to divide the causes of productivity psychologically into those *he* can manipulate and is responsible for manipulating, and those that are "inevitable" from his point of view. But the wider the range of experience with which a given production process is compared, the fewer will be the inevitable aspects. Administrative attention entirely organized by routine data collection and problems of subordinates will not investigate these inevitable conditions.

The main devices for ensuring outside comparisons in the Venezuelan plant were scholarships to foreign countries and steel plants and the hiring of foreign experts. The foreign experts, of course, disagreed among themselves, partly depending on which country's productive processes were compared with the plant. Libraries were small and inaccessible to many of the personnel, and tended to be run on the principle that "a book stolen is a book lost" instead of the much more realistic principle for technical libraries that "a book stolen is a book in use." Only catalogues seemed to be quite freely available, presumably because they did not have to be bought.

(4) *Advantages and Disadvantages of Periodic Decision Requirements.* The periodic decision requirements of high management, e.g., at budget time, tended to lengthen the planning time span briefly and superficially within the tube factory. Presumably, its main values are for decisions taken at higher levels. The attitude of production managers seemed to be that the budget is something that can get you into trouble (e.g., if you underestimate requirements) but not a planning tool of any use to them directly, nor a stimulus to detailed cost–benefit studies of requirements.

(5) *Limitations of Administrative Initiative.* The value of administrative initiative depends on the cost of mistakes. Some administrative systems are set up primarily to *avoid mistakes* (the criminal court system is supposed to be set up this way). Others are set up to *achieve success*, and would not fire a man for his mistakes if they are more than balanced by his successes. Obviously, court systems need to discourage initiative and innovation on the part of lower court judges, because most such initiatives will be mistakes. Obviously, it would be fatal to try to run a factory with the majestic delays of the court. But one must realize that most initiatives fail, for one reason or another, and that when the cost of failure is very high, caution needs to be applied with regard to implementation of initiatives. One cannot let every foreman experiment with a blast furnace to see if he can get it to work better.

The Mix of Administrative Strategies

The overall efficiency of an industrial administration will be determined by the accuracy with which it locates those causes of high productivity that can be operated on most easily and cheaply. The likelihood of high efficiency depends, in the first place, on whether the scarce resources of administrative attention and energy are focused on those causes which in fact determine productivity. In the second place, it depends on whether administrators can make a rational decision about how to modify the causes once their attention has been rationally focused. Thus, the adaptation of a set of strategies for focusing attention on the causal system that is really in operation is the first step in rational administration. The second step is to see that the analysis carried out is as nearly rational possible, and this involves competent personnel, adequate data with which to work, and sometimes the application on special techniques of rational decisions.

In general, the most rational administrative system will combine the attention-focusing strategies in some systematic manner. For instance, routine data collection on the main indexes of success in raising productivity are taken as *measures of performance* of production personnel by their superiors. Bad performanance on one or more of the indexes, or on the general index of costs of fabrication per ton, becomes a problem to the people responsible for that performance. This sets in operation the much more responsive "problems of subordinates" strategy of focusing attention within the shop. If subordinates do not pose the right problems, then the superintendent tends to be pushed toward requesting "studies" by staff departments or toward inducing higher management to bring in consultants. A complete study of an administrative system would have to include the rules of thumb by which people decide when to switch basic strategies for focusing attention, and the frequencies with which problems cause such switches to go one way or another. One of the fundamental functions of the authority and status systems of organizations is to provide such a switching system among strategies for focusing attention.

The Meaning of the Example

The purpose of introducing this example is primarily to destroy two common misconceptions. The first is that routine administration and innovation are radically distinct—that they answer different problems and are treated by different administrative principles. The problem we have analyzed is an ideal—typical routine problem: to keep the production line running. That it is not routine, in fact, is shown by the failure of the best efforts of very good men to solve this problem more than 35% of the time. In order to solve it, industrial administrators must search for major and minor innovations that will give them better control over some of the causes of successful routine production. Thus, when we study innovative behavior in what follows, we are studying the solution of the problem of making the plant run at all. *Only by innovation can the routine problems of producing steel pipe be solved.* To apply the routine procedures of the Traffic Inspector would be to fail to solve the routine problems of industry.

The second misconception is that "policy" and "administration" are different sorts of things. We will range in this book from the political situation of industry as a whole to how often a man reports on his performance to his superior. What ties these apparently disparate things together is their impact on the overall functioning systems of human action, such as that previously described. The description ties together the different actions by their common *technical* impact. The technical details are not important for the sociology that follows. What is important is the vision of how basic policy decisions (e.g., from what country to buy capital equipment, and hence repair parts) and small administrative details (e.g., how closely the maintenance department estimates how many repair parts will be needed) intertwine in reality.

An implicit product of the analysis of the example is an outline of the set of problems generated by an interdependent technical system. By viewing the problem of industrial administration as one of finding and acting on the causes of low productivity, we have located a set of structural and functional aspects of administrative organization, whose quality will determine industrial productivity. If we were to ask an "entrepreneur" of the classical theory of economic development to set up a system of organizational arrangements of human actions that could run a production line efficiently, the outline of administrative requirements would be a description of his role responsibilities. Figure 1.1 and Table 1.1 provide a summary of what we have said such an entrepreneur must do.

Figure 1.1 gives an overall picture of what such an administrative system must do. The core of the system is the technology (Box 1), the causal system to be manipulated. The causes are the causes of high productivity. The first thing the "entrepreneur" must set up is a system for monitoring and coding information on this causal system in terms of what actions are likely to have to be taken (Box 2). This system must correspond to the strategies of focusing attention and making decisions in common use in the system. Then he must set up a structure for focusing attention on the problems identified in that information (Box 3). This administrative analysis system must then be hooked to the authority system that can carry the proposed solutions into effect (Box 4). These decisions and actions then result in the manipulation of the technical system.

Table 1.1 specifies the elements that go in each of the boxes of Figure 1.1 for the administrative system for reducing delays on the hot rolling line of the tube mill at Matanzas. It differs from the picture presented in the preceding text by

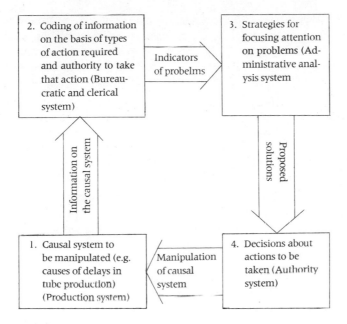

Figure 1.1 *Overall Structure of Production Administrative Feedback Systems*

extracting from the discussions of technology, information, and attention-focusing some of the related elements of the authority system (Part IV).

The Problem of This Book

How can a government and society that produces the traffic inspector of San Felix produce an administrative system that can reduce delays in a pipe mill? It seems to me that this is the central question of economic development, for the line will not run at all with the traditional governmental administration. The *Inspectoría* in San Felix does not compete with the Department of Motor Vehicles in Glen Burnie, Maryland (where I renewed my license by mail while the events I previously described were taking place). But the steel plant in the Venezuelan Guayana does compete with the steel plant at Sparrow's Point, Maryland. It is probably most irritating to Venezuelans to pay $20 for the idiotic process that results in the receipt of a driver's license, but there is no doubt that the job will get done, somehow. There is real doubt that the job of industrialization will get done. Yet, the Venezuelans were in fact running an administrative system in the steel mills that did fairly well in minimizing delays on the seamless

TABLE 1.1

Some Elements of the Boxes in Figure 1.1 as Manifested in the Tube Mill at Matanzas, Venezuela

---

  I. *Elements of the Technical Causal System as Related to Delays*
    A. Design
      1. Which product—overall design
      2. Large modifications
      3. Small modifications
    B. Maintenance
      1. Preventive
      2. Emergency
    C. Scheduling
      1. Daily
      2. Product mix—long term
    D. Personnel
      1. Quality
      2. Quantity, scheduling

  II. *Elements of the Coding System of Delays*
    A. As Cost
    B. As Responsibility
    C. By machine and motive system
    D. As ordering unit for purchases
      1. Parts
      2. Capital
    E. As manning requirement

 III. *Ways of Structuring Attention*
    A. Routine data collection
    B. Problems of subordinates
    C. Studies
    D. Outside comparisons, experts and books
    E. Periodic decision requirements
    F. Administrative initiative

 IV. *Authority System*
    A. Hierarchical division of decision by size of investment
    B. Functional specialization by type of action to be taken
    C. Line structure of subordination—supervision
    D. Staff structures of specialists in innovations
    E. Authoritative organization of information systems (e.g., accounting, quality control)

---

tube line. The problem of this book is to explore the social factors that determine how well such industrial administrative problems are solved.

To repeat how I propose to do this, I will apply an intellectual strategy first used to study economic efficiency by Max Weber in his studies of the origins of "rational bourgeois capitalism." What Weber did (for instance, in *The Pro-*

testant Ethic and the Spirit of Capitalism) was to break the problem into two parts. First, he outlined a set of behavior patterns in economic life which *would result* in economic activity being highly rational. He adopted this model mainly from classical economics. For instance, costs and returns of an economic activity have to be calculated in money terms, or else the firm will choose to do things which are "unprofitable" from the point of view of the market. Or, workers must obey the decisions taken by an entrepreneur on economic grounds, whether or not the entrepreneur is a traditional lord. These component behaviors of a capitalist— rational economy then become dependent variables to be explained.

The second part of the analysis consists of locating the causes in the social structure of the variations in these dependent variables. For instance, as long as the calculation of money returns was considered to be money grubbing and not fit for an honorable man to do, it was very difficult to obtain both commercial integrity and also careful calculation. Protestant theology and sect organization were, according to Weber's argument, causes of variation in the degree to which calculation in money terms could legitimately be carried out by honorable men; sects did this mainly by giving social status to worldly "callings." Calculation of the cost of labor in money terms, and the passage of authority to successful innovators were both facilitated by the development of "formally free labor," whereby the worker did not have tenure in his job (as the typical peasant, for instance, did) and the master did not own the workers (as slave owners did).

That is, Weber's fundamental innovation was to conceive of the *degree of rationality* of economic life as a variable. Where classical economists assumed . men were rational, and most of the critics of these assumptions pointed to love, hate, and ignorance as part of the human condition, Weber observed that men are more rational under some circumstances than under others. If we wanted to understand the radical increase in economic efficiency during the industrial revolution, we had to study the social determinants of the degree of economic rationality.

Two other innovations followed from this fundamental one—and allowed this abstract scheme to be specified with enough empirical content so that Weber was to become the founding father of the sociological theory of economic development. The first of these innovations was to borrow from the classical economists the conception of rationality as a *property of a system*, rather than primarily a property of individual psychology. The crucial point is not that men should not hate, love, or be ignorant, but rather that there should be structural and normative devices to isolate economic action from these influences. The specification of the conditions of economic rationality thus becomes an aspect of the social structure of economic administration.

The second innovation was the description of ideal types of social structures, such as bureaucratic administration of the firm, which maximize one or another aspect of this structural rationality. Bureaucracy, for instance, maximizes *discipline*, the degree to which actions taken by subordinates are determined by the decisions of the entrepreneur. The component variables of the ideal type concept of bureaucracy are chosen in such a way that the greater the degree of their presence, the more disciplined the action of the organization.

Our first problem, then, is to specify the features of administrative behavior and structure that result in efficient industrial administration. Our second is to take these variables, rather than efficiency as such, as the dependent variables and explore their social sources.[5]

The Cognitive Component of Administrative Rationality

Clearly one aspect of administrative rationality is to have a "correct" diagnosis of the causal system to be manipulated. All the motivation to produce steel pipe will be of little avail if the system cannot predict correctly which repair parts will be needed in what quantities at what time, or if a furnace is so designed that once a bent pipe gets into it, the furnace has to be cooled and dismantled to get it out. What can we say in a general way about the nature of this cognitive problem?

The most important feature of this problem in that it is constantly changing. In the United States, for example, technical change results in increases of productivity of around 3% per year on the average. This means that in the ordinary course of events, a productive process that does not change will be about 75% as efficient as it could be after 10 years, or about 56% as efficient as it could be after 20 years, even if it started at the most advanced level of technology. In most underdeveloped countries, it will not have started at the highest level of efficiency, but at a considerably lower level than that found in more advanced countries.

This implies that rationality in manipulating a technical system cannot be achieved without constant and substantial innovation. The rate of innovation necessary in poorer countries, if they are to hope to compete with more advanced countries, has to be even higher. As with all technical innovation, the main part will be borrowed from elsewhere. Technical innovations, if they are very substantial, usually have to be made only once.

The very substantial effects of technical stagnation even for a decade or two make the rate of innovation the key variable in the rationality of industrial administration. There is very little one can do which will improve the efficiency

5. There is, of course, the risk that we will choose the wrong variables. In that case, this book will be a more or less interesting study of behavior in economic life with little relevance to economic development. The crucial parts of the logical structure of the book are, therefore, the theoretical chapters of each section, Chapters 2, 5, and 7.

of an administrative system as much as keeping up with the development of worldwide technical culture. The other cognitive problems of running the enterprise also have to be solved, of course, but the key factor in the cognitive rationality of an industrial administrative system is that set of processes which determines the rate of innovation. The fundamental characteristic of a rational industrial administration is that it innovates constantly, usually by borrowing.

Usually the process of innovation has several separate elements. First, the problem to be solved comes to administrative attention either through routine data collection, because it is a problem within someone's responsibility, through a special study, or in some other way. Usually, at the same time, the general nature of the solution is anticipated. (In fact, many things are seen as "problems" for the first time when somebody becomes convinced that there is a solution. One of the reasons that staff departments are organized according to the nature of the solutions they are competent to propose and analyze is that such specialized departments see the problems to which their solutions are relevant.) A proposed innovation is planned and developed, specified in such a way that it fits the concrete situation. Depending on how substantial the investment and reorganization implied by the innovation, there is a more or less detailed evaluation in terms of costs and returns, and a final decision is made. Then, the introduction of the innovation has to be carried out, and the bugs taken out of it by minor "adjustive" innovations.

For most technical innovations of any complexity, each of these stages involves a common type of cognitive behavior—more or less systematic thinking about systematically collected data. Consequently, the behavior patterns whose social sources we need to locate are systematic thinking and data collection related to innovation. In the usual case, much of the information about possible innovations will come from outside the organization, so a crucial aspect of this process will be contact with outside sources of ideas and information. Part II of this book is directed to the analysis of the sociology of thinking and data collection in economic life. We will be especially concerned with the *quantity* of thinking about innovations that goes on in different structures and different roles, filled by different types of men.

The Motivational Component of Administrative Rationality

It is clear that the Inspector of Traffic in San Felix could not possibly do his job so badly if he were trying to do it well. Thus, besides making a correct diagnosis of what is ailing a system, administrations need to put effort into the cure. Consequently, we want to know the social sources of administrative effort.

The ideal type of capitalism, presented in microeconomic theory, involves the assumption that the entrepreneur either makes all the crucial economic decisions himself or specifies the criteria by which his subordinates make the decisions. This is where the motivational energy to run a capitalist economy is supposed to come from. Yet in advanced capitalist societies, the entrepreneur is a committee that does not itself collect most of the profits (in most enterprises), and production decisions are not usually made by the committee in any case. In government enterprises, including two of the steel plants we shall be studying here and formerly including the third before it was sold to private interests, this capitalist notion of motivational energy is even more appropriate. There is, of course, no inherent reason that the voters should have any more difficulty motivating efficiency in the directors of socialist enterprises than the stockholders have in motivating the board of directors in private corporations. Nor is there any inherent reason the mechanisms of control which a socialist directorate holds over the men who actually make production decisions should be any less effective than those held by a private directorate.

A clue to the source of motivational energy in industrial administration was given by Weber. Weber noted that industrialization depended on the bureaucratic administration of production, the arrangement of administrative tasks into roles for a set of officials arranged hierarchically. Then in his general discussions of bureaucracy, he suggested two structural provisions which tended to secure the motivation for the performance of these roles. These were the temporal organization of these hierarchical roles (so that they formed a *career* for a given man) and the differentiation of rewards received in bureaucratic roles from all rewards claimed on any other basis. Payment in money, full-time occupancy of the role of officials, the elimination of kinship in recruitment and promotion, etc., all serve to separate claims on the administration from all claims based on grounds other than performance. The organization of hierarchically ordered roles into career sequences serves other functions besides motivation—for instance, it provides more experienced men in positions of authority. The differentiation of rewards also does things besides allowing the reward system to be based purely on performance. For instance, it keeps officials from the temptation to introduce nonorganizational considerations into their organizational decisions. But clearly one function of both these arrangements is to provide career rewards for officials and to allow the organization to make these dependent on the level of performance of organizational duties.

From the point of view of the individual, the career organization of roles in a bureaucracy appears as a life plan in which he expects to get future reward for good performance and for improving his competence. The psychological dimensions corresponding to Weber's structural specifications are that, first, he should expect to have higher status in the future, and second, he should expect that status to depend on his performance and competence, rather than on kinship, political, moral, or other irrelevant grounds. Since our primary concern here is the source of motivational energy, we will concentrate on men's subjective view of their prospects and on their perceptions of the criteria on which their careers depend. We will expect men's motivation to do their job well to depend on whether they think there are rewards in prospect for them and on whether they think those rewards will depend on their merit.

Politics and Administrative Structure

Our basic assumption in the fourth part of this book is that the preference for the truth and the desire to do a job well are precarious and weak motivations, easily undermined if not isolated from sources of cognitive prejudice or alternative rewards. The arrangement of the social order so that such weak motivations govern men's thoughts and actions in a job is a delicate matter. What are the social structures in which the rare phenomenon of collective social action guided by reason and calculation can happen fairly frequently? (This is one way of formulating the problem that Weber treated in most of his work.) Many of the structural features of industrial administration depend on the larger social structure in which they are embedded. In poorer countries at the present time they depend, in particular, on the structure and orientation of governments, which are generally responsible both for the legal and financial creation of large-scale enterprises and also for shaping the labor market institutions (schools, trade unions, pensions, the structure of seniority rights, etc.) which guide the construction of the status system of organizations.

Notions about what sorts of status systems are just and what the rights of various men ought to be, are the focus of modern political conflict. The growth of large organizations inevitably brings up the political problem of defining the rights and obligations of new roles, those of administrators and workers. The new middle class of administrators bears a different relation to the received legal order for determining the political status of social classes than does the petty bourgeois middle class, for that received order is mainly directed to the distribution of property rights. The workers bear a different relation to the received regulation of status because their rights and duties are specified by powerful bureaucracies rather than individual lords and because their conditions of work facilitate political and trade union organization.

The fate of the status order within industrial administration depends in great measure on the fate of the claims of social classes in the political order. And the fate of the political order depends in considerable degree on the political energies generated by the growth of industrial bureaucracies.

The Marxists have argued for several generations about what it means for political life, that the men who bear authority in industrial matters are no longer related to the political system directly through property institutions but rather through the labor contract. Their answers range from the proposition that industrial administrators become essentially proletarians, with the same interest in attacking the institutions of property as other proletarians, to the proposition that they are merely paid lackeys of property interests.

The non-Marxist arguments on the same question generally turn around the question of the relative importance of high status versus economic interest in the determination of political attitudes. American sociologists argue that the existing political order tends to guarantee all types of high status, and that therefore any kind of high status, bureaucratic or property, tends to produce conservatism. Further, men of high status have many things to make them happy—autonomy and discretion in their work, big incomes, prestige, a sense of participation in determining their own conditions of life. Workers, on the other hand, have the reverse of these things that make men happy, and by Pascal's principle that men with a pain in their bowels go out to change the world, they oppose the present political order.

But there are reasons to think that the status-leads-to-conservatism formulation of the problem misses the central dynamics of the politics of modernization. Trotsky has suggested that the political problems of modernization depend on the nature of the preexisting political and social order, and that the introduction of modern economic management into a reactionary order creates special tensions in the political system. We can think of this as follows. Modernization always involves the political order in the following problems:

1. The political incorporation of the industrial and urban working class and their organizations into the policy-making apparatus of the state. This is because industrial workers can organize and are encouraged to organize by their conditions of work and by the universalism of the status system of the factory. The larger the enterprises, the more acute this pressure is for incorporation.
2. The problem of national economic policy—of protection for industries, of fiscal policy, of backing for the currency—and the execution of the necessary activities for following such a national policy throughout the country.
3. Intervention on the local scene, into businesses and local politics, to enforce political decisions about the status order—especially rights of organization of workers, rights of citizenship, rights to social security, and obligations to the tax authorities.
4. The encouragement of specific activities, industrial and commercial, thought to be critical for the success of overall economic policies.

All of these problems involve the nationalization and politicalization of local enterprise status systems. They all involve the responsiveness and regulation of individual activities by socially established standards. They involve the growth of politically defended rights that are not property rights. They involve the organization of interest groups to affect political policy, and also of bureaucracies to intervene in local systems of activity.

This nationalization, reorientation, and reorganization of political activity may be opposed by groups in the population with orientations and interests incompatible with it. The institutions of social security, trade union recognition, progressive taxation, universal suffrage, and government regulation of business may come tardily and weakly after a great deal of violent opposition (as in Czarist Russia), or they may come early and strongly, as they typically have done in the socialist countries, both democratic and dictatorial.

Many of these issues have an overtone of equalization and leftism about them, but many of them do not. There is, for example, very little evidence that the system of social security in the United States equalizes incomes among the social classes (though, of course, it equalizes incomes somewhat among different age groups).[6] Yet, conflicts about social security played a central role in some rather bitter class political struggles in the United States. What was being struggled over was not so much equalization as reorganization of the stratification system by the government, by bureaucratic intervention. This conflict ranged the party of property against the party of the workers, although it had to do with the bureaucratization of status systems more than with the redistribution of income.

In short, it seems that because property holders have been associated with certain views about the proper organization of society, both Marxists and non-Marxists have been deceived into thinking that the motor of the political conflict was a division of interests. What we hope to do is to analyze the attitudes of the new and old middle classes on those questions crucial for the reorganization of traditional politics into modern bureaucratic politics. For the reorganization of politics is at least an apparently inevitable concomitant of industrialization, and this reorganization is probably a requirement for political peace in a society where men work mainly in bureaucracies. On the questions of reorganization of national political life into more modern forms, the new middle classes of our sample have a much more favorable attitude than the old petty bourgeoisie.

The Sources of Evidence

Most of the evidence presented in this book was collected by Rene Marder and myself during a year and a summer of fieldwork in three South American countries: Chile, Argentina, and Venezuela. The basic object of the study was to obtain firm data for a systematic comparison of the cognitive, motivational, and political life of industrial bureaucracy with the life of nonbureaucratic

6. For example, see Harold L. Wilensky and Charles N. Lebeaux, *Industrial Society and Social Welfare*. New York: The Free Press, 1965, especially pp. 158–160. The industrial society referred to in this book is the United States.

middle-class economic organizations. To do this, we combined a random sample of people living in middle-class housing in the cities near three steel plants with a stratified sample of middle-class industrial administrators. The samples were constructed in as nearly identical a fashion as we could manage in the three countries.

Each of the three sites of investigation was selected because it had a steel plant as a major part of its industrial base. These steel plants were of approximately the same size, with about 5000 workers, and all were involved in the processing of steel from ore to finished and semifinished products. This comparability of the plants, together with the comparability of the structure of the sample, was designed to let us compare the three countries. We hoped to be able to sort out those features of the industrial social structure which changed with variations in national culture and social structure.

The sample in the steel plant was stratified in such a way as to oversample substantially the top executives, and consequently, to undersample lower-level clerical and administrative employees. Thus, in the sample as a whole, we have very substantially oversampled industrial bureaucratic employees, and oversampled the top executives even more. We have included those industrial employees who turned up in the random sample together with the industrial employees from the special steel plant sample.

Each individual selected was interviewed with an interview schedule. He was generally given the printed version of the schedule so that he could follow the questions as they were asked. Since most of the interviewing was done by professional sociologists, the results may be influenced more than usual by our preconceptions of what we would find. Nonprofessional interviewers would not be likely to bring to their work many preconceptions about the effects of career organization or about the politics of modernization, whereas we obviously did. We did not have the preconceptions of interviewers to set against and cancel out our own theoretical presuppositions. This also means that we found out many things in the interviews that we would not have found out otherwise.

Because the objective of the study was to study the impact of social forces on the activities that make up middle-class occupational life, we made some special modifications of survey technology to handle reports of activities. The data on time spent in different types of activities during a day's work rest on a modification of the time-budget technique, of asking people what they did during each hour of the day. We ran into many problems of interviewing and analysis with these data which were unfamiliar to us. From a comparison of the results of this process with our observations of activities in the same administrative structures, I would judge that they bear approximately the same relation to the "reality" of activities as attitude questions of the agree—disagree type bear to the "reality" of men's psychological predispositions. The relation is not too close, but it is close enough to locate aggregate patterns.

The rate of nonresponse was higher when we interviewed in the home, as we did for all the nonindustrial middle-class people and the industrial administrators in Argentina. Our aim was to have about 75 people from the middle-class males of the steel plants in each country, and 75 middle-class male heads of households from middle-class housing. Our achievements after some difficulties and ad hoc adjustments were 136 interviews in Chile, 142 in Argentina, and 124 in Venezuela, for a total sample of 402 interviews. Details are presented in the Appendix on Method, along with various arguments about the methodological procedures followed.

PART II

Cognition and Bureaucratic Structure

CHAPTER **2**

Written and Oral Social Systems—
Cosmopolitanism and Localism

Modernism and Intellectual Life

Max Weber conceived of modernization as being dominated by the "rationalization" of social life. By "rationalization" he meant the application of *systematized intelligence*, or *intellectually organized doctrine*, to the regulation of social activity. The rationalization of religious traditions involves the systematic intellectual organization of theology, and the guiding of religious practice by that theology. The rationalization of law involves systematizing legal doctrine and governing legal decisions by that doctrine. The rationalization of empirical lore into science involves its intellectual organization into a systematic conceptual structure, and the guiding of experiments by theory. The rationalization of music involves systems of notation, theories and standards of harmony, and increasing guidance of musical production by such systems and theory. The rationalization of economic life involves setting up systematic dictates or norms for efficient productive activity, and then governing factories or commerce by them. Weber emphasized, especially, the analysis of activities in terms of money and the control of such activities in terms of financial accounts.[1]

1. On law, see Max Weber, *Law in Economy and Society*. Cambridge, Massachusetts: Harvard University Press, 1954, especially pp. 198–223. On science, "Science as a Vocation," in H. H. Gerth and C. Wright Mills (Eds.), *From Max Weber: Essays in Sociology*. New York: Oxford University Press, 1946, pp. 138–142. On music, "Die rationalen und soziologischen Grundlagen der Musik," in *Wirtschaft und Gesellschaft*. Tubingen: J. C. B. Mohr, Paul Siebeck, 1956, pp. 877–923. On economy, in Frank H. Knight, *General Economic History*. New York: Greenberg, 1927, pp. 343–370.

Thus, the distinctive features of modern life derive from the fact that a large share of social activity is governed by bodies of systematic abstract doctrine. This doctrinal or theoretical component of social action is generally developed, systematized, and tested by a group of specialists in doctrines: scholars, men of science, theologians, writers of legal textbooks, literary critics, political theorists, newspaper commentators, military general staffs, and the like. Such specialists in doctrine usually have ultimate control over the content of the educational system. They teach the teachers of teachers.

The government of activities by doctrines is the primary function of bureaucracy. The foundation of the dominance of professions in modern society is competence in a specialized body of abstract knowledge, systematized and taught by scholars in professional schools. Science, education, bureaucratic administration, the professions—these distinctive features of modern life are primarily concerned with developing, transmitting, and governing activities by bodies of systematized intelligence. The study of modernization is, therefore, in large measure the study of the social role of systematized intelligence and its application to daily affairs.

The observations of Weber, and of other scholars since, suggest that rationalization is intimately tied to reading and writing as forms of social intercourse. Scholarship and education, which become far more important with modernization, are distinctive in using writing for the major part of communication. We might almost take the definition of the word "scholar" to be "a man who writes about a specialized body of knowledge or doctrine." Weber defined "bureaucracy" as a system that keeps written files.[2]

Hence the sociology of reading and writing, and of written social interaction, is crucial to the study of modernization. Clearly, also, the people who routinely read and write, people in "middle-class" occupations, are a strategic group for any understanding of modernization.

Our purpose in this chapter is to outline a theory of the social psychology and sociology of written social interaction, particularly with respect to the adequacy of cognition. First, we will discuss the distinctive psychological features of written interaction. Then, we will examine the distinctive features of social systems with large components of written social interaction. Finally, we will discuss the differentiation of people in a given concrete system according to their degree of involvement in supralocal systems of interaction, which are generally written.

The reason we develop this theory here is that we will be studying the cognitive behavior of industrial bureaucrats as compared to other middle-class people in Chapters 3 and 4. We will be arguing that the distinctive features of cognition in the three steel plants derive in large measure from the different

2. For example, see H. H. Gerth and C. W. Mills (Eds.), *From Max Weber.* p. 197.

role of reading, writing, and calculation in these plants as compared to the administration of traditional economic activities. That is, to solve the sorts of technical problems outlined in the introduction requires an organized system of cognitive behavior in steel plants. We will be trying to show that the organization of this system depends on the adequacy of paper flows and of thought about written documents. In order to link the fact about the predominance of written interaction in bureaucracies to the central concern of the book, industrial efficiency, we need now to make a theoretical argument connecting written communications with cognitive effectiveness.

Written social interaction, as a social—psychological phenomenon, is distinguished from oral interaction by many characteristics deriving from the nature of writing. Written communications are generally more abstract, shorn of much expressive content, of status considerations except those relevant to action on the issue, and of irrelevant concrete detail. Writing preserves the cognitive elements of an interaction in immutable form, allowing its extension in time. Writing allows the construction of algorithms, or physical arrangements of the elements of a communication, so that aspects of a problem can be considered in a systematic order—the algorithms of mathematics and accounting are special cases. Written messages are portable, allowing interaction without spatial constraints. They do not interfere with each other, allowing for a greater variety of recipients and simultaneous interaction. Messages may be scanned, rewritten, or called back before being transmitted, favoring deliberation and checking of the message. Reinforcement on the basis of interaction is more likely to be deliberate and germane to the issue at hand.

If all this is so, we would expect that those who participate much in written communication will differ systematically from those who participate little. The main effect of this differentiation is to involve people in more extended social systems than their local concrete system—its effect is a "cosmopolitanizing" effect. We will argue that people who participate more in written interaction have more innovativeness, for the concrete features of local systems seem less inevitable and alternatives seem more psychologically real; greater abstractness of thought about the local system, isolating the essential causal and economic relations from the buzzing confusion of concrete reality; greater liberalism and tolerance of diverse opinions about the local scene; a clearer conception of the local system as manipulable and controllable, and hence an attitude of "instrumental activism"; and a greater tendency to judge people and issues by standards germane to the issue at hand—greater universalism and performance orientation.

Some Main Features of Written Social Interaction

Consider first why it is that most arithmetical and mathematical computations are carried out in writing, and why mathematics instruction depends so much on the blackboard. This is an illuminating case, because mathematics is an extreme case of abstract thinking and because computation and mathematical reasoning are central to the operation of industrial bureaucracies and form a core segment of the training of the engineers and accountants who run them.

The act of writing for answering a mathematics problem is an act of abstraction, pruning away the irrelevancies from a problem. Concrete machines, people and their emotions, emphases of the voice, status considerations, and the like, tend to disappear from the written formulation of a problem. In view of the limited capacity of the human mind, such abstraction is essential for computation. In addition, the tendency of perception to be influenced by irrelevancies is reduced by this process of abstraction. The great emphasis on numbers and mathematics in industrial administration is undoubtedly a device to enable administrators to treat the complex of concrete activities and people as an abstract system of causal and economic relations. Of course, the abstraction must preserve the essential features of the system if it is to be useful, just as is the case in setting up a mathematical problem for solution. Physical diagrams and cost statistics are probably the most important abstractions in industrial administration.

The act of writing preserves the elements of the problem in relatively immutable form, not as easily misperceived or misremembered as oral stimuli. The capacity to recall elements accurately enables one, in turn, to forget them while concentrating on something else. Writing allows one to think about one thing at a time.

Writing allows the construction of algorithms, methods of step-by-step calculation of complex problems, or systematic physical organization of the elements of thought. This takes advantage of the preservation of elements to enable one to carry out an orderly and systematic scanning of all elements to locate exactly the relevance of each and to specify the missing ones. The most important algorithm in industrial administration is probably double-entry bookkeeping, followed closely by mathematical algorithms in engineering and graphical algorithms used to analyze the time path of performance statistics.

The written version of a problem is portable without any change in the elements, and can be transferred to others with a low degree of error. Students can carry a mathematics problem home, and it will still be the same problem. Furthermore, the error of transfer can be rechecked by visual scanning by the originator of the problem. This allows much longer chains of communication without loss of information, and allows problems to be solved in different environments than those in which they originated.

Written communications do not interfere with each other, are not "noise" for other messages in the same system. This noise-free character of sets of written communications allows the same communications system to bring together more individuals on more different problems simultaneously, each going at his own speed and making his own mistakes. This means that written communication is much more selective in the recipients of information.

A message may be scanned, rewritten, considered for long periods of time (without the social burden of having a waiting listener), and then canceled after all. Each of these processes is much more difficult with oral communication. Inaccuracies or bad judgment in the "emission" of stimuli are much less common with written communication. A mathematics professor can check beforehand whether the problems have a solution, and the student can check his solution before turning it in.

The delay between emission of responses and reinforcement (reward or punishment for the communication) is longer with written communication. Further, for all these reasons, the reinforcement is far more likely to be for relevant, rather than irrelevant, aspects of the communication.

Social Systems with Written Components

The peculiarities of written interaction allow social systems to develop differently if they have written components than if they are entirely oral. One of the distinctive features of bureaucratic industrial administration, as we will see in detail in the following chapters, is a far greater reliance on written communications. We can perhaps understand the significance of this by considering what this means for systems of social interaction generally.

Let us consider a number of social systems which are distinguished by a large written component to see what their distinguishing features are: science and scholarship in contrast to lore; formal education in contrast to apprenticeship; modern law and contractual relationships in contrast to customary law and gentlemen's agreements; modern monetary and banking systems in contrast to barter systems; bureaucracy in contrast to prebureaucratic administrations; statistical control in authority systems in contrast to personal supervision; mass news media in contrast to rumor; the "great tradition" in peasant societies in contrast to the "little tradition;"[3] mail order retailers as compared to local retailers, and so forth.[4]

We must be careful not to exaggerate the differences. An educational system does not usually run exclusively on books. Instead, we deliberately put into the

---

3. See Robert Redfield, *The Little Community* and *Peasant Society and Culture*. Chicago: University of Chicago Press, 1960, Chapter IV of *Peasant Society* especially pp. 41–43. The "great tradition" is the body of high culture carried by elites, the "little tradition" is the body of folklore or popular culture carried by peasants.

4. Most of the above examples have been treated by Max Weber in various places under the general name of "rationalization." See Footnote 1.

system oral contact between teachers and students. Given that this is by far the most expensive component in the system, it must serve an important purpose or it would be eliminated.[5] Clearly, in all the systems mentioned, oral contacts play crucial roles. However, as long as this is kept in mind, the features which distinguish all the more written systems from all the more oral ones can be attributed largely to the distinctive features of written interaction.

Written systems are much less dependent on physical arrangements. The primary function of "rooms" (as compared to "space" not divided into rooms) is to isolate oral interactions from each other. The oral part of education cannot manage without the systematic allocation of rooms to it. Much written interaction needs only "space," as for instance desks in a library. Mass media are much less dependent on physical contact between people than are rumors; clerks processing written materials are more likely to work in large "spaces" than executives who must confer in "rooms." Contracts can tie together physically dispersed firms; international boundaries are crossed more cheaply by technical magazines than by consultants; mail order houses have national markets for much cheaper goods than do retailers depending on oral sales talks; "great traditions" tie together nations made up of distinct local "folk traditions," and so forth.

Written systems can provide a larger number of people with the same information at one time. This is perhaps clearest with the mass media and with mass education, but it is also true that cost accounts in a bureaucracy are more widely distributed than oral communications about technical difficulties, written laws are more easily administered uniformly throughout a nation, and prices or interest rates affect more people uniformly in a modern monetary system than in barter systems.

Written systems of interaction are less time-dependent than oral systems.

---

5. The more advanced the student, the more we do indeed eliminate such expensive interpersonal components. The main advantages of oral communication seem to be related to three features. First, the speed and inexpensiveness of oral communication, once people are in the same room, increase the chances of immediate feedback. Therefore, misunderstandings are more easily found, relevant aspects of the problem which one man has not noticed are more likely to be mentioned by another, and new ideas can be introduced before a man gets committed to a cognitive set by writing it down. Second, combined with immediacy of feedback, is the greater expressive content of the communication, and consequently its greater capacity to serve as a reinforcer of an action. It is easier to encourage or discourage someone in oral interaction. Third, and closely related to the second aspect, oral communications are definitely attached to concrete individuals, and consequently reinforcement of activity is always also reinforcement for interacting with a particular individual. Thus, oral social interaction is the main source of creation of social bonds and solidarity.

Perhaps this last feature explains why sociologists have concentrated on oral interaction, for many sociologists believe that systems of social action are mainly created by social bonds and social solidarity. But industrial plants are mainly created by mutual convenience and common relations to a productive purpose, rather than by solidarity. Consequently, the social psychology appropriate for explaining them will be different. In some ways, the advantages of oral communication are the reverse of the advantages of written communication, and they serve opposite social functions.

People can "emit" a communication which can be "received" years, or even centuries, later. This means, among other things, that groups with written communications are likely to have much longer "histories"—more of the past is available to influence current interaction. Laws and contracts can remain stable over longer periods of time, allowing a longer period for planning privileges and obligations. Accounts from the past can guide budgeting for the future. The total amount of information in the system can grow in a cumulative fashion, and still all be available. The long delays in producing books or educational materials become profitable (both intellectually and commercially) because they can be used to guide others' actions and thoughts over a longer period. Hopefully, a book produced at leisure is more reflective than an oral stimulus produced on the spot. In administrative systems data can be analyzed, reanalyzed, abstracted in a different way, and then reanalyzed again, without constantly referring back to the original source of data. In general, deliberation and calculation become more possible and fruitful, because the input of information does not decay in quality with time, and the output of analysis can govern future behavior for a longer time.

We have emphasized the advantages in extensiveness of systems with written components. But each of these characteristics of written social systems also allows them to be *more selective* and hence, *more specialized*. Because written interaction does not depend as much on physical arrangements, the recipient of a message may be selected, or select himself, on grounds other than physical convenience. Because masses of people can be reached cheaply, each message received tends to be cheaper to the recipient. Hence, he can select from a wider variety whatever is relevant to his problem. Because written messages do not decay as rapidly, relevant information or thought can reach a man when he needs it—when he is working on a problem to which it is relevant. Of course conversely, when everyone needs immediate information to react fast to an emergency, oral communication is much better. Compare the example in Chapter 1 of emergency versus preventive maintenance. Written communications therefore make the division of intellectual labor much more possible.

In an industrial bureaucracy, for example, the cost–benefit analysis for a potential innovation can be made in the controller's office, its physical arrangement considered in engineering, its manning requirements considered in industrial engineering, the scheduling and costing of purchases to carry it out decided in purchasing, and the impact on production scheduling of its installation minimized in production control. Furthermore, these intellectual operations can be scheduled in any order that seems strategic, funneled to the most competent man without disturbing that man's neighbors at each point, and crucial data may be rechecked at any point by direct investigation without holding up any of the many people involved.

This same sort of division of intellectual labor is perhaps even more marked in science and scholarship, in education, in the complicated cataloguing system of libraries as opposed to theaters. It also clearly distinguishes "great traditions" from "little traditions," modern law from customary law, and modern monetary systems from barter systems. In a modern bank, money has as many different "statuses" as the people of Newburyport, each handled by a specialist in that kind of money.

In intellectual life as well as economic life, the degree of division of labor is determined by the size of the market. The market for an idea or piece of information is expanded spatially, temporally, and in the number of its recipients through written communications.

Written systems are much more likely to be governed by considerations germane to the issue at hand. Personal likes and dislikes, irrelevant status considerations, irrelevant details of concrete situations, urgency, excitement, and the passions, generally, are much less likely to be built into cost accounting systems or engineering drawings than into oral communications. Much irrelevant information is communicated subliminally in oral communication, and the systematic control of a communication by its purpose is much more difficult. The abstractness and general germaneness of written communications, their greater deliberation, and the greater precision and discrimination of reinforcement by others, all tend to make the written part of status systems, for example, far more universalistic and performance oriented. A rough guide for the empirical researcher is to find the universalistic parts of the structure by examining the written status and reward system and the particularistic parts by examining oral interaction.

This has a number of important implications. First, commitments undertaken in writing are likely to be for specific performances rather than for generalized support. Strangers and people who distrust each other can far more often agree on specific exchanges of pay for performances than on what course of action they both favor overall. Second, it means that rewards and punishments can be allocated on grounds germane to the course of action, so that "learning" can make action more efficient rather than divert it. Third, each man's task is cognitively simpler, because he need not abstract the germane elements from the jumble of things that come through in an oral interview. Fourth, all the germane elements can be scanned by some systematic algorithm, because the scanning process does not have to adapt to a changing mix of irrelevancies.

Thus, bureaucratic administration is generally more "universalistic" than prebureaucratic administration, written law more universalistic than customary law, schools more than apprenticeships, science and scholarship more than lore, news more than rumor, and probably, generally, "great traditions" more than "little traditions." The universalism of modern monetary systems, and the way they corrode all "idyllic patriarchal relations," has been a topic of social commentary at least since early modern times.[6]

6. See Talcott Parsons, *The Social System.* Glencoe, Illinois: The Free Press, 1951, pp. 101–112.

Cosmopolitans and Locals

In many studies of local, concrete systems of interaction, we find a strong differentiation of the group according to their degree of involvement with larger systems. The people involved in larger systems behave in a systematically different way than those thoroughly embedded in the local system. They march to a more distant drum.

This differentiation has been located in street corner gangs,[7] in systems of community influence,[8] in Middle Eastern, Mexican, and Russian villages,[9] in colleges and universities,[10] in the diffusion of innovation in American rural life,[11] and in local medical communities,[12] in the American military establishment,[13] in the professional staffs of industrial bureaucracies,[14] in local community power systems,[15] in trade union bureaucracies,[16] in the Russian Bolshevik Party at the time of the Russian Revolution,[17] in international banking,[18] in

7. William F. Whyte, *Street Corner Society: The Social Structure of an Italian Slum.* Chicago. University of Chicago Press, 1961, pp. 12, 206—214, 259.

8. Robert K. Merton, "Patterns of Influence." In Paul Lazarsfeld and Frank Stanton (Eds.), *Communications Research. 1948—1949.* New York: Harper and Brothers, 1949, pp. 189—202.

9. Daniel Lerner and Lucille W. Pevsner, *The Passage of Traditional Society.* Glencoe, Illinois: The Free Press, 1958, especially pp. 23—28 on the chief and the grocer. John H. Kunkel, Economic Autonomy and Social Change in Mexican Villages. *Economic Development and Cultural Change,* **X**(1), 1961, pp 51—63. Leon Trotsky, *History of the Russian Revolution.* Ann Arbor: University of Michigan Press (Copyright 1932 by Simon and Schuster), Vol. III, pp. 19—22.

10. Paul F. Lazarsfeld and Wagner Thielens, Jr., *The Academic Mind.* Glencoe, Illinois: The Free Press, 1958, pp. 140—144, 262—265. Alvin W. Gouldner, Cosmopolitans and Locals: Towards an Analysis of Latent Social Roles. *Administrative Science Quarterly,* **II,** 1957—1958 281—306 and 444—480. Theodore Caplow and Reece J. McGee, *The Academic Market Place.* New York: Basic Books, 1958, pp. 182—208. William Garvey, *et al.,* American Psychological Association, Project on Scientific Information Exchange in Psychology, Reports (various publications from 1963 to 1966). Washington, D.C.: American Psychological Association.

11. Herbert F. Lionberger, *Adoption of New Ideas and Practices.* Ames, Iowa: Iowa State University Press, 1960.

12. James S. Coleman, Herbert Menzel, and Elihu Katz, Social Processes in Physicians' Adoption of a New Drug. *Journal of Chronic Diseases,* **9** (1), 1959, 1—19, especially graphs on pp. 6—7.

13. Morris Janowitz, *The Professional Soldier.* Glencoe, Illinois: The Free Press, 1960, pp. 150—172, Chapter 8, "The Elite Nucleus."

14. William Kornhauser and Warren Hagstrom, *Scientists in Industry.* Berkeley: University of California Press, 1962.

15. Robert O. Schulze, "The Bifurcation of Power in a Satelite City." In Morris Janowitz (Eds.), *Community Political Systems.* Glencoe, Illinois: The Free Press, 1951, pp. 19—73.

16. Harold L. Wilensky, *Intellectuals in Labor Unions.* Glencoe, Illinois: The Free Press, 1956, Chapter VII and pp. 205—208.

17. V. I. Lenin, "April Theses." In *Collected Works.* Moscow: Foreign Languages Publishers, 1960, Vol. 24, pp. 21—26.

18. Count Egon Caesar Corti, *The Rise of the House of Rothschild.* New York: Blue Ribbon Books, 1929, pp. 26—27.

ethnic and nationality groups.[19] That is, every social system is internally differentiated by the degree of "local embeddedness" of different people in it. It is convenient to adopt Merton's term (see Footnote 8) for this differentiation, and to speak of "cosmopolitans" and "locals."

By cosmopolitans, we mean people who are in contact with, attached to, or influenced by events and communications from outside the local, concrete system of social relations. It is not at all surprising to find that cosmopolitans travel more and that they are far more involved in systems of written communications than locals. They read more, write more, and migrate more. Their jobs are more often classified as "professional" or "intellectual," and if they do not have intellectual jobs, they are more likely to be intellectual leaders on the local scene. Often their local status is precarious for these reasons: Their migration more often involves them in ethnic minority status, their rejection of local verities and their concern with the welfare of outsiders make them locally disloyal, and their distinct cosmopolitan style of life and thought corrupts local standards. What can we expect, then, about the behavior of cosmopolitans in local social systems? We would expect any differences to be related to education, to migration history, to attachments outside the local system, and to current reading and writing behavior.

We expect cosmopolitans to be less likely to regard features of the local system as inevitable. Cosmopolitans will more often have seen, and been attached sentimentally to, other systems that work differently. They are more likely to have been exposed through reading to alternative ways of doing things. They have contacts to explore these alternatives once they become interested. Their sentimental and economic attachments to local structures are much less likely to be identified with local peculiarities, since their recruitment is more likely to have been on grounds germane to the goals of the enterprise, and since they have psychologically real opportunities of the same sort elsewhere. That is, cosmopolitans are far more likely to have been recruited universalistically. They are more likely to depend on their performance for continued attachment to the local system, since they do not have any ascriptive status in it. For all these reasons, we will expect cosmopolitans to be more intellectually and psychologically prepared to introduce innovations in a local system.

Thus we will expect first, *that innovative behavior will be more common among cosmopolitans*. This is so commonly accepted in science and scholarship as to be trivial: The great innovators in science are those who move on the national international scene; publication is ordinarily taken *sine die* as a measure of innovation; common myth has it that scholars recruited into local offices as

19. Arthur L. Stinchcombe, "Social Structure and Organizations." In James March (Ed.), *Handbook of Organizations*. Chicago: Rand McNally, 1964, pp. 185–191 and the literature cited there, especially Karl Deutsch, *Nationalism and Social Communication*. New York: Wiley, 1953.

deans or supervisors of undergraduate programs are those who fail in scientific innovation; scientific conventions, not intra-university seminars, are recognized as central scientific institutions. Likewise, it has been established that cosmopolitans, as defined by several of the criteria are more likely to innovate in agricultural practices,[20] and in medicine.[21] Janowitz has shown that responsiveness to shifts in the world political situation affect the policies advocated by those with experience in nonmilitary assignments, in embassies, etc. (cosmopolitans) more than they affect men with careers purely inside the military establishment, e.g., combat leaders (locals).[22] The German word for "metropolis" is *Weltstadt*, or "world city," which communicates much better than our word the cosmopolitan character of London, New York, Paris, Berlin or Tokyo. These *Weltstädte* are centers of fashion innovations, scientific progress, innovations in business,[23] literary production and artistic innovation, and of new political movements.[24] In the street corner gang studied by Whyte, it was Doc, the cosmopolitan with attachments outside the gang, who introduced the use of the settlement house, political activity, and other innovations into the life of the group.[25] The role of minority ethnic and religious migrants in introducing innovations in various societies has been documented in banking, cuisine, agriculture, industry, science, military practice, and so forth.[26]

A second feature produced partly by the cosmopolitan's detachment from the local system and his knowledge of others in a facility in abstracting the essential

20. Herbert F. Lionberger, *Ideas and Practices*.

21. James S. Coleman, *et al. Journal of Chronic Diseases*, **9** (1), 1959, 1—19.

22. Morris Janowitz, *The Professional Soldier*.

23. Raymond Vernon, *Metropolis 1985* Cambridge, Massachusetts: Harvard Univ. Press, 1960, pp. 68—78.

24. For instance Lenin, Trotsky, and Castro spent years in exile, developing the bases of their revolutionary movements in cosmopolitan centers: London, Zurich, New York, and Mexico, D.F. The role of Western-educated men in anticolonial political movements—a role so well known that documentation would be trivial—provides further evidence for the relation of political innovation to cosmopolitanism.

25. William F. Whyte, *Street Corner Society*, pp. 3—12.

26. Examples: the Jews in banking, cf. Count Corti, *House of Rothschild*; various American ethnic groups in American cuisine, cf. F. M. Farmer, *The Fannie Farmer Cookbook* (Boston: Little, Brown, 1965); the Italians in Argentine industry, cf. Thomas C. Cochran and Reuben E. Reina, *Entrepreneurship in Argentine Culture, Torcuato di Tella and SIAM* (Philadelphia: University of Pennsylvania, 1962), and Gino Germani, *Política y Sociedad en una Epoca de Transición* (Buenos Aires: Paidos, 1962); various European refugees in the development of American high energy physics, cf. Robert Jungk, *Brighter Than a Thousand Suns* (London: Victor Gollancz, Ltd. in association with R. Hart Davis, 1958); for military practice, aside from the role of German experts in American rocket development, see for instance Thomas B. Cochrane and H. R. Fox Bourne, *The Life of Thomas Lord Cochrane* (London: Richard Bentley, 1869), Vol. 1. Aristotle offers a more ancient example; born in Macedonia he had studied in half a dozen Aegean cities before he produced his philosophy. Most of his work was done in Athens where he "lived as an alien without political rights"; see Richard McKeon, *The Basic Works of Aristotle*. New York: Random House, 1941, pp. xiii—xvi.

features from irrelevant local detail. This is facilitated also because he more often writes to others about it, and hence abstracts for them, and has been trained to use various devices for abstraction (mathematics, accounting, mechanical drawing, etc.). Thus, we would expect to find cosmopolitans disproportionately represented in activities that depend on abstractions, e.g., science;[27] the handling of money and pieces of paper that stand for different kinds of money in banking, accounting, stockbroking; strategic planning as opposed to tactics in the military; and generally, the more theoretical, teaching branches of law, medicine, the clergy, and other professions.

Because they understand the alternatives, cosmopolitans are much more likely to conceive of the present concrete system as controllable or manipulable. They are therefore much more likely to believe that men can control their destinies in a particular local system. And also, since the supra-local system makes sense to them, they can conceive of manipulating it. This sense of mastery over the world and over one's fate is, in turn, crucial in learning. Seeman and others have shown in various experiments that men who believe that they can control things learn new material more rapidly.[28] This means that cosmopolitans are likely to be more active in trying to manipulate the environment, to learn more rapidly from the environment, and especially to be more active toward, and learn more from and about, the supralocal environment. Cosmopolitans have been shown to be more politically active,[29] to try out new strategies,[30] and generally to have that attitude or value which Parsons has called "instrumental activism."[31]

These effects of cosmopolitanism have been cognitive. But there are also extremely important attitudinal consequences. A cosmopolitan is far more likely than a local to know that people who act and believe differently from himself are really people, with human qualities and reasoning processes. Hence,

27. Thorstein Veblen, "The Intellectual Preeminence of Jews in Modern Europe." In Leon Ardgrooni (Ed.), *Essays in Our Changing Order*. New York: Viking Press, 1945, pp. 219–231.

28. Melvin Seeman, Alienation and Social Learning in a Reformatory. *The American Journal of Sociology*, **69**, 1963, 270–284; cf. James S. Coleman's results in *Equality of Educational Opportunity*. Washington, D.C.: United States Office of Education, 1966, Chapter 3.

29. Melvin Seeman, On the Meaning of Alienation. *The American Sociological Review*, **24**, 1959, 783–791; Herbert McCloskey and John H. Schaar, Psychological Dimensions of Anomie. *The American Sociological Review*, **30**, 1965, 14–40. Linda Mirin and Arthur L. Stinchcombe, "The Political Mobilization of Mexican Peasants" (unpublished manuscript); Karl Deutsch, *Nationalism*; Daniel Lerner, *et al.*, *Traditional Society*, pp. 54–64.

30. See the innovation literature cited previously.

31. Talcott Parsons, *Structure and Process in Modern Societies*. Glencoe, Illinois: The Free Press, 1960, pp. 172–173, 311. Parsons thinks this attitude or value is caused by religious belief or national culture, which seems to me a most unlikely hypothesis. Parsons' hypothesis is not well supported by our data, as there is no appreciable attitudinal difference between Catholics and Protestants in our sample.

he is more likely to be tolerant of diversity. For example, education, living in metropolitan areas, living in areas with large numbers of migrants, and community associational leadership, are all related to support for civil liberties for Communists in the United States. These same variables are also related to the probability of having known a self-proclaimed Communist.[32] The notion of education as a "broadening" experience has the same implications. Knowing that the backward ancient Greeks were often brilliant reasoning men, that Lenin had an argument that he believed, that Natasha could love Peter even if he were fat and ineffectual, all open the mind to the variety of human experience. And Lerner found in the Middle East that people who could read and write were able to imagine themselves in the social roles of others. For instance, literates could answer the question: What would you do if you were President? But illiterates would tend to say: But that's impossible.[33]

Since cosmopolitans are more likely to be engaged in written interaction, with its characteristic relevance to the matter at hand, and since their attitude toward social action is characterized by "instrumental activism," we will expect them usually to be more universalistic and performance oriented. Ordinarily, kinship, race, ethnicity, and disagreement on irrelevant matters will play less role in their judgments of people and affairs. In politics, they should be more oriented toward issues and less oriented toward personal characteristics of candidates than the general population. They are likely to be the chief supporters of universalistic innovations in organizational status systems such as psychometric tests, performance or cost measurements of executives or of professors, recruitment to higher levels from outside the organization, and the like. Since they are more often recruited to local systems on universalistic-performance grounds, their interests lead them to support the more universalistic parts of the status system. They are more likely to believe that a man's knowledge of abstract causal and economic relations is more important than his acquaintance with local details and personnel. We thus come to the ironic proposition that an attachment to the outside can provide the chief support for disciplined achievement of the goals of local systems.

Innovativeness, facility with abstractions, liberalism, instrumental activism, and universalism—these tend to be produced by a cosmopolitan style of life, cosmopolitan social attachments, and that facility in written interaction which is a usual basis for cosmopolitanism. But beyond this, it would be difficult to find a better description of the traits necessary to industrial entrepreneurs. If these relations are at all strong, the role of cosmopolitanism in entrepreneurial activity will be very important.

32. Samuel A. Stouffer, *Communism, Conformity and Civil Liberties*. Garden City, New York: Doubleday, 1955, pp. 25–57, especially p. 51 for leaders; for education p. 93. See pages 175–185 for variables related to having known a Communist.
33. Daniel Lerner *et al. Traditional Society*, p. 24.

Recapitulation of the Argument of This Chapter

If the analysis in Chapter 1 about the contrast in administrative problems between modern industrial management and traditional economic activities is correct, then the dominant role of written interaction in steel plants cannot be explained merely by the fact that they are big. Only with written systems of interaction can we expect the complex problems of interdependent production to receive cognitively adequate solutions. The functional necessity of a system of written social interaction explains the common "bureaucratic" features that we find in the steel industry everywhere in the world.

To understand the central phenomenon of industrial bureaucracy, we have to study the social psychology of reading and writing in industrial administration. Hierarchical authority, often taken as the cornerstone of bureaucratic administration, will not make the plant go. The sociology of adequate cognition *by a social system*, that is, by the administration *as a whole*, is the central problem before us. Except for Weber's treatment of "rationalization," there has been very little theoretical study of the adequacy of cognition of a social system. This is probably because cognition has been erroneously conceived of as an individual process.[34]

By the "adequacy of cognition" of a system, we mean adequacy in the diagnosis of difficulties, adequacy in collecting and using data for the control of economic activity, adequacy of the evaluation of alternative proposals, adequacy of the search for alternatives, adequacy of focus on the essential aspects of a problem rather than irrelevancies, etc. *Our argument claims that such cognitive adequacy of a social system depends on its use of written social interaction. This independence has three main components: the cognitive advantages of written interaction as such, the systemic advantages of social systems with written components, and the cognitive advantages of the kind of people (cosmopolitans) who engage in supra local written communication.* Or to put it another way, written communication has advantages for adequate cognition on the cultural level (in the content of written social interaction), on the social system level (in the organization of cognitive effort that it facilitates), and on the personality level (in the orientations toward the world it induces in its participants).

The analysis of entrepreneurship in a bureaucracy, and probably entrepreneurship generally, must concentrate on the analysis of written social interaction: on reading, writing, studying, calculating, drawing, and planning. Analysis of such written interaction has been largely ignored in sociological writing except in the more empiricist branches (public opinion analysis, especially), because in spite of its tremendous influence on systems of social action, it has not been built into the theoretical structure of the social pyschology we have usually used. We have concentrated on the "informal" (i.e., oral) aspects of organizations rather

34. Max Weber, works cited in Footnote 1.

than the "formal" (i.e., largely written) aspects. Men never sit down to figure things out about pieces of paper in our sociology of organizations.

Appendix

SOCIALIZATION VERSUS EDUCATION—
THE CREATIVE PERSONALITY VERSUS
THE CREATIVE SOCIAL ROLE

Innovativeness, abstraction, liberalism, instrumental activism, and universalism sound very much like the character traits associated with "creative personalities."[35] Entrepreneurship has been attributed to "creative personalities," traced to socialization of a type that would not produce the opposite, "authoritarian personalities."[36] Our emphasis on written interaction, on migration, and on education as the creators of these behavior characteristics seems to challenge the evidence on personality types from the relevant literature.[37] It will be useful to discuss more fully the issues involved here.

First, the personality literature may be conceived of as being directed to two separate questions: (1) Which of the people in a local group will be more likely to be "creative personalities"? (2) How many "creative personalities" are there likely to be in a given group? To these we can add a third question: (3) How adequately does the number of "creative personalities" predict the amount of creative activity within the group?

For instance, if we are studying scientific innovativeness, we can observe that: (1) Some kinds of people, from certain backgrounds, are more likely to be creative scientists; (2) *Perhaps*, the higher the number of these kinds of people in a population, the more creative scientists there will be; and (3) Most scientific innovations are made by people paid a salary to make them, while "creative personalities" who are not professional scientists make very few. For instance, first-born sons are more likely to be creative scientists. With the decline in family size, there have been more first-born sons recently than a century ago, and perhaps this has facilitated the growth of science. But first-born sons outside the scientific professions do very little creative scientific work; it therefore seems

35. See, for instance, the literature cited by Everett Hagen, *On the Theory of Social Change*. Homewood, Illinois: Dorsey Press, 1962.
36. Everett Hagen, *ibid.*
37. Besides the literature cited above, see Milton Rokeach, *The Open and Closed Mind*. New York: Basic Books, 1960; Herbert McCloskey and John H. Schaar, *American Sociological Review*, **30**, 1965, 14–40, and numerous studies of the "authoritarian personality."

likely that the growth of scientific professions rather than the increase in the proportion of all men who are first-born sons explains the historical development of creativity.

If we wish to test whether some personality or background variables aid in success in a role, it would be appropriate to study the covariation between personality characteristics and innovative behavior among individuals. If we wish to test the second hypothesis, that a larger number of appropriate personalities cause a higher rate of innovation, we should study rates or means of personality characteristics in a population as related to rates or means of innovation. If we wish to test the third hypothesis, that people make innovations because they are paid to, it would be appropriate to use the relation of individuals to a relevant social structure as an independent variable from which to predict their innovative behavior, or to relate aggregate rates of such structural conditions (e.g. the number of professional scientists) to aggregate innovative behavior. Each of these research operations is logically and practically autonomous, and they can all have positive, zero, or negative results independently of how the others come out.[38]

Further, there is considerable doubt about what the cause of adult "personality" variations are. It seems very unlikely that, say, 20 years of exposure to interaction in classrooms, with textbooks, examinations, and papers as the principal incidents of interaction, would not affect people's permanent "personality dispositions." In classrooms they are treated with considerable universalism and performance orientation, with considerable "fairness." Fair treatment affects personalities. In education, in addition, a variety of strange types of people, Napoleons and Newtons, James Joyces and G. B. Shaws, become "introjected" as ego-ideals. In schools men choose visions of their personal future, especially in occupational life, in quite a different fashion than they choose a vision of what it means to be a father in the family. These school-based visions govern their disciplining of impulses by "reality," especially during

---

38. Many people of a psychological bent do not see how the individual and aggregate results can go in different directions. Perhaps a clear example would be the following. Consider a town with a given stock of housing. Within that town, richer people live in better houses. A sudden shutting down of the main factory in town may drastically reduce everyone's income, but still leave the relatively better-off people in the better houses. In this case, a correlation at the individual level between wealth and housing would not predict, over the short run at least, what would happen to housing if the aggregate level of wealth decreased. Similarly, paying more people a salary for making scientific innovations may increase the aggregate level of innovations, even though more creative people always go into science and even though the proportion of creative people remains the same or declines. Conversely, shutting down universities would decrease the rate of innovation, even if creative people become more numerous.

the working day.[39] That is, even if personality explains innovativeness, education rather than family life may explain personality.

Clearly, insofar as education has an effect on "personality," we would expect it to be in the direction of innovativeness, abstraction, liberalism, instrumental activism, and universalism. We would also expect education to qualify and incline people to participate in written interaction, which in turn should produce such patterns of behavior. All this is not surprising, because education is exactly one form of written interaction system. We would expect education to have the same effect on behavior as does post-educational written interaction. Hence, from a theoretical point of view, the effects of education on personality need not be separated from the effects of current cosmopolitan interaction (much of our empirical analysis that follows will treat them together). Part of the "personality" differences in creativity, then, are theoretically speaking, the same as cosmopolitanism. But in the one case, we are looking at the effect of past participation in cosmopolitan, written systems of social interaction; in the other, we are looking at the effects of current participation.

Insofar as the personality literature does not deal with effects of education on personality (and I think it partly does not), the former considerations focus the area of dispute on *that part of* personality formation that takes place outside adult written social interaction. That is, if personalities are admitted to be formed mainly in school, then there is no difference between a personality explanation of innovativeness and a cosmopolitanism explanation. The question Hagen poses then may be rephrased as: Does oral interaction vary enough *among families, communities, or ethnic groups* to make substantial differences in the aggregate level of "creative" behavior, and is this variation large compared to the variation caused by education's effect on personality and cosmopolitanism's effects on current behavior?[40]

---

39. Ego-functioning in psychoanalytic theory refers to relating impulses and moral principles to "reality." It was Erik Erikson's great innovation to perceive that the significant part of "reality" is the future, especially in his "The Problem of Ego Identity." In *Identity and the Life Cycle* (New York: International Universities Press, 1959), pp. 101–164. The "reality" of any situation from a psychological point of view, is what *will happen* if a person takes various courses of action. Hence, the determinants of ego-functioning are largely visions of the future. These visions can vary in: (1) accuracy, (2) intensity, (3) style of inferring the future from the present, (4) degree and direction of distortion by impulses or superego demands, (5) the models (especially older people) who represent and reify the personal future, and so forth. The preceding point is that the "reality" to which people adapt in schools is different in all these aspects from the "reality" of the family. Most students of the impact of education on personality have been concerned mainly with superego effects, which are apparently small. The effect of education on the "reality" which people adapt to is held here to be powerful. See my *Rebellion in a High School* (Chicago: Quadrangle Books, 1964).

40. Stinchcombe, *Rebellion*.

A third area of dispute is raised if we consider Hagen's, Max Weber's, and Werner Sombart's, analysis of the economic role of certain minority ethnic and religious groups.[41] Hagen's argument is that certain kinds of minority status tend to change patterns of family interaction in such a way as to produce more creative personalities. Weber argues that peculiarities of religious organization and theology may produce "instrumental activism." Sombart hypothesizes that peculiarities in the culture and status of Jews, among others, produced innovative behavior. We could construct alternative explanations in terms of cosmopolitanism.

Discrimination and moral noninclusion in local systems would tend to orient members of minorities to events elsewhere, to solidarities with people involved in different concrete systems, and the like. Hence they would be more cosmopolitan. Precariousness of status in a local system, combined with solidarity over a wider area with co-religionists, would tend to produce more politically induced migration. Jews, European sectarian Protestants, and other "guest peoples" have a longer history of such cosmopolitanizing migrations. In every country for which Sorokin provided data, foreigners or migrants were more likely to live in cosmopolitan environments.[42] Hence, in particular, migrating minority groups will be more often in metropolises and in port cities where commerce and industry are likely to develop. Several of the specific groups analyzed by these writers have been characterized by a religious tradition that enjoined reading and writing. This is especially the case with Protestant sectarians and Jews. Reading and writing are central components in a cosmopolitan style of life.

Durkheim showed that for Catholics and Protestants, the smaller a religious minority, the more education they got.[43] Thus, the pressure to participate in cosmopolitan interaction even seems to affect children of minority groups. The smaller the minority, the more preferable is universalistic interaction with the school as compared to interaction with peers of different ethnicity.

Weber, in his analysis of the effects of American sects on capitalism, emphasized the importance of such sects for inducing commercial trust and reliability in paying debts. A minority group member in a new place, a place outside his local community, is more likely to be able to find someone he can trust in commercial dealings, and who will trust him with credit, among his co-religionists

41. E. Hagen, *Theory of Social Change.* Max Weber, *The Protestant Ethic and the Spirit of Capitalism.* New York: Charles Scribner's Sons, 1958; and "The Protestant Sects and the Spirit of Capitalism." In H. H. Gerth and C. W. Mills (trans.), *From Max Weber,* pp. 302—322; Werner Sombart, *The Jews and Modern Capitalism.* Glencoe, Illinois: The Free Press, 1951.

42. Pitirim Sorokin, Carl C. Zimmerman, and Charles J. Galpen, *A Systematic Source Book in Rural—Urban Sociology.* Minneapolis: University of Minnesota Press, 1930—1932, Vol. 1, pp. 203—212.

43. *Suicide.* Glencoe, Illinois: The Free Press, 1951, p. 168.

or *paisanos*. Since industrial and commercial development to a considerable extent involves constructing supra-local exchange systems, the advantage of a commercial tie to the outside may greatly facilitate entrepreneurship.

Thus, on many different grounds, we would expect the minorities discussed to be more cosmopolitan. If cosmopolitanism itself produces a pattern of instrumentally active innovation, we would expect the "spirit of capitalism" more often among them.[44]

To state the same point in a more theoretical way, an ethnic or religious minority is not only a set of families or congregations which socializes people in a different way from the majority. It is also a set of people with a distinctive, precarious relation to local systems and distinctive supra-local solidarities and experiences. It is not clear which of these is more important for the innovative behavior of such minorities.

44. Besides being leftist, radical movements are also innovations. Perhaps part of the greater radicalism of minorities can be explained by their greater cosmopolitanism as well as their reaction to ethnic oppression. Cosmopolitanism may also explain the greater appeal of radical movements to college students than to their peers outside college. On the general effects of channels of communication in radicalization, see Andre Siegfried, *Tableau Politique de la France de l'Ouest* Paris: Armand Colin, 1913.

CHAPTER 3

Bureacratic Structure
and Innovative Behavior

If we wish to understand how a social structure fulfills some function, such as analysis of the problems of production, we need to analyze the system of activities that constitutes the structure. In this chapter our purpose is to describe the system of cognitive activities that go on in heavy industrial bureaucracies, and to compare it with the structure of such activities in the nonindustrial middle classes of the same cities. In particular, we want to analyze the interrelation between cognitive activities and the hierarchical structure of industrial bureaucracy. For the most obvious structural feature of industrial bureaucracies, the feature which has formed the basis of most of the theory about them, is their hierarchical character. We have to study the interrelation between rationality and hierarchy in order to find what is distinctive about bureaucratic social structures. Surveys in the past have often been studies of verbal intent rather than of activities, which is one reason that functional analysis and statistical research methodology have not come together. We have attempted here to measure the structure of activities, using survey methods so as to gain the advantages of a cheaper technique than direct observation of activities.

The central source of data for this analysis is a modified time-budget of the last previous full working day for the people interviewed. We went through each hour of the working day, including any work done at home, and asked specifically what the respondent was doing. People have a rather hard time reconstructing the previous day, for usually they do not plan their day's activities in detail, but rather respond to concrete exigencies. Thus, they have no cognitive picture of their activity. They can probably tell as accurately what they will be doing during the next 2 hours, as they can reconstruct 2 hours of activity during the previous day. Many people started reconstructing the previous day out of their own general idea of what they usually did, and only by cross examination did it turn out that yesterday they had done something different. This tendency will introduce a bias in the direction of people's stereotypes of their jobs, and we are sure that we have not eliminated all of it.

Furthermore, we coded the materials to the nearest quarter hour; none of the figures for any individual, therefore, will be more accurate than the nearest 8 minutes. However, these measurement errors will tend to cancel, so the means for a group of people will be somewhat more accurate than for an individual.

We also asked who people communicated with during each hour. We hoped in this way to get at the general structure of communications behavior. Such communications were coded in terms of the hierarchical or nonhierarchical relation of the recipient of communication to the man being interviewed, and his relation to the organization (inside, outside customer, and other outsider). Here, we shall consider only inside communications. This is, of course, a very rough measure of the communication structure.

On the Measurement of Structure

Most studies of organizational structure, except direct observational studies, use either occupational statistics or information on hierarchical arrangements (organization charts, etc.). Occupational statistics describe a role by its name. Organization charts describe a role by certain of its formal role relations—especially authority relations. The information we have on people's occupations and hierarchical positions will not be used; instead we will use time-budget data. The reason is that they give much more precise information about the structure of activities than do the more traditional measures.

The traditional occupational and hierarchical measures have the rhetorical advantage of not pretending to be very precise. For instance, later, we will contrast the steel plants by how often high executives report to their superiors. We will find that the Argentines say they talked to their superiors much more often than did men in the Chilean and Venezuelan plants. The traditional measure of how closely a man is supervised is the span of control of his superior. It is clear, I think, that the number of consultations per day is a much better measure of hierarchical relations than the span of control. But the number of consultations per day pretends to be a very precise measure of behavior, while the span of control measures certain abstract features of role relations—

abstracted by the people themselves. One can think of a lot more reasons that a figure on the number of consultations per day might be in error than one can think of a figure on the number of subordinates a man has. The span of control, then, is a measure that is unlikely to be in error, but likely to tell us very little about the relations between superior and inferior. The number of consultations per day is very likely to be in error, but tells us a good deal.

The reason for this is that we do not really understand hierarchy very well. The fact that a man is someone's formal superior does not tell us much about their role relations. No doubt most university professors have had a funny feeling when a credit application asks for their immediate supervisor at work. A department chairman in a university is, of course, often an errand boy to get things for professors from the administration, rather than a work supervisor. But even though hierarchical position tells us very little about the activities in the structure, it tells us exactly what it pretends to tell us without much chance of mistake. Even though the word "supervisor" rings false for a university department chairman, everyone in the university will agree about who a man's immediate supervisor is. The organization chart tells us very little, but what it does tell us, people agree on. On the other hand, it is quite clear that very often university professors would forget when and how long they talked to their supervisor yesterday.

We have a situation then in which data with small validity about hierarchy have been accepted because of their high reliability. Although a description of actual communications behavior is obviously much superior to a description of formal authority structures, the numbers that will appear in tables of communications behavior will clearly have more error in the original data than would numbers about spans of control (I have some spans of control—they do not show much difference between the plants).

The same situation of substituting reliability for validity holds for occupational statistics. Roughly 17–22% of people will give a different occupation on reinterviews,[1] but they usually give an occupational name that falls in the same general category. (More especially, they tend to give another occupational name with about the same rank, so that the reliability of measurement of occupational rank is very high.) That is, there is relatively high agreement on the correct name to give a man's occupation, and the social rank of his occupation is quite reliably measured by the name he gives. This social rank in turn is quite highly correlated with a number of other things of interest to sociologists, such as his IQ, his years of education, the rank of his previous jobs, his race, and his social class of origin.

But now if we ask how well the name of a man's occupation describes the role he plays in the organization he works for, the answer is, not very well. One has only to think of the immense variety of activities of different men who have

1. Peter Blau and Otis D. Duncan, *The American Occupational Structure*. New York: Wiley, 1967.

the census occupational name of "college professors and instructors not else-where classified." Some people with the occupational name "clerk" are really sort of subordinate executives, while others merely keep ledgers or type. Two men both be called, and call themselves, *"ingeniero,"* but one may be essentially a draftsman, while the other is essentially a foreman for highly skilled craftsmen.

Everybody knows all this, of course, so no one would expect that the three plants, which have roughly the same numbers of engineers, clerks, foremen, etc., therefore have the same structure of administrative activity. Since there is no pretension, there is no objection to the gross inaccuracy of occupational names as measures of the activity carried out.

If a man wanted to say that people with engineering educations are more often "engineers" than are others, it would be regarded as trivial but unlikely to be in error. If he wanted to say, as I will want to say, that men with engineering educations spend more of their time thinking about innovations than do uneducated people, then the definition of thinking, the problem of misreporting, errors of memory, motivated distortion of what they were doing, and so on, all become more pressing. Because I want to say specifically what it is that the occupational name "engineer" described in the different plants, the shelter of safe triviality is not open to me. I will try to describe as well as I can the sources of error in the sort of data I will use here, but I will do so in the conviction that they are the best data on the comparative structure of different organizations that presently exist.

The Time-Budget Interview

Because of the inaccuracy of currently used measures of organizational structure, we needed to come closer to the activities of the people than occupational names or organization charts let us do. But it would clearly be very difficult to get a comparable set of data from three different steel plants and from nonsteel middle-class people by direct observation. As far as I know, of all direct observational studies of organizations, none has tried to collect comparable observations from more than one organization. The main reason for this is clearly that observation is very expensive. It is expensive first because the observer has to sit there. But even more, it is expensive because a high degree of trust has to be established between the observer and the observed. This is one of the things that makes sampling in a systematic way very difficult in observational studies.

We therefore decided to experiment with a time-budget interview. Since we had no experience with this form of data, we decided to allow the people themselves to describe what they were doing during various times during the previous day. They used the common-sense language of their work: "I was in a conference"; "I was inspecting the work on the heavy crane in the port"; "I was working at the drawing board." When this description seemed on a common-sense basis not clear to the interviewer, he probed. For instance, he would ask: "What was the conference about?" "What sort of work was being done on the crane?" "What project were you drawing for?" We probed systematically for work outside working hours (including thinking). We also probed for all communication outside the immediate work group during each hour of the day, and asked specifically about communications with superiors for each hour.

The basic data then are common-sense descriptions of the main activity carried out during each working hour of the last previous full working day. People mainly described their activity by the dominant intention or the purpose that was uppermost in their minds during that hour. That is, people were giving us vocabularies of motive, descriptions of the purposes that justified their actions. Such vocabularies undoubtedly understate random and instinctual and habitual aspects of action, the immediate responsive part of action, and the like. People never pick their noses, for example, in our interviews. But of course semi-instinctual actions like nose-picking are not a very important variable in organizational structure, however important they might be in particular ritual situations.

Aside from this distortion in the direction of justifiable actions, there are quantitative inaccuracies in the data because of our asking about hour-long lumps of time, and because of faults of memory. There are also great variations among people in the richness and detail of their memories, in the habitual circumstantiality with which they describe themselves, and so forth.

So much for the original data. We then coded these common-sense descriptions *into categories of interest to our theories.* It is very important to realize that people did not categorize their own actions; they did not tell us that they spent 1 hour in innovation, 3 hours in thought, and 1 hour on personal affairs. An entry in our table of an hour of "innovative activity" would be described by a man as "working on plans for a change in the size of the opening of a furnace." An hour of "contact with clients" was described by a phrase like "waiting on customers." Many of these activities, of course, fall into several categories. "Writing a report on a study of materials handling (for planned change in materials handling)" would be both coded "intellectual activity" and "innovation." "Supervising the installation of a new machine" would be both "visual supervision" and work on an "innovation."

In most cases the coding was fairly clear. There are fuzzy areas, of course, but it is difficult to say that a man who says he was drawing plans for a new installation was not engaged in "innovation" and "definitely intellectual" activity. If another says he was waiting on customers in the shop, it is hard to make him out either innovating or doing "definitely intellectual" activity. We did not make systematic studies of coding reliability, but all interviews were checked by two coders, and the second coder had the final say.

We did discover that people who gave the same occupational names did very different sorts of things. There is a broad correlation between occupations and activities, of course. But, and this is crucial for us, the errors in occupation names as descriptions of activities are closely related to differences among organizations. For instance, we found very marked differences in what "administrator—engineers" did in different plants. The occupational name of technical executive denotes a rank and an educational background, not a role. Since we had data to show that occupational statistics and organization charts were worse data than the time-budget data, the imperfections of the time-budget interview loomed less large.

Some further technical material on the use of time-budget interviews appears in the Appendix on Method. Clearly, much work remains to be done on the technical features of such data—especially validity studies correlating interview reports with actual observations.

Classification by Structural Position

We wanted to contrast the activities of industrial bureaucrats with the rest of the middle class, so we constructed in each of the three countries (Chile, Argentina, and Venezuela) a special sample of steel plant employees and a random sample of the city middle class. The special sample was made up of three levels, approximately the top 5% of administrators, the next 20%, and the bottom 75%. We sampled an equal number of individuals from each of these three levels. In addition, some steel plant employees were picked up in the random city sample, and in Venezuela some 14 employees of modern North American iron mining bureaucracies were also picked up in the random sample. We added these to the "industrial" samples of each country. Thus, the city samples were "purified" of all but a very few industrial bureaucrats. The nonindustrial samples from the three countries were combined so as to provide a base line for analysis of industrial bureaucracy. The total sample was then divided into four groups for our present purposes. The first group we will call "employees," although there are a few self-employed artisans and professionals among them. They are a *nonentrepreneurial* (and nongeneral manager) group, with either one or no level of subordinates under their authority. They are very similar to the "low" industrial bureaucratic group in their formal position.

The other employed nonindustrial group we have called "bureaucrats." They are employed people with two or more levels of subordinates below them, but they are not general managers. That is, they stand in a hierarchical relationship in an organization that has at least four levels of authority, and they are in the third or higher level. They are quite comparable in structural position to the intermediate level industrial bureaucrats.

The other two groups in the city nonindustrial category are entrepreneurs and general managers, who are not artisans or free professionals. One group we will call "small businessmen," because they have either one or no level of employees below them. The other group we will call "larger businessmen," because they have two or more levels in the hierarchy below them.

In each country, the industrial middle-class members who were picked up in the random sample were all classified as either low or intermediate line employees. This means that a few high executives or staff people will have been classified among the low and intermediate line. It also means that the low and intermediate line industrial bureaucrats in Venezuela represent two industrial bureaucracies, the majority from the steel plant and a minority from the highly modern North American iron mining companies.

In the special steel industry sample, we classified as "low" (line) employees those who belonged in the bottom 75% in terms of salary and who had one or no levels of subordinates below them. (In Argentina, the sample was drawn by level on an organization chart, since salary data were not available to us.) This group, then, included such people as clerks, foremen, and a few salaried manual workers (especially crane operators in Chile). In total, the majority of the "lows" came from the special steel industry sample, and only a minority from the city sample. The latter group were all industrial bureaucratic employees who had one or no levels of hierarchy under their command.

The "intermediate" (line) employees were those with low or intermediate salaries (i.e., the bottom 95% of middle-class steel employees), who have two or more levels of hierarchy in the chain of command below them, plus a few industrial bureaucrats from the city sample with two or more levels below them.

The "high" group included none from the city sample. It includes only those in the highest (top 5%) salary group. If such high-salaried people had three or more hierarchical levels below them, they were considered "high executives."

This leaves the intermediate salaried group with one or no level below them, and the high salaried group with two or less levels below. Such high status combined with low hierarchical control was taken to indicate a "staff" position. This definition makes sense in terms of the results of the analysis.

These operational classifications are outlined in Table 3.1 for easy reference. The main place where things are not quite what they seem in the tables is in the Venezuelan low and intermediate category, where a highly cost conscious, modern iron mining company has apparently cut out a lot of intermediate positions. Hence, many of the 14 people from the iron mining companies should probably have been classified as high executives or staff people, and at any rate, do not characterize the steel plant itself. There are just too few for separate analysis.

Let me here anticipate the main patterns of the empirical results to follow, in the form of propositions:

TABLE 3.1

**Criteria of Classification of Structural Groups for
Analysis of Time-Budgets, and Base Numbers for
Tables of Mean Hours Spent on Various Activities**

| | Industrial bureaucrats | |
City nonindustrial	Chile and Argentina	Venezuela
Employees Employed men with 0–1 levels below, and self-employed professionals and artisans with 0–1 levels below, not in steel or iron mining, all three countries (65)	*Low* Employees with low pay rates from special steel sample with 0–1 levels below, plus steel employees in city sample with 0–1 levels below (Chile 24, Argentina, 42)	Same as Chile and Argentina, plus iron mining employees with 0–1 levels below (26)
Bureaucrats Employed with 2 or more levels below, not in steel or iron mining, all three countries (20)	*Intermediate* Employees with low or intermediate pay in special steel sample, with 2 or more levels below, and steel employees in city sample with 2 or more levels below (Chile, 21, Argentina. 13)	Same as Chile and Argentina, plus iron mining employees with 2 or more levels below (27)
	High Employees with high pay rates in special steel sample, with 3 or more levels below (Chile 20, Argentina 23)	Same as Chile and Argentina (19)
	Staff Employees with intermediate pay rates with 0–1 levels below, and employees with high pay rates with 0–2 levels below (Chile 10, Argentina 15)	Same as Chile and Argentina (17)
Small business Commercial or industrial entrepreneurs or general managers, with 0–1 levels below, all three countries (39)		
Larger business Commercial or industrial entrepreneurs or general managers., with 2 or more levels below, all three countries (17)		

I. *Propositions about industrial bureaucracies as compared to traditional middle-class activities.*
   A. Bureaucracies spend more time working on innovations.
   B. Bureaucracies spend more time on intellectual activities of reading, writing, and calculating.
   C. Bureaucracies spend more time on routine written communication.
   D. Bureaucracies spend more time on oral lateral or nonhierarchical communication within the organization.
   E. Bureaucracies spend more time on hierarchical communication.

In sum, the internal communications density of industrial bureaucracies is much higher, and much of that communication is about innovations.

II. *Propositions about hierarchy.*
   A. The greater the hierarchical organization of communications, the more pressure on higher executives to supervise, and the less time for thought and innovation.
   B. Consequently, staff structures (combinations of high status and few subordinates) are specialized in thought and innovation.
   C. Also consequently, the more meetings are substituted for hierarchical communication, the more time for thought and innovation among higher executives.
   D. These propositions combine to produce a structure most capable of innovative administration in the Chilean plant, next in the Venezuelan, and last in the Argentine plant. This structural result is compatible with the observed time spent on innovative activity in the three plants.

Innovative Activity and Bureaucracy

In Table 3.2 are data on the number of hours spent during the last full working day in any kind of activity working on innovations. This includes any work on expansions or improvements of procedures, studying problems in order to think of innovations, drawing plans for technical changes, manual work installing new machines, or visual supervision of such work, calculations connected with any of these, studying catalogues to select new tools, etc. The most striking feature of the data, compared to much past theory of innovative activity, is the poor showing of entrepreneurs as compared to bureaucrats, whether industrial or nonindustrial. Every group of industrial bureaucrats, and the bureaucratic officials in the city, spent more time on innovations than did the small businessmen. Every bureaucratic group, except the low and intermediate line in industrial Argentina, exceeded the larger businessmen. High steel bureaucratic officials spent from two to six times as much time working on innovations as did the larger entrepreneurs. The staff in the industrial bureaucracies spent from four to seven times as much time as the larger entrepreneurs.

TABLE 3.2

Hours Worked on Proposed Innovations during Last Working Day[a]

City nonindustrial			Industrial bureaucrats		
				Chile	Argentina	Venezuela
Employees	.00	Low	0.68	0.18	0.59
Bureaucrats	.46	Intermediate	0.43	0.12	0.63
		High	1.99	0.58	0.83
		Staff	1.72	1.20	2.34
Small business	.09				
Larger business	.29				

[a]The number of interviews on which each average is based may be obtained from Table 3.1, for this and other tables without base numbers in this chapter.

If "working on innovations" has any relation to the introduction of innovations, we are called on to make a fundamental revision in our notions of the sources of economic growth. If economic growth takes place mainly by means of innovations (and since Schumpeter,[2] this is generally agreed), then Table 3.2 shows that bureaucracies are the main source of economic growth. If larger firms have "economies of scale" which make them "more efficient," Table 3.2 suggests that a major "economy of scale" is more rapid innovation. The stereotype of rigid, stultifying "bureaucrats" preserving traditional forms, while vigorous, manly "entrepreneurs" make innovations, is not only not valid, it is the opposite of the truth. Bureaucracies are evidently the main source of change and innovation.[3]

This implies that most of the theories of economic development are looking at the wrong people when they theorize about entrepreneurship. Hence we ought to see whether it makes sense in terms of the larger patterns of economic growth.

First, we may note that large-scale bureaucracy is a distinctive feature of modern Western societies, which have been a main source of technical and

2. Joseph A. Schumpeter, for example, in *Capitalism, Socialism and Democracy*. New York: Harper, 1950, pp. 81–86.

3. The image I have drawn of the "entrepreneurship" approach to economic development is a caricature. It is implicit, for example, in the indexes of success of an achievement training program in Chapter 8 of D. C. McLelland and others, *Motivating Economic Achievement*. New York: Free Press of Macmillan, 1969, pp. 205–231, in the criteria of choice of innovators in Everett E. Hagen, *Theory of Social Change*, pp. 294–309, in the discussion in J. A. Schumpeter, *Capitalism, Socialism and Democracy*, pp. 131–39, on the decline of the entrepreneurial function as innovation becomes routinized (i.e., bureaucratized). In the first two cases, bureaucratic structures are defined out of existence as sources of innovation, leaving only individual men. In the case of Schumpeter, innovations stop being entrepreneurship when done by bureaucracies.

economic innovation. That is, economies characterized by high bureaucrat- ization are also characterized by high rates of innovation.

Second, within the advanced societies, the newer, more technically sophis- ticated industries are more likely to be highly bureaucratized. The highly inno- vative motor vehicle, airplane, air transport, chemical, electrical, electronic, computer, and steel industries have long hierarchies of paid officials, numerous clerks, and other bureaucratic trappings. The nonbureaucratic industries sound like a roll call of less technically sophisticated, less innovative industries: retail trade, construction, agriculture, intracity transportation, and the like.

Third, it is a common observation that much of the thrust for economic development in poorer countries comes from the government. All the steel plants in our study were started as government operations (though the Chilean one had been sold to private investors and has now been renationalized). The government is usually one of the first structures to be bureaucratized. It appears that the main bureaucratic structure in poorer countries, although not primarily an economic organization, is a main source of economic innovations. Actually, when evaluated by the proportion of new jobs created, governments in advanced countries are also main sources of innovation.

Fourth, in the United States, those industries (outside the free professions) which employ the most "professional, technical, and kindred" workers are highly bureaucratized.[4] This is significant because a main function of employed professionals, engineers especially, is to create and evaluate innovations. The correlation between the rate of growth of industries and the proportion of their staff that is professional is very high. This suggests that professional workers do cause innovation. Thus, the bureaucratic character of professionals' places of employment is associated with apparent innovativeness.

Fifth, data on the kinds of people recruited to entrepreneurial roles do not suggest that the principle of selection is mainly innovative capacity. Non- bureaucratic businessmen are generally less educated, older, have more experi- ence in manual occupations, and tend to support archaic and reactionary social forms.[5] In these ways, they show little prospect of being innovators.

Thus, the gross patterns of economic development also suggest that bureau- cracy and innovation go together, reinforcing our conclusion from Table 3.2. If innovation takes place in less developed economies, then, it will probably have little to do with "entrepreneurship" in the classical sense and a great deal to do with the activities of bureaucracies. People studying the origins and character of entrepreneurs are mainly studying how traditional, noninnovative industries

4. See the data presented in my "Social Structure and Organizations." In James March (Ed.), *Handbook of Organizations*. Chicago: Rand McNally, 1965, p. 156.
5. See for example the data on the origins and careers of small businessmen scattered throughout S. M. Lipset and R. Bendix, *Social Mobility in Industrial Societies*. Berkeley and Los Angeles: University of California Press, 1959.

come to be manned at the managerial level. This is, of course, a very important topic. But it should not be confused with the study of economic development.

The Structure of Bureaucracy and Innovative Activity

In addition to this gross finding about the bureaucratic locus of innovation, several features of the internal structuring of innovative activity in industrial bureaucracies deserve notice. First, in every country, the high industrial executives are more involved in innovation than the low and intermediate executives. All of the high executives have at least three levels of hierarchy under them, and are in charge of ongoing activities; yet despite this the job of innovation is so central that it forms a main part of their job.

This is particularly true in Chile, where the plant has been in operation about a decade. This suggests, though it does not prove, that *when routine operations are still innovations*, they involve the top executives, as they do in Argentina and Venezuela. When routine operations become really routine, the pressure of innovation requirements, and the necessity for innovations to be treated by the most talented, experienced, and weighty people causes a drift in the direction of executive involvement in "entrepreneurship." We will treat some related data on this problem later in this chapter.

The "staff" in the table, it will be recalled, are defined purely in status-system terms. They are highly paid men without many levels of subordinates. This positional definition has clearly identified a group with a distinctive role. In all cases, they are more involved in innovations than low and intermediate line officials, and, except in Chile, more involved than the high executives. This suggests that innovative activity is, by its very nature, interfered with by the requirements of supervising a system. We showed in the previous paragraph that the higher an industrial bureaucrat's status, the more time he spends on innovation. But within each status, the fewer subordinates he has, the more time he spends on innovations. Probably the noninnovative role of entrepreneurs is closely related to their being too involved in the supervision of the work force. The dilemma that these contradictory forces create for the organization is "solved" by creating staff structures, i.e., deliberately created high status positions without too many inferiors. The line-staff structure, thus, is intimately related to the institutionalization of innovative activity.

In the light of this argument, the concentration of high Chilean executives on innovations becomes even more interesting. These men have many levels of subordinates yet work on long-range plans. The exact dynamics of this, and of the somewhat lower concentration of Argentine and Venezuelan executives on innovation, will be a focus of attention in what follows.[6]

6. For future reference, we should note that in every position, the Argentine bureaucracy is less involved in innovation.

Bureaucracy and Reading and Writing

Max Weber chose as one of the defining characteristics of bureaucracy the presence of written files. Our analysis in the preceding chapter suggests a close sociological relation between innovation and written social interaction. In this chapter, we have shown that there is a close relation between bureaucracy and innovation. This appears to be a set of mutually compatible propositions. Let us study a little more closely the relations of written communication behavior to the structural variables we have been analyzing.

In Table 3.3, we give the working hours spent in reading, writing, thinking, drawing, calculating, or other clearly intellectual activity. This does *not* include office routine, filling in forms, answering correspondence, or other written interaction without a clearly intellectual character. The distinction between routine and intellectual work was made through a combination of the interviewee's comments and the coder's judgment. We cannot have too much confidence in this division, as anyone who has worked with both intelligent and dull secretaries doing his "routine" written interaction will testify. But the rough outlines of the pattern of clearly intellectual reading and writing can be obtained. Practically all of this intellectual activity was connected with pieces of

TABLE 3.3

Hours Spent in Reading, Writing, Studying, or other Clearly Intellectual Activity, Not Office Routine or Correspondence[a]

City nonindustrial		Industrial bureaucrats			
			Chile	Argentina	Venezuela
Employees	0.12	Low	0.53	0.85	1.72
Bureaucrats	1.52	Intermediate	0.37	1.00	1.35
		High	1.42	1.12	0.66
		Staff	1.90	1.92	2.65
Small business	0.32				
Larger business	0.75				

[a]Again the numbers on which each mean is based may be obtained from Table 3.1. A more complete analysis of this table is contained in the Appendix on Method, where the mean and variance of each occupational group is broken down into a part due to variations in the proportion doing any of the activity, and the mean and standard deviation of those who do some of it, and then the active group is further analyzed to take account of the skew distribution of time spent. Unfortunately, the statistical treatment of these distributions is quite complex and unfamiliar to most readers. I have made the choice of not doubling the size of the tables and their exposition, and of not engaging in statistical instruction at this point, in order to get on with the argument. The standard deviations of the above figures, as explained in the Appendix, are essentially meaningless, and not usable for statistical inference.

paper, though a little thinking was done during visual inspection or just sitting. Basically, people only think for extended periods in the context of written materials.

The pattern in Table 3.3 corresponds quite closely to that in Table 3.2. The group that rates highest in the city is the bureaucratic officials, followed by the larger businessmen. Among industrial administrators, staff people clearly engage in more intellectual activity. Among the high executives, the Chileans again stand out. Of course, it must be remembered that many of the same working hours appear in the two tables—that is, working on innovations is proportionately far more intellectual activity, thinking about pieces of paper. The main exceptions to this correspondence are two. In Venezuela, a moderate positive relation between innovation and rank is replaced by a sharp negative relation between intellectual activity and rank. In Chile, the relatively high involvement in innovation of low and intermediate line officials does not involve them in so much clearly intellectual activity. Except for low and intermediate line officials in Chile and high executives in Venezuela, all groups of bureaucrats engage in more intellectual activity than does the group of larger businessmen. All bureaucrats without exception do more intellectual work than small businessmen. The staff in each country spend approximately 2–3 hours a day in clearly intellectual activities—reading, writing, and studying. The staff is clearly an intellectual institution, with top executives and city bureaucratic officials close behind (except in Venezuela). Intellectual use of reading and writing is clearly *positively* related to hierarchy, both among employed people and among entrepreneurs, except in Venezuela. Managing people and managing economically productive systems creates intellectual problems. But with the long lines of authority and complex technical systems of industrial bureaucracies, the intellectual problems become so sizable that the specialization of higher executives in intellectual operations is not enough. Special staff thinking apparatus, without subordinates, are added to the structure.

The generation and receiving of routine data create a somewhat different pattern. In Table 3.4, we report hours spent in "routine" written interaction. Among bureaucrats there is a clear curvilinear relation. The low-level administrators, many of them clerks, generate data in the system, deal with the correspondence of the executives, and keep payroll records. But the high executives also spend considerable time, averaging about an hour a day, on routine paper processing. The data originated at the bottom are received, routed, and validated at the top. This same validation of routine communications occupies a substantial part of larger entrepreneurs' time.

The overall relation between bureaucratic structure and written communication is best obtained by summing Tables 3.3 and 3.4. This is done in Table 3.5. In the city, we see a sharp relation to hierarchy, with both bureaucrats and larger businessmen much more engaged in written social interaction. Among

TABLE 3.4

Hours Spent in Paper Processing, Office Routine, Correspondence, Signing Papers

			Industrial bureaucrats		
City nonindustrial			Chile	Argentina	Venezuela
Employees	0.81	Low	1.42	1.51	1.88
Bureaucrats	0.51	Intermediate	0.54	0.23	0.63
		High	0.71	1.18	1.22
		Staff	2.15	0.48	0.79
Small business	0.26				
Larger business	1.00				

industrial bureaucrats, the staff is always either highest or is approximately equaled by the low-level line (clerks and foremen) and the high executives. The least involved in written interaction are intermediate-level line supervisors. We will see later that they are heavily engaged in visual supervision and in distributing work, nonwritten forms of interaction. Excluding them, all the industrial bureaucratic groups are more involved in written interaction than any of the entrepreneurs or the employees, and most of them more than city bureaucrats. City bureaucrats, low-level industrial employees, high-level steel executives, and staff, all spend from one-fourth to one-half of their working time receiving, considering, or originating written communications. The highest groups are those most involved with innovations (except for the top Venezuelan executives). Not only, then, is there a broad correspondence between written interaction and innovation, but the correspondence also extends pretty well to the details. And our evidence bears out Weber's selection of both hierarchy and written social interaction as defining criteria of bureaucracy. Hierarchies, especially long hierarchies like steel plants, run by means of writing and reading.

TABLE 3.5

Hours Spent in Written Interaction (Sums of Tables 3.3 and 3.4)

			Industrial bureaucrats		
City nonindustrial			Chile	Argentina	Venezuela
Employees	0.93	Low	1.95	2.36	3.60
Bureaucrats	2.03	Intermediate	0.91	1.23	1.98
		High	2.13	2.30	1.88
		Staff	4.05	2.40	3.44
Small business	0.58				
Larger business	1.75				

Patterns of Nonhierarchical Communication

We can gain further evidence on the cognitive nature of an activity from the structure of oral communication it induces. Hierarchical communication is generally oriented to the *legitimacy* of a message. Nonhierarchical communication is more often oriented to *problem-solving*, reflecting the variety of contacts required by data collection, coordination, and planning activities. We have two alternative measures of nonhierarchical communication activities: meetings with more than two people, and individual communications outside the immediate work group with men who are neither inferiors nor superiors in an organizational sense. The hours spent in meetings are reported in Table 3.6; the hours in which individual nonhierarchical communication took place at least once are reported in Table. 3.7.

Table 3.6 shows clearly that meetings are a distinctive feature of higher bureaucratic management. The only people who spend significant time in meetings are the city bureaucrats (with two or more levels of subordinates) and industrial bureaucrats above the bottom level. This is also the social location of innovative activity and thinking, as we have previously seen. The highest figures are for the Chilean top executives and the Chilean staff. The pattern is quite similar to the distribution of innovative activity, except for the peculiar lack of meetings in the highly innovative Venezuelan bureaucracy. (In Venezuela, there was a positive antimeeting sentiment. People felt they wasted their time in meetings.)

If we are right in thinking that the inherent pressure of cognitive problems produces nonhierarchical communication, then the failure to use meetings in Venezuela should produce a heavy pressure for individual nonhierarchical communication. This is what shows up in Table 3.7. During nearly half of the hours of a working day, Venezuelan high executives contact someone in the

TABLE 3.6

Hours Spent on Last Working Day in Meetings (of More Than Two People)

City nonindustrial			Industrial bureaucrats		
			Chile	Argentina	Venezuela
Employees	0.16	Low	0.00	0.01	0.02
Bureaucrats	0.60	Intermediate	0.96	0.40	0.96
		High	2.01	1.99	0.87
		Staff	1.85	0.30	0.00
Small business	0.10				
Larger business	0				

TABLE 3.7

Number of Hours in Which Nonhierarchical Individual Communication
Took Place Outside the Immediate Work Group

City nonindustrial			Industrial bureaucrats		
			Chile	Argentina	Venezuela
Employees	0.36	Low	0.56	0.10	1.48
Bureaucrats	0.30	Intermediate	0.96	0.35	1.78
		High	0.81	2.14	3.63
		Staff	1.20	0.52	1.85
Small business	0				
Larger business	0				

plant with whom they do not have hierarchical relations. All other levels in
Venezuela are also characterized by high levels of extra-work-group contact on
an individual basis. Among the Chilean high executives, who are so meeting-
prone, less than an average of one hour a day has a lateral, extra-work-group
contact. This suggests that meetings and individual lateral contacts are, to some
extent, functional alternatives.

It is likely that much of an individual's time in a meeting is wasted—more
than in an individual communication. He hears things with no relevance to his
work. On the other hand, an hour with one individual communication in it
probably does not represent as much total communication as goes on in an
hour of meetings. If, despite these difficulties, we add the hours in meetings to
the hours in which an individual lateral communication took place, we get the
pattern of Table 3.8.

Table 3.8 shows that the total number of hours in which lateral communica-

TABLE 3.8

Hours Spent in Meetings or in Which Nonhierarchical Communication
Took Place (Sums of Tables 3.6 and 3.7)

City nonindustrial			Industrial bureaucrats		
			Chile	Argentina	Venezuela
Employee	0.52	Low	0.56	0.11	1.50
Bureaucrats	0.90	Intermediate	1.93	0.75	1.74
		High	2.82	4.13	3.50
		Staff	3.05	0.82	1.85
Small business	0.10				
Larger business	0				

tion took place is farily similar between Chile and Venezuela, the two countries with high innovative activity in Table 3.1. The different segments of the bureaucracy are solidly tied together by about two to three hours daily in which lateral communication takes place, at the intermediate and higher levels of the hierarchy.

Now certain peculiarities of the Argentine plant begin to take on a clear pattern. The Argentine staff, specializing in innovation, are communicatively isolated from the rest of the administrative apparatus. This may be because they enjoy a lower status in the Argentine plant—almost all of them are in the "intermediate" rank. All but one of the highly placed top Argentine sample have three or more levels below them, i.e., only one of them is "staff." The top executives themselves are highly involved in lateral communication, but evidently only with each other. The knitting together of the subparts of the organization at lower levels is weak, and the general level of communication from staff to line is low. The whole system is thus likely to be hierarchically oriented rather than problem oriented. This lack of problem orientation is found to be related to low levels of innovativeness. In Table 3.1, we showed that the Argentine plant had the least work on innovations of the industrial bureaucracies. These peculiarities will be illuminated if we examine hierarchical communications behavior.

Hierarchical Communications Behavior Upward

In our survey data we have two separate indicators of the upward orientation of communication behavior. The first is the number of hours during the last working day in which the interviewees reported having talked (not in meetings) with their superiors. This pattern is reported in Table 3.9. The most striking characteristic of this table is the contrast between the nonindustrial and the

TABLE 3.9

Number of Hours in Which Communication with Superiors (not in Meetings) Took Place

City nonindustrial			Industrial bureaucrats		
			Chile	Argentina	Venezuela
Employees	0.28	Low	0.69	0.36	1.18
Bureaucrats	0.46	Intermediate	0.68	1.17	1.41
		High	0.32	1.06	0.78
		Staff	0.70	0.23	1.28
Small business	0				
Larger business	0				

industrial employees (communication to superiors is irrelevant to businessmen). That is, not only is lateral communication within the organization more frequent in industrial bureaucracy; hierarchical communication is *also* more prevalent. The overall oral communications density of industrial bureaucracy is much higher than in the middle classes generally. (So is the overall written communications density, as we saw in Table 3.5.) The tight integration of a complex technical system evidently requires a good deal more communication of all kinds, and most of the day of an industrial administrator is spent in some kind of communication with someone else inside the organization.

Beyond this gross pattern, we can note several peculiarities of the different hierarchical communications patterns in the different bureaucracies. First, no subgroup in the Chilean bureaucracy communicated as frequently individually with their superiors as did the least communicative among the Venezuelans. This probably indicates two things. First, probably, *meetings are functional equivalents of hierarchical communication as well as of lateral communication*. Second, the greater age of the Chilean operation probably makes subordinate executives more competent to handle their own problems and leads them less often to seek advice or approval from their superiors.

We can hypothesize that the strong hierarchy in the Venezuelan plant indicates, essentially, that top executives are doing much of the work of their subordinates, which the Chileans do not have to do. It may also be that meetings have a greater effect in socializing subordinates to consider their work from the point of view of the requirements of the system as a whole, so that they become more competent to run their own work compatibly.

In both the Chilean and the Venezuelan plants, the group with lowest levels of communication with superiors are the high executives, with the staff and lower line groups all about equal. The Argentine plant shows a completely different pattern. First, the staff group, which we have seen had a very low level of lateral communication has also a low level of hierarchical communication. The staff appears to be essentially isolated, without substantial connection to the operation of the plant. The Argentine staff's superiors, who would be mostly the high executives, do not apparently have time to communicate with them, either laterally or as subordinates individually. This in turn seems to be related to the high executives' low involvement in innovation, presumably as both cause and effect. The high executives, not being involved and interested in innovation, do not need communication with the staff who are the source of specialized innovative work. But conversely, not being in communication with the sources of innovations, they do not get involved in innovative activity. In addition, the high executives in Argentina are in very frequent communication with their superiors, nearly as much so as the intermediate group.

The structures we have seen evidently have to do with contrasting philosophies of responsibility and hierarchy in the different industrial bureaucracies.

We asked each respondent: "How frequently do you have to report about your work to your superiors, or how often do your superiors inspect what you do?" The responses were coded from 2 to 8 (1 meant that the person had no superiors), ranging from "never" (2) to "every little while" or "always" (8). The mean code is reported in Table 3.10 for each of the structural groups.

Again, the weaker hierarchical organization of the city middle class shows up in Table 3.10, as in Table 3.9. These figures could be affected considerably by the few artisans and free professionals who had no superiors.

In the industrial bureaucracies, we see both in Chile and Venezuela a sharp decline in the normative frequency of reporting to one's superiors with an increase in rank. The low steel bureaucrats are supposed to report, on the average, nearly once a day (a mean code of 7 would indicate a normative frequency of once a day). The high executives are normatively supposed to report to their superiors between once every week (a mean code of 6 would be once a week) and once a month (a mean code of 5). The staff is apparently expected to report, on the average, about once a week. (Incidentally, a comparison of Table 3.9 with 3.10 shows that the norms about reporting and consulting superiors are poor predictors of the actual contact, if reports of actual contacts are reasonably good measures of what happens.)

But the Argentines are apparently organized according to a "mystique of command," which may be related to the military tradition under which the army-run Argentine plant operates. Top executives with three levels of authority below them are normatively expected to report every day to their superiors. Instead of being delegated authority, which they can in turn delegate, with some periodic review, they are expected to report their day's accomplishments to their superiors. In every case, the Argentine code is higher (i.e., frequency of

TABLE 3.10

Mean Code on Frequency of Reporting to Superiors or Being Inspected by Them[a]

City nonindustrial		Industrial bureaucrats		
		Chile	Argentina	Venezuela
Employees	5.00	Low	6.20	7.24	6.00
Bureaucrats	4.70	Intermediate	6.96	6.85	6.80
		High	6.71	6.87	6.59
		Staff	5.05	6.93	5.74
Small business	1.00				
Larger business	1.00				

[a]Code: 1,2 = Never; 4 = every few months; 5 = every month; 6 = every week; 7-once a day; 8-every little while or always.

reporting is greater) than in either of the other two plants. There is no substantial decline in frequency of reporting with rank.

This sharp upward orientation, or mystique of command, evidently focuses the solution of all problems of coordination among the top executives. This probably explains the extraordinarily sharp differentiation of the Argentine high executives in lateral communication (see Table 3.8); they spend more than five times as much time in lateral communication as does the next highest group (staff or intermediate line). In Chile, the high executives spend about the same time as the staff; in Venezuela the executives spend about twice as much time as the staff.

Thus, apparently, we can rank the three plants roughly in terms of the predominance of hierarchy in their communications systems: first Argentina, then Venezuela, and last Chile. This predominance of hierarchy apparently influences several other aspects of the overall structure of the communications system and the cognitive focus of it.

First, the higher the degree of hierarchical orientation, the greater the degree to which lateral coordination will be concentrated at the level of high executives. With low hierarchical orientation, both the staff and the intermediate line are heavily involved in lateral communication through meetings or individual contacts. In particular, the involvement of intermediate line managers in meetings seems to be a sensitive indicator of the hierarchical dimension.

Second, the higher the degree of hierarchical orientation, the greater the amount of time spent at the top of the hierarchy on office routine, signing papers, and correspondence (see Table 3.4) and the less the time devoted to thinking, studying, or other clearly intellectual activity (see Table 3.3).

Third, and directly related to both of these, the greater the degree of hierarchical orientation of the communication system, the smaller the proportion of time spent in innovation by the high executives.

Hierarchical Pressure on Executives from Below

At first blush, it seems that hierarchical communication downward should be the same as upward, merely looked at the other way around. But the pyramidal structure of hierarchies means that when looking upward, one is looking through the large end of a telescope, while looking downward one magnifies the details. A superior usually spends more time in downward communication than an inferior spends in upward communication. This means that there is an inherent tendency of heirarchy to produce communications pressure from below on hierarchical superiors. This pressure tends to squeeze everything else out of the executive's day: free time during work, leisure outside of work, long-range planning, thinking and studying, and the like.

We would expect this squeeze to be stronger, the more upward communica-

TABLE 3.11

Hours Spent in Visual Supervision, Inspection Trips, Visual Studying of Plant Operations

City nonindustrial			Industrial bureaucrats		
			Chile	Argentina	Venezuela
Employees	1.05	Low	0.92	1.26	1.51
Bureaucrats	1.35	Intermediate	3.77	3.98	2.98
		High	0.99	2.45	4.72
		Staff	0.50	2.63	1.52
Small business	0.82				
Larger business	3.12				

tion there is—the more hierarchical the orientation of the communication system. This can be observed in the (few) meetings that are held in the Venezuelan plant. Many meetings I observed there were disrupted because the crucial people were either called away, or taken out of the conversation, by "urgent" problems presented by subordinates. A call would come through to the chairman of the meeting from one of his subordinates. The rest of the people would wait around, or fall into individual conversations about something else while the chairman dealt with the urgent problem. During the course of an hour meeting, as much as 20—30 minutes would often be "wasted" in this fashion. This explains in large measure the antimeeting feeling in the Venezuelan plant.

We can see this pressure of hierarchical orientation in Tables 3.11 and 3.12. In Table 3.11, we give the hours spent in visual inspection of work processes by people at different levels in the hierarchy. In the nonindustrial groups, we see a clear differentiation by levels of subordinates: Bureaucrats with two or more

TABLE 3.12

Hours Spent Planning Work for Self and Others, and in Distributing Work

City nonindustrial			Industrial bureaucrats		
			Chile	Argentina	Venezuela
Employees	0.16	Low	0.62	0.26	0.24
Bureaucrats	1.18	Intermediate	1.95	1.52	1.37
		High	0.70	1.94	1.46
		Staff	0.80	0.47	0.73
Small business	0.50				
Larger business	0.82				

levels of subordinates spend more time in visual supervision than employees with one or no levels below them, and larger businessmen with two or more levels of subordinates spend nearly four times as much time in visual supervision as smaller businessmen.

Among the industrial bureaucrats, we find in every case a sharp differentiation between the intermediate and lower levels, between people with two or more levels of subordinates and those with one or no level below them. The intermediate executives spend from two to four times as much time in visual supervision, inspection, and visual data collection on the work process.

But among the high executives, we find a sharp differentiation among the plants rather than among hierarchical levels. The less hierarchically oriented Chilean plant produced little pressure on executives to collect their own data on the work process, to go out and check up on their subordinates, or generally to *originate* communication with subordinates (visual inspection is a device for originating communication with subordinates). In the Venezuelan industrial structure, where the level of upward communication from the bottom two levels was so high (see Table 3.9), the level of visual supervision by high executives is extraordinarily high, running to nearly 5 hours per day.

The Argentine plant, pervaded by the mystique of hierarchy, has an intermediate level of visual supervision. This is compatible with the low amount of upward communication at the low levels, and may indicate merely the overloading of the communications capacity of the top executives. If they must do all the coordination for different departments of the plant (see Table 3.8), and are themselves responsible for communicating daily with their own superiors (see Tables 3.9 and 3.10), they may not have any time left for communication downward. Still, they spend nearly two and one-half times as much time in visual supervision as the Chileans.

In Table 3.12, we report the hours spent planning one's work or in dividing up work among subordinates and telling them what to do. Distribution of work probably occurs also during the time spent on visual supervision, but Table 3.12 reports time exclusively devoted to dividing up the work.

In the industrial plants, the intermediate level executives are, again, very substantially above the low-level employees in time devoted to distribution of work. But again the Chilean executives show evidence of a much lower level of hierarchical orientation, with the Venezuelan executives in an intermediate position, and the Argentines at the top. The combined result, then, is for the hierarchical orientation of the Venezuelan and Argentine administrative apparatus to put pressure on the high executives to spend about half of their working day in downward communication, either through visual supervision or the distribution of work. This pressure is very substantially reduced for the Chilean high executives, occupying less than 2 hours a day of their time.

The hierarchical pressure is, in each case, considerably less on the staff. It will be recalled that the staff are *defined* here by a combination of high status and few levels of subordinates. It is fairly clear that the relief from the pressure of upward communication is primarily responsible for their capacity to engage more in innovating activity, thinking, studying, and planning. When high executives are relieved of some of this pressure, as they are in Chile, they can also engage in innovating activity, and in longer-range planning, thinking, and studying.

Inspection of the staff figures in Table 3.11 suggests one source of the pressure toward a hierarchical orientation of the communication system. We note that the staff in Venezuela, and even more in Argentina, are much more highly oriented to visual inspection of the production process. Both of these plants are much newer than the Chilean plant, which has been in production for about a decade. The figures suggest that the process of data collection on routine operations is not well enough developed yet in these two for planning work to be able to get along primarily on written data. Perhaps also, the intermediate level supervisors are not yet sufficiently experienced and cannot describe their problems so that staff people (or higher executives) can understand them without making their own diagnoses. One high executive in the Venezuelan plant commented that he had to serve as a sort of general foreman, and did not have time for his own special responsibilities.

The effects of hierarchical pressure show up in several ways. First, there is a general moral pressure of subordinates which reduces the time spent during working hours on personal affairs, recreation, bull sessions, coffee breaks, and the like. Table 3.13 presents the hours spent on personal affairs or recreation of this kind during working hours. In the city, among both employed people and businessmen, the average time devoted to personal affairs by men with one or no level of subordinates was more than 30 minutes; those with two or more levels below them spent about 15 minutes. In the industrial bureaucracies, the staff in every case spent more time than high and intermediate line executives

TABLE 3.13

Hours Spent on Personal Affairs and Recreation during Work Hours

City nonindustrial		Industrial bureaucrats		
		Chile	Argentina	Venezuela
Employees	0.53	Low	0.12	1.04	0.30
Bureaucrats	0.28	Intermediate	0.12	0.38	0.16
		High	0.05	0.09	0.21
		Staff	0.42	0.62	0.28
Small business	0.67				
Larger business	0.12				

TABLE 3.14

Total Hours Worked on Last Full Working Day before Interview

			Industrial bureaucrats		
City nonindustrial			Chile	Argentina	Venezuela
Employees	8.88	Low	7.55	8.88	8.84
Bureaucrats	9.08	Intermediate	8.36	8.58	9.23
		High	8.28	9.05	10.68
		Staff	8.92	8.90	8.41
Small business	10.83				
Larger business	9.21				

on personal affairs, and the lowest hierarchical level, in every case but Chile, spent more time than the higher hierarchical levels on personal affairs. And in every case except Venezuela, the high executives spent least time of all.

However, the hierarchical pressure shows up most clearly in the extension of the working day and the working week. Table 3.14 presents the hours worked on the last full working day before the interview. The most marked differentiation is among the high executives. In Chile they had worked a "normal" working day of a little over 8 hours, about the same as the staff and intermediate line. In Argentina, they had worked slightly more time than the staff or intermediate line. In Venezuela, they had worked over an hour longer than the staff and intermediate line.

The same sort of differentiation shows up in the answers to the question of how long the respondents usually worked during a week. Again, the Chilean high executives worked approximately the same length of time as the staff or intermediate line; the Argentine executives somewhat longer; the Venezuelan executives considerably longer (see Table 3.15).

TABLE 3.15

Average Hours Worked per Week on Principal Job

			Industrial bureaucrats		
City nonindustrial			Chile	Argentina	Venezuela
Employees	49.7	Low	50.5	45.6	46.5
Bureaucrats	45.7	Intermediate	51.6	47.9	50.6
		High	50.6	53.7	63.3
		Staff	50.6	44.4	50.4
Small business	58.2				
Larger business	52.2				

TABLE 3.16

Percentage Who Say That Their Work Sometimes Makes Them
Nervous or Tense

City nonindustrial		Industrial bureaucrats (countries combined)	
Employees	35% (65)	Low	44% (92)
Bureaucrats	70% (20)	Intermediate	56% (61)
		High	60% (62)
		Staff	40% (42)
Small business	56% (39)		
Larger business	65% (17)		

This hierarchical pressure shows up again, though somewhat irregularly, in the amount of attention people have to pay to their work. In Table 3.16, we report the percentage of respondents who answered "yes" to the question: "Do you have to pay so much attention to your work that you get nervous or tense?" Since this is merely a yes or no question, we have combined the three industrial plants to get some stability in the percentages. In all cases, those with two or more levels of subordinates (the city bureaucrats and large businessmen, and the intermediate and high executives in the industrial bureaucracies) are more likely to report nervousness or tenseness at work.

The pattern of results is quite clear. Indicators of downward communication, such as visual inspection and distribution of work, are more characteristic of men who have subordinates. These same indicators are much higher for the top executives of the more hierarchically oriented Venezuelan and Argentine administrations. Various indicators suggest that the funneling effect of hierarchy creates more pressure on men with subordinates. Men with subordinates more often report that their work sometimes makes them nervous or tense and they spend less of the working day on their personal affairs and relaxing. This pressure tends to produce longer working days and longer working weeks; and the pressure to lengthen the working day and working week is apparently considerably stronger in the more hierarchically oriented Venezuelan and Argentine plants.

We take it that this is one of the main sources of the lower level of involvement in innovation of the high Argentine and Venezuelan executives. Just as personal affairs and leisure time become invaded by hierarchical pressures, so does time for thinking about the more long-range problems and about innovations. Moreover, it may well be, as suggested by Gouldner in *Wildcat Strike*,[7] that a strong hierarchical orientation, *combined* with considerable attempts at innova-

7. Alvin W. Gouldner, *Wildcat Strike*. Yellow Springs, Ohio: Antioch, 1954.

tion (absent in the Argentine plant), induces pressure for detailed visual supervision by high executives.

Innovations themselves create problems at the working level. The stronger the hierarchical orientation of the communication system, the more likely it is that the high executives will have to deal with the urgent problems created by innovations. This would explain the exceptionally high pressure on the Venezuelan executives, for the general level of innovative activity is relatively high, even though the high Venezuelan executives themselves spend considerably less time on innovations than the Chileans (though considerably more than the Argentines). These innovations presumably create more urgent problems in the Venezuelan than in the Argentine plant, though perhaps not as much as in the Chilean plant. But in the last, these problems tend to be taken care of; that is, the executives and staff do not have to supervise visually the solution to problems, nor distribute the shifting work load among their subordinates.

In sum, then, this analysis suggests the pattern for the origin of hierarchical pressures on high executives that is outlined in Table 3.17.

TABLE 3.17

Hypothetical Sources of Hierarchical Pressure from Subordinates on High Executives or Bureaucratic Officials

	City bureaucrats	Industrial high executives		
		Chile	Argentina	Venezuela
Innovations creating urgent problems for subordinates	Low	High	Low	High
Hierarchical orientation of communication	Low	Low	Very high	High
Pressures on high executives (product of rows 1 and 2)	Very low	Low	High	Very high
Hours worked week (see Table 3.15)	45.7	50.6	53.7	63.3

The Dilemma of the Ivory Tower in Industry

The Argentine plant employs a staff that occupies a position essentially similar to that implied in the word "ivory tower." They are heavily engaged in work on innovations, but no one else in the plant is so engaged—their "innovations" are not having an effect in modifying what goes on in the plant. This is apparently because the staff forms a communications isolate: We showed in the tables on written, lateral, and hierarchical communication, that they have much lower rates of communication than the staff groups in the other countries. They have created the conditions for thinking and innovative work at the expense of their relations to the reality of the functioning of the plant. As a result (either of this itself or of the causes that produce it), the operative plant personnel in Argentina are less involved in innovation than operative personnel in either of the other plants.

In Venezuela, the staff is innovative and connected with plant operations by multiple communication channels. As a direct or indirect result, there is a great deal of innovative activity. But the hierarchical orientation of the plant creates fantastic pressures on the high executives, requiring them to solve the day-to-day problems created by this innovative activity, so that they have time to pay only minimal attention to the analysis of the innovations themselves. This creates a sharp differentiation in the style of work between the staff and the high executives. The executives are in the hurly-burly of practical affairs, they work harder, they are always out on the floor watching. The staff are more leisured, more reflective, more "impractical." Each innovation is trouble for the executive, an additional burden on his already overextended powers. In Venezuela, the details of innovations cannot be as carefully and reflectively analyzed by the man who is ultimately responsible for the results as they can in Chile, and the innovations are probably less likely to carry the full weight of authority of the man in charge.

In Chile, this dilemma has been cut through by a rather radical cutting of the hierarchical pattern. This cutting probably has two sources. First, the subordinates in the older Chilean plant are more experienced, and they can probably handle more problems themselves. Second, there is the tradition of extensive "nonhierarchical" communication in meetings, which apparently substitute for both individual lateral communication and individual hierarchical communication. This, so to speak, brings the top executives *into* the ivory tower, puts the weight of their authority behind the innovations which they have themselves analyzed in considerable detail, and still leaves them with enough detachment from operations that they can sometimes stay home over the weekend.

This weakening of the strong hierarchical pattern is accompanied, or perhaps caused, by a difference in the philosophy of command and responsibility. The idea, as shown in Table 3.10, that executives can take care of themselves for longer periods of time is widely distributed in the Chilean plant. Chilean bureaucrats were less likely to have known of someone who had been fired from a position of responsibility, and this also indicates a generalized trust that other people are perfectly capable of doing their jobs. If they are not, the plant executives can have a meeting to help solve their problems, and then they can get by.

This intimate interrelation between the focus of high executives on innovative problems and decentralization as an organizational philosophy has been noted by Chandler in his study of the administrative history of several of the great American industrial giants.[8] The creation of a central, full-time top executive staff which would concentrate on "entrepreneurial" innovative prob-lems was connected in the American industries with the cutting of the hier-archical orientation of communication on operative problems, just as it appears to be in the Latin American steel industries. The formation of relatively auton-omous operating divisions, and the differentiation of the role of managing these divisions from that of central long-range planning, were preconditions for the top executive staff concentration on problems of innovation. This de-centralization could take place only when cost statistics and market statistics became accurate measuring rods for the autonomous subdivisions.

The dilemma is that of detaching the consideration of innovations from hierarchical pressures, without thereby detaching the innovations themselves so completely from the hierarchy that they do not get instituted. In Chile, this dilemma is resolved by partly detaching the top executives from the supervisory hierarchy, through a series of devices of delegation, meetings, and the like, so that the hierarchical pressure is taken off sufficiently that they can consider innovations. What is the likelihood that the other two plants will reach the same resolution?

It seems that the military mystique of command in the Argentine plant makes it unlikely that such a resolution will take place there, unless ultimate control over the plant falls into other hands than the army. Aside from the data presented here, this is also indicated by the paucity of devices for objective measurement of performance in the Argentine plant. It seems that, psychologically, if a man is controlled carefully by his superior in all the details of his work, then he does not need to be controlled by cost accounts.

The cost accounting system in Venezuela is relatively advanced and accurate, and the prices of finished products, which form the basis of control, are much more closely related to economic prices than they are in Argentina. (In Vene-zuela, the prices are set approximately in keeping with world market prices, and the inefficiencies of the plant relative to world producers are absorbed by a subsidy. In Argentina, there are special national prices supported by protective arrangements.)

The delegation of authority depends on accurate measurement of perfor-mance by "objective" techniques. A cost account, related in a realistic fashion to actual efficiency by realistic prices for each of the products, is a good substitute for a superior. The Venezuelan plant has made a heavy investment in foreign consultants in cost accounting, and it has given a very high rank to the chief accountant (he is at the same rank in the overall organization as the general manager of the plant); these are the people who provide the performance measurement basis for the delegation of authority. Our data show that this

---

8. Alfred D. Chandler, *Structure and Strategy*. Cambridge, Massachusetts: MIT, 1962.

delegation of authority has already gone considerably further in Venezuela than it has in Argentina.

On the basis of these data and arguments, then, we would expect the Argentine plant to fall further and further behind the world standard of efficiency, as it fails to introduce innovations at a reasonable rate to keep up with world developments. The Venezuelan plant we would expect to approach the world standard of efficiency, and we would also expect it to undergo some structural changes in the direction of greater detachment of the top executives from operating problems and more involvement in innovative activity. The Chilean plant was already returning a profit: It was selling its steel at about the same price as that paid for U.S. steel delivered in the country, while paying some of the highest wages among nonforeign industrial firms. In sum, we would predict from these data that in another decade, the price of steel will be considerably higher in Argentina than in Chile or Venezuela, and that the Venezuelan and Chilean plants will both be solvent.

CHAPTER 4

The Social Sources
of Individual Rationality

The inclination toward intellectual analysis, as we have shown, is heavily dependent on the characteristics of the *roles* people have in the administration. People with many levels of subordinates often carry such severe burdens that they cannot spend as many hours a day in thinking as staff people can. But presumably there are variations among people, as well as among roles, in the inclination to think, in the inclination to treat each concrete difficulty as a problem capable of rational solution. This chapter is directed toward finding *the social sources of the disposition to treat problems rationally*, the disposition that Parsons has so aptly named "instrumental activism."[1]

The general strategy here is straightforward. First, we will outline some elements of individual rational dispositions, of the inclination to treat problems of experience in a rational fashion. This is essentially an explication of an empirically derived scale. The scale was obtained by item-to-total item analysis and elimination of the weaker items. We started with a group of items thought to measure a "modernistic" *Weltanschauung*. Most of these items were derived from studies by Joseph Kahl.[2] Since the details of this empiricist procedure do not establish the theoretical rationale which I use to justify the scale, and since all the estimates of correlations are biased upward by the structure of the sample

1. See *Structure and Process*, pp. 172–173, 311.
2. Joseph Kahl, *The Measurement of Modernism*. Austin: Univ. of Texas Press, 1968.

and by taking advantage of chance in the elimination procedure, no knowledge would be added by giving the scale construction data.

We will then elaborate our ideas about the sources of variation in rationality of attitude in people's biographies. On this basis, we will construct a "modernism predictor" scale that combines educational experience with measures of cosmopolitanism of biography.

Our next task will be to explore the relation between these biographical factors and the disposition toward rationality. This will then prepare the ground for exploring how cosmopolitan and educational biographical characteristics, and modernism of attitudes are distributed in the role system described in Chapter 3.

We will want to know, of course, how psychological and biographical determinants of rationality are integrated with the system of cognitive and supervisory activities that form the basis of economic administration. Modernism or rationality of attitudes is significant for modernism of economic activities only if it influences how these activities are carried out. It must be studied, therefore, in relation to the activities and communication processes by which economic activities are in fact administered.

The disposition to resolve problems rationally may be considered to have the following four components:

(1) The disposition to regard other people as fundamentally understandable, predictable, and manipulable by rational means. The conviction that people will be responsive to the role requirements of their positions, and that they are not a source of irregular and unpredictable negative motives, is a primary requirement of any administration on a large scale, because large-scale administration is conducted by people who are mutually strangers.
(2) The disposition to differentiate decisions made at work from various primordial, primary-group considerations.
(3) An activist, nonfatalist attitude which regards the world as fundamentally predictable and controllable by planned activity. That is, the preceding two conditions tend to render other people predictable, but rationality also involves the assumption that outcomes generally can be controlled.
(4) A disposition to use cosmopolitan sources of information and ideas in the solution of local problems—especially a disposition to read and study.

(1) *Trust in Others.*   Of all the causal determinants of the outcomes of activities, people are the most complex, difficult to control, and self-directed. In addition, perhaps because of the way men are socialized, other people's activities and motives are most likely to arouse emotional reactions: fear, love, anger, obligation, and anxiety. People's approach toward other people, then, is crucial

for predicting the rationality with which they will treat problems of cooperative action. The misbehavior of a machine is obviously a cognitive problem, not one of fear, anger, hatred, or bad will. Emotions enter into the administrative process mainly when the problem is one of the misbehavior of people. Hence, regarding people as trustworthy and predictable is an elementary requirement for a rational approach to administrative action.

Men's attitudes toward the behavior of other people seem to cut across the distinction between intimate and impersonal relations. Broadly speaking, the man who finds his wife mysterious and unpredictable also finds strangers unpredictable. If he cannot plan a course of activity in which his wife has a part, because he expects that she will bring in unpredictable motives, he likewise cannot trust the motives of strangers. In the scale analysis that we carried out with a series of items on trusting of other people, we found that questions about trust in relatives and friends are closely related to questions about trust in strangers. Probably this is because we learn our attitudes toward the behavior of strangers from the behavior of people we know well. The behavior of friends and relatives is crucial to our fate in day-to-day affairs, so we learn most rapidly from them. We have included four items to measure this orientation toward others in our scale of modernism; all of them are statements with which the respondent can agree or disagree, and all of them call for agreement as the most "distrustful" response. These statements are:

> *The majority of people repay kindness with ingratitude.*
>
> *It's not good to let your relatives know everything about your life, for they can take advantage of you.*
>
> *It's not good to let your friends know everything about your life, for they can take advantage of you.*
>
> *One can only have confidence in those he knows well.*

The man who agrees with all of these statements must confront social interaction with fear and trembling. He must have great difficulty in working out concerted social action, because he needs constant guarantees that others will do as they say, and he probably does not believe the guarantees. The fundamental unpredictability of other people's motives, implied by such a distrustful view of others, interferes greatly with the adminstration of large-scale concerted action.

(2) *Differentiation of Work from Familial Considerations.*   Weber emphasized the degree to which rational administration, "bureaucracy," depended on the differentiation of role behavior in administration from familial, local, and friend-

ship ties. To the degree that people are appropriately socialized for work in modern administrative structures, they should be *personally* inclined to differentiate their administrative activity from these primordial ties. If, as Weber argues, structural differentiation is so important for ensuring the predictability, rationality, and discipline of role behavior in administration, then the psychological inclination not to mix business with affection should also be important. The item analysis left two items in the scale which seem to tap this dimension of the rational disposition:

In looking for employment, one ought to find a job near his parents, even if this implies losing a good opportunity elsewhere.

To be happy, one ought to behave as other people want, even if he has to repress his own ideas.

The inclination to mix familial matters with employment decisions and the inclination to decide problems according to the drift of opinion among associates should both diminish the inclination to treat administrative problems without fear or favor.

(3) *Activism.* One of the items that remained in the scale seems to tap an activist, controlling, attitude toward the world in general. Planning involves a belief that the world is fundamentally controllable. This item is:

Making plans only brings unhappiness, because plans are always hard to realize.

(4) *Orientation toward Sources of Knowledge.* Rationality would not amount to much if solutions had to be created anew with every new problem. The body of relevant knowledge is cosmopolitanized by means of writing. The chief advantage of modern societies, as compared with primitive societies, is that the body of knowledge is much larger. But if men solve their problems as individuals, without reference to that body of knowledge, we can expect approximately a primitive level of performance. The inclination to seek knowledge where it is, namely in written materials, is an essential component of rational behavior. We had several scale items on communications behavior, from which the one that was selected out by item analysis was the number of books which the respondent reported having in his home. Probably this is because systematic organization of knowledge in relation to a series of problems is most characteristic of the book form of publication. Hence, the inclination to read books and to buy books and keep them, reflects rather accurately a positive attitude toward the use of a cosmopolitan body of knowledge. We gave a weight of 2 to this item

if the respondent reported more than 300 books in his home, 1 if he reported between 20 and 300, and 0 if he reported 20 or less.

Our selection of items by an empiricist procedure of item-to-total correlation has produced a set of attitudinal and behavioral variables that seems to measure a predisposition to use rational methods in the solution of problems. The scale has a high degree of internal consistency for this sample. Comparison with the work of Kahl suggests that the items on trust of others have more discriminating power in the middle-class sample than in the population as a whole.[3]

Biography and Rationality

A social structure at any given time can be conceived as a cross section of flows from various other social structures: flows of people, flows of goods, flows of ideas. Cities in their ethnic aspect are cross sections of migration flows of families from different origins. Populations are flows of living entities from birth to death. Organizations are cross sections of flows through the labor market.

In each of these social structures, these flows are significant because people are affected by their place in them. If we look at them from the point of view of the individual, these flows are biographies. A man's origin before he came to the city (or better, the origin of his family) is a determinent of his ethnic role in the city. A man's age in a population structure is a critical determinant of his behavior, especially of his behavior in introducing new births into the population and in his entry into the labor market. A man's participation in previous social systems is a determinant of his disposition in his present organization.

Our purpose in this section is to examine the impact of the origins of men on their dispositions to rationality within the organization. Then we will deal with the structural aspects of this flow, that is, where men *from* different structures end up in the structure of the factory. We are interested first in the psychological connections between biographical characteristics and rational or "modern" predispositions, and then in the flow of men with those predispositions into administrative roles.

Two features of men's biographies seem to be crucial. The first is education. Education is explicitly organized around bodies of rationalized and systematized knowledge, mostly of an instrumental kind. People are much more likely to read in schools than in spontaneous interaction. They are much more likely

3. Kahl, *Measurement of Modernism*, p. 39. Kahl himself finds this result. The program that I have handy will not compute a split-half reliability with weighted items, but the computation on a related scale dichotomizing the number of books gives an estimated reliability of .62. This is an overestimate because of the way items were selected with the same sample so as to maximize reliability.

to read nonfiction when their reading is determined by the educational system rather than by personal impulse or spontaneous social groups. Educated people's reading usually has a larger nonfictional component. This systematic knowledge-oriented character of social interaction in schools distinguishes schools from most other kinds of social interaction.

This may seem like a trivial point, but like many trivial points it has great implications. There is a general conception that the role of education is to stuff a certain amount of relevant knowledge into the mind of the student. But, first, the evidence that people still know, when they are mature adults, what they learned in school is rather shaky. Second, it usually turns out that the knowledge they have learned does not apply exactly to their problems. I think that what *is* "learned" and what does have a permanent effect is not, for instance, knowledge about the Renaissance in Italy, but the *disposition* to find out about the Renaissance by reading books. This behavior pattern, once learned, is reinforced in everyday life by its success in solving problems. Knowledge of the Renaissance is not usually reinforced.

The second critical biographical feature seems to be sheer variety in the number of social systems in which people have been deeply engaged. Such engagement renders intelligible and predictable the motives and beliefs of others, and forms a basis for trusting their motives. It renders believable, also, alternative ways of doing things, as we discussed in Chapter 2, and consequently inclines people to find out about these other ways of doing things. For our purposes, education was measured merely by asking people how much schooling they had completed; "cosmopolitanism," or the variety of biographical experience with other social systems, was measured by a combination of questions selected by an item-to-total correlation criterion. These may be summarized under the following headings: (1) the number of friendship attachments to people living in other places, (2) the migration history of the family, (3) the cosmopolitanism of the city in which a man's early years were spent, and (4) his current traveling behavior in his work.

(1) *The Distribution of Friendships.* Deep involvement in social systems tends to shape the context of friendship formation. Those systems in which one has formed friendships are likely to be those which have had the greatest socializing effect on the individual. Consequently, the *present* distribution of friendships probably measures fairly accurately the depth of psychological involvement in *past* social systems. The core of our scale of "biographical" cosmopolitanism is an indirect measure of involvement in other social systems, the frequency with which "best friends" live in other cities. We asked the place of residence of the three best friends of each respondent. For each of his friends who lived outside the steel city region, the respondent received one point on the scale of biographical cosmopolitanism.

(2) *Migration History.*   We would expect that the migration of families or individuals would produce a network of attachments to, and knowledge of, social systems beyond the local one. By summing two items, we arranged it so that a man whose family had migrated to the area before the birth of his parents received no points; one whose parents had migrated before he was born, or who himself had migrated more than 20 years ago, was given one point; one who had migrated, with or without his parents, between 4 and 20 years ago, received two points; and one who had migrated (usually without his parents) 3 or less years ago received three points. Essentially, then, this component of the cosmopolitanism scale is a measure of the recency of familial contact with another social system, insofar as this is determined by migration.

(3) *Cosmopolitanism of Early Socialization.*   We asked each respondent the size of the city he had lived in when he was 15 years old. The variety of social systems to which one is exposed in early childhood depends on the complexity of the urban structure in which one is raised. A respondent got two points if his city was a major urban center with a population of over 500,000; one point if it was a city of between 25,000 and 500,000; no points if it was less than 25,000.

(4) *Current Contacts.*   Finally, a few people traveled frequently to the capital city in the course of their work. The cumulative impact of this travel, or better, the impact of the involvement in another social system that it implies, measures a more current form of cosmopolitanism.

These items form a scale of high reliability in the sample. All can be thought of as measuring a single underlying characteristic of a man's biography. They all measure social involvement in other social systems by friendship attachment to another system, by having lived in the other systems, or by now working in a role that moves him physically to other systems. Even though some of the measures are of current behavior, as is the case with friendship and travel, they seem to reflect the character of the biography which a man brings to the local social system.

The Interaction of Education and Cosmopolitanism

Let us consider a component of the rational attitude, studying, which is not included in the scale of modernism of attitudes, to explore how the components of biography, education, and cosmopolitanism, interact to produce rational behavior. We asked each respondent whether he had studied anything, or was studying anything at the time, for the purpose of having more success at work. Studying is, of course, systematic preparation for being rational. Table 4.1 reports the percentage of respondents who had studied outside of work, after having left school.

TABLE 4.1

The Percentage Who Have Studied for Success at Work after Leaving School, Varies with Both Cosmopolitanism and Education

	Education		
Biography	Secondary or less	More than secondary, less than univ. grad.	University graduate
Locals	42% (93)	61% (28)	— (7)[a]
Intermediate	56% (61)	88% (41)	85% (32)
Cosmopolitans	71% (28)	90% (42)	90% (67)

[a]Too few cases for meaningful percentage.

The cosmopolitanism scale was broken approximately in thirds with scores of 0–3, low; 4–5, medium; 6–8, high. Three people did not answer the education questions and were eliminated from the following analysis. "No answers" to items in the cosmopolitanism scale were scored as local. Clearly both cosmopolitanism of biography and education produce independent effects on studying behavior. Among those with secondary or less education, cosmopolitanism of biography makes a 29% difference in the number who set out systematically to furnish their minds. The same order of effect also holds for those who have shown sufficient motivation to go to school after secondary graduation. On the other hand, at any given level of cosmopolitanism of biography, an education beyond secondary school gives a strong push toward systematic improvement of one's cognitive capacities.

The same broad additive effect of education and cosmopolitan biography occurs with a number of dependent variables, including such things as reading newspapers from outside the area, and the various individual items on the scale of attitudinal and behavioral modernism already discussed. Apparently, there is usually a stronger difference between university graduates and all others than appears in Table 4.1 (Table 4.1 was selected for presentation to show this exceptional pattern.)

What this means, then, is that the sorts of experiences measured by the cosmopolitanism scale produce the same pattern of cognitive and attitudinal behavior as does education. The more education, *or* the more migration, the more modern one's attitudes and behavior. This suggests that we might construct a combined "modernism of background" scale by adding together some weighted function of years of schooling and a weighted function of cosmopolitanism.

We did this by using the categories in Table 4.1. Locals received no points, intermediates one point, and cosmopolitans two points. Those with less than secondary education received no points; those with more than secondary, but less than university received one point; and those with a university degree got a special weight of three points. Thus, a university degree was weighted more heavily. Table 4.2 gives the scale scores of the cells in Table 4.1.

The correlation between this scale on modernism of background and the other on modernism of attitudes and behavior (discussed earlier in this chapter) is .58. For the scales themselves, this is an estimate of their minimum validity in the sample, because the content of the two scales is sufficiently different that the high correlation between them validates each.

But more important from our point of view, this high correlation suggests the mechanism by which an orientation toward modernism is generated. Consequently, it suggests at a more fundamental level what the "modern" attitude really consists of.

TABLE 4.2

Modernism of Background Scale Scores

	Education		
Biography	Less than secondary	Secondary, no degree	University degree
Locals	0	1	3
Intermediate	1	2	4
Cosmopolitans	2	3	5

Number of cases in each scale position, eliminating three cases with no information on education:

Scale score	Number
0	93
1	89
2	69
3	49
4	32
5	67
	399

The Predisposition to Abstract

When we look at naturally occurring cognitive behavior, we are not trying to study the same thing that intelligence tests try to study. Intelligence tests, by setting up a specially motivated situation, quite deliberately try to avoid the "interference" of such motivational factors as the predisposition to solve mathematics problems for fun. Such tests predict quite well how students will behave, for it predicts from a test situation in which people are expected to solve mathematics problems, to a classroom situation where they are also expected to solve mathematics problems. Hence, the intelligence test measures the capacity to solve abstract problems, given the inclination. But the predisposition to abstract in daily life is a mixture of both inclination and capacity.

Men abstract in an intelligence test, because they are presented with abstract problems, are told that they are expected to solve them, and know they will be graded by abstract features of the answer. This kind of situational expectation to abstract is built into educational institutions, legal and political institutions, cost accounting systems, engineering practice, and so forth. But after we have accounted for as much variation in everyday cognitive behavior as possible by a combination of intelligence and situational expectations, is there anything left to explain by predispositional factors? And if there is, what would be the types of biography that would produce the inclination to abstract? Our purpose so far in this chapter has been to locate this predisposition through some of its effects, and then to study its sources in men's biographies. The rest of this chapter will explore the effects of this predisposition on men's cognitive behavior.

Let us summarize the argument so far. Our main point has been that the complex of modern attitudes and behavior so often found associated with modern societies, and with the most modern sections within societies, is a matter of cognitive style, of *Weltanschauung*. The central feature of this cognitive style is that it interprets the experience of everyday life in terms of abstract conceptual schemes. In these abstract conceptions, the causes of the experience, and alternative ways of manipulating it, may be unobservable. Causes and alternatives are learned only through reading, writing, and calculating.

One fundamental aspect of this world view or cognitive style is that other people's behavior becomes interpretable. The actions played out by others on the stage can be conceived of as part of a sensible life pattern of the others, and as part of an organizational system of actions. The more another's behavior is abstracted from its concrete significance to our situational motives and anxieties, and interpreted from the point of view of his biography, his interests, his organizational position, the less that behavior seems stubborn, evil, or irrational. This, of course, merely translates into the language of measurable variables the adage: "To know all is to forgive all."

Men whose cognitive style leads them to forgive more people will experience social life as more benign. Partly this is because they understand the evil that is done to them. But partly, it is because less evil is done to them; social life becomes in fact more benign to those who diagnose correctly what other people are up to. Social life, to a man with little inclination to abstract, is one damn thing after another—much of it painful. Social life to a man who abstracts is the stoical experience of what he expected anyway. The amount of pain and frustration may be the same. Hence, trust in others, and the perception of the behavior of others as understandable and benign, can be thought of as one effect of the inclination to abstract—to apply to experience frames of reference which are not present in the situation of action. This is not, of course, the only way that trust in others can be interpreted. To justify such an interpretation we must explore both the other elements of a modern *Weltanschauung*, and the biographical sources of trust in others.

Now let us consider what the relation between the inclination to abstract and the motivational force of primordial ties—family, neighborhood, and age groups—compared to the motivational force of careers or ideals. If a man experiences life as it comes, its meaning will be organized in terms of the crucial social ties through which he has emotionally significant relations. These are the family, the territory, and the age groups with whom he is socialized; perhaps we should add the work group. But careers and ideals are organized around causal forces that have extensions into the future and into the past. The future and the past are creations of the abstracting process. No one can experience the future. The meaning of the past in terms of the future can be created only by abstracting. Hence, the motivational force of careers, and of ideals, depends on the vigor of abstraction. Only if present experience is selectively perceived in terms of the future, can the future endow it with motivational significance. Careers and ideals are both mechanisms that make the future motivationally significant. Hence, the decline of primordial motivations is tied to the inclination to abstract.

In the same way, the meaning of plans is given by the future. Activism involves the conception of present activity in terms of its causal impact on the future. The conception that the world is manipulable depends on the causal analysis of past and present experience. The inclination to causal analysis requires an inclination to abstract, for most of daily life has an insignificant effect on the future.

Finally, reading and writing almost invariably involve greater abstraction than other forms of social interaction. One need only compare the subtlety of biographical and motivational explanation in the average novel, intended to be read, with the crudity of the plot motivation in the average drama, intended to be heard and seen.[4] The inclination to read and study reflects an inclination to abstract.

All we have shown here is that one can conceive the complex of modern attitudes as the result of a cognitive style. But in order for this to be convincing,

---

4. Very few artists are talented in both media. Of those who made a living from drama, the only one who occurs to me as a leading prose writer is George Bernard Shaw and the people in Shaw's prose are pasteboard characters, unreal capitalists, poor people, and even unreal other playwrights. See his *The Quintessence of Ibsenism* (New York: Hill and Wang, 1958). Of those who made a living writing novels, it is hard to find a really talented playwright—Tolstoy perhaps. See also the discussion of the difference in structure between oral narrative poetry and written narratives in Robert Scholes and Robert Kellogg, *The Nature of Narrative* (London: Oxford Univ. Press, 1966, pp. 17–56).

we have to show that causes which should produce the inclination to abstract do indeed produce a modern attitude. Clearly the major logical potential cause of the inclination to abstract is education. Education takes as its aim the teaching of schemes of abstraction, and it provides the tools for manipulating and communicating abstractions.

The problem here is that education is too good a variable—it explains too much. We know that education measures at least the following variables: social class of origin, achievement motivation, intelligence, experience in the metropolis, region, or country of birth, ethnicity, occupational achievement, and income. Knowing how many things influence the amount of education, or are influenced by it, it would be rather surprising to find an attitude that was not related to education. But that, in turn, means that the strong positive relation we find between education and a modern *Weltanschauung* supports our notion very weakly. There are so many mechanisms by which education could produce modernism that we have little confidence that we have found the right one. Nevertheless, it is at least in keeping with the professed aims of schooling that it would increase the inclination to abstract. And it is in keeping with the data that it does indeed produce that result.

But a more interesting and persuasive argument can be constructed if we consider the degree of cosmopolitanism of a person. Our proposal is that a biography of deep involvement in a variety of social systems will produce an inclination to abstract from the details of present experience. Various indicators of deep involvement in other systems can be used. If people have friends in other social systems, they are likely to have been deeply involved in them. If people speak the language of another system they have probably been in communication with its members. If people have lived in other social systems, they are more likely to have experienced how those social systems worked. If people keep up contact with another system, it indicates continuing involvement.

It turns out that these indicators of the degree of involvement with other social systems hang together empirically in our sample.[5]

It also turns out that the modernism attitude complex is quite well predicted by cosmopolitanism of background, even when we control for education. The question we face, then, is why such indicators of cosmopolitanism as the number of best friends who live elsewhere are correlated with a complex of attitudes which are also correlated with education.

---

5. They also hang together quite closely with education. For various reasons, too tedious to outline here, this study overall cannot at all be thought of as indicating the degree to which migration, education, urbanism of origin, and occupation hang together. If that were of interest, the correlations in the middle-class random sample might give a clue. In the sample as a whole, our sampling procedure might cause correlations even if, in the country as a whole, the correlations were zero. Migration is very tricky to deal with in a local sample.

The explanation I suggest is that a variety of involvements in other social systems encourages a man to abstract from his current experience. After a man moves from a system that had his commitment, he interprets the new system in terms of the old. But this involves abstracting from his past experience those elements which explain the difference. And it involves abstracting what is essentially different about the new system. We have all met the man who has just moved and who is constantly saying: "At _____ we used to do it differently." But when he was at _____ he did not realize it was such a different way of doing things.

I suggest, then, that a man with a biography of variety in social involvements will experience his environment differently. This difference will be in the direction of abstraction, of interpreting an experience in terms of the past, of the future, of the distant, of notions from books and magazines. It frees men of complacency with their immediate reaction and it convinces them that to understand one's experience, one has to study it. This suggestion is not, of course, a new one. It is the explanation that Thorstein Veblen gave for "The Intellectual Preeminence of Jews in Modern Europe."[6] What I suggest, essentially, is that Veblen's theory of the intellectual preeminence of European Jews also explains why people with friends elsewhere are more likely to take adult education courses.

All of this has been a rather heavy intellectual superstructure to explain why some attitude items fall into a scale, why some background items fall into another scale, and why these scales are highly correlated. That set of facts has to be explained, to be sure. But it would be more convincing if we could show that the background scale, and the attitude scale, actually predict the pattern of cognitive behavior of men at work. That is, we can presumably obtain better measures of how much abstracting behavior men carry out than whether they trust their relatives or pursue a career even when it takes them away from their relatives. Even though some color of reality might be given to these attitudes as measures of cognitive style, the tones are rather pastel. With the scales in hand, then, let us explore cognitive behavior in the work role.

Structural Position and Individual Rationality

We now wish to consider the relation between the structure of administrative activity outlined in Chapter 3 and the social foundations for a rational use of the intellect, outlined so far in this chapter. A convenient way to start is to consider the social location of the kinds of people identified by high values of the "modernism predictor scale" developed in this chapter. The proportion "high" (3, 4, or 5) on this scale, for the structural groups discussed in Chapter 3 is given in Table 4.3 in Columns (1) and (3).

6. Thorstein Veblen, *Essays in Our Changing Order*. New York: Viking, 1945, pp. 219–231.

TABLE 4.3

The Relationship among Structural Position, Modernism of Background (Columns 1 and 3), Modernism of Attitudes and Behavior (Columns 2 and 4) (Percentage "High" on Each Dependent Variable)[a]

	City nonindustrial			Industrial		
	(1) Percentage "High"	(2) Percentage "High"		(3) Percentage "High"	(4) Percentage "High"
Status	mod. back.	modernism	Status	mod. back.	modernism
Employees	15 (65)	17 (65)	Low industrial	12 (92)	16 (92)
Bureaucrats	55 (20)	30 (20)	Intermediate	43 (61)	46 (61)
			High executive	90 (62)	81 (62)
			Staff	55 (42)	50 (42)
Small business	10 (39)	10 (39)			
Larger business	41 (17)	35 (17)			

[a] The numbers in parentheses are the number of cases on which the percentage is based. The definitions of the structural variables are outlined in Table 3.1.

It is clear that some of the main selective criteria of the economic system in general are tapped by this modernism of biography variable. In the city, both bureaucrats and larger businessmen are more cosmopolitan and educated than those without subordinates. In the plants (the three countries are considered together here), the low-ranking people are as little cosmopolitan and educated as the employees and small businessmen of the city, but the intermediate line and high executives are much higher. The staff is the only group without many levels of subordinates who show the educational and migration background and cosmopolitan attachments that produce "modern" attitudes and intellectual behavior.

In view of the high correlation between this cosmopolitanism—education "modernism predictor" and the composite attitudinal index of rational use of the intellect, which we have called "modernism," it is not surprising that the proportions "high" on modernism in the various groups is quite similar to the proportion "high" on the modernism predictor. This percentage is given in Columns (2) and (4) in Table 4.3. It is clear that we are talking about the same things when we talk of cosmopolitan—educated structural groups and when we talk of groups with "modern" attitudes toward planning and the use of the intellect.

What Table 4.3 shows, then, is a strong empirical relationship among three theoretically distinct variables: (1) hierarchical and industrial position in the productive process; (2) educational and migration biographical factors in the individual, and his resulting social attachments to supralocal systems of social action; and (3) his attitude toward planning, intellectual autonomy, ascriptive familial attachments, the reliability of people, and his relation to books. Present economic and administrative position, background and biography, and behavior and attitudes toward rational use of the intellect in social life, are tightly empirically linked.

The problem now is to explain the mechanism by which the link between background and attitudes, discussed previously, is related to a man's role in the economy in the way indicated by Table 4.3. We want, so to speak, an outline of the physiology of the economy to explain how people with a cosmopolitan— educated background are concentrated so highly in certain structural positions in the economy. We presume that this is because they are the appropriate kinds of people to carry out the activities corresponding to that structural position. A clue to what kind of people they are, and hence what advantages they might bring to a structural position, is the complex of attitudes and behavior measured by the "modernism" scale. And a clue to why such orientation and behavior will be crucial in certain roles is the pattern of activity which we found associated with these roles in Chapter 3.

Modernism and Cognitive Activities

There are two possible alternative theories about the relation between administrative position and modernism. First, we might think that the statuses determined both the type of people qualified for them, and also the cognitive activities. That is, it could be that we hire engineers (who happen to be modern in outlook) for staff and executive positions. Then we tell all engineers and executives (regardless of origin) that they must think and plan. Or second, it might be that we recruit a modernized, cosmopolitan person because we require the sort of cognitive behavior that he will naturally be inclined to carry out.

In the first case, we will expect all people of equivalent status to have equivalent role behavior, regardless of their background and attitudes. In the second case, we will expect people of equivalent status to behave differently, according to their background. The key place to look for differences between these two expectations is in the areas of cognitive behavior itself, especially reading, writing, calculating, drawing, and other sharply intellectual activities. We will also expect differences in work on innovations and in the committee problem-solving style of communication. Because of the strong relations between background and status, we will of course have difficulty finding people with equivalent backgrounds in different statuses.

Table 4.4 reports hours spent in various sharply intellectual activities, mostly having to do with thinking about written communications. In every case but one (city employees), there is a strong relation between the background variables

TABLE 4.4

Hours Spent in Intellectual Activity (Thinking, Reading, Writing, Calculating, Drawing), by Status and "Modernism Predictor" (Education and Cosmopolitanism)

| | City nonindustrial | | | | Industrial | | |
| | Modernism predictor | | | | Modernism predictor | | |
Status	Low	Med.	High	Status	Low	Med.	High
Employees	0.20 (25)	0 (34)	0.25 (10)	Low	0.49 (38)	0.88 (43)	3.34 (11)
Bureaucrats	[a] (1)	0.56 (8)	2.36 (11)	Intermediate line	[a] (6)	0.69 (29)	1.39 (26)
				High executive	[a] (0)	[a] (6)	1.07 (56)
				Staff	[a] (3)	1.17 (16)	3.13 (23)
Small business	0.06 (18)	0.44 (17)	[a] (4)				
Larger business	[a] (3)	0.43 (7)	1.39 (7)				

[a] Less than seven cases; averages meaningless.

which predict modernism and the amount of intellectual activity.[7] This shows up even among owners of businesses, who have created their own roles for themselves, so it is unlikely to be because of the role-requirements of positions.

This effect of background is particularly striking for the highly modern people in industry. There the pattern is almost exactly the reverse of what would be expected on the basis of the first role requirement theory; for that role most recruited from among more modernized men, the high executives, is the role in which such modernized men spend the least time in intellectual activity (but compare Table 4.6). Probably, this is because of the pressure of hierarchical communication from subordinates, discussed in Chapter 3. Subordinates' problems tend to push contemplation and study out of the lives of their superiors.

There is evidence here, therefore, that education, and the variety of attachments to different social systems produced by it and by other factors, have an independent causal impact on the shape of cognitive life in industrial bureaucracies. The amount of intellectual activity in such bureaucracies cannot be predicted very well from the requirements of the roles in them. People apparently do not think about written materials just because they are paid to do so. They also think about them because of the kind of men they are.

Table 4.5 shows that this patterning of intellectual activity corresponds rather closely to the patterning of work on innovations. The pattern is not as clear in the city, perhaps indictating that our measure of innovation is not as appropriate for commerce as for industry.[8] Within the industrial firms, however, the relation of modernism of background to innovative activity is clear and strong, and overrides any relation of innovation to hierarchical rank. Only the staff statuses produce a markedly higher proportion of time in innovation, among people of equal modernism.

Table 4.6 reports the amount of time spent in that form of organizational communication most appropriate for solving cognitive problems, the "meeting." In each case, except among the city bureaucrats and large businessmen, the committee style of communications behavior is more prevalent among the more modernized men. As we might expect, however, communications behavior is

7. The exception is not significant, since we are talking about a difference between no intellectual activity and 12 minutes a day. It does show the emptiness of the usual low-paying middle-class job, which discourages thought even among those predisposed toward it.

8. There could be two difficulties. First, it may be that the central commercial innovative practice is starting new firms, and that consequently innovative activity is much more concentrated during that part of a man's life when he starts a firm. By sampling fluctuations, we may have missed all but one or two of those rare bursts of concentrated innovation. Second, commerce and professional practice both involve manipulating people rather than things, and procedures for handling clients may be changed by detailed responsive feedback mechanisms (involving visual supervision) rather than by redesigning formal procedures or machines. If so, the distinction between administration and innovation would be difficult to make in the city.

TABLE 4.5

Hours Spent on Innovations (Expansions, Improvement of Procedures, New Machines, etc.), by Status and "Modernism Predictor"

City nonindustrial

Status	Modernism predictor		
	Low	Med.	High
Employees	0 (25)	0 (34)	0 (10)
Bureaucrats	a (1)	0.50 (8)	0.48 (11)
Small business	0 (18)	0.12 (17)	a (4)
Large business	a (3)	0.71 (7)	0 (7)

Industrial

Status	Modernism predictor		
	Low	Med.	High
Low	0.20 (38)	0.38 (43)	1.39 (11)
Intermediate line	a (6)	0.26 (29)	0.77 (26)
High executive	a (0)	a (6)	1.20 (56)
Staff	a (3)	0.61 (16)	2.84 (23)

[a]Less than seven cases; averages meaningless.

TABLE 4.6

Hours Spent in Meetings with More Than Two People, by Status and "Modernism Predictor"

	City nonindustrial				Industrial		
	Modernism predictor				Modernism predictor		
Status	Low	Med.	High	Status	Low	Med.	High
Employees	0 (25)	0.19 (34)	0.38 (10)	Low	0.01 (38)	0 (43)	0.05 (11)
Bureaucrats	[a] (1)	0.75 (8)	0.54 (11)	Intermediate line	[a] (6)	0.43 (29)	0.92 (26)
				High executive	[a] (0)	[a] (6)	1.71 (56)
Small business	0. (18)	0.24 (17)	[a] (4)	Staff	[a] (3)	0.19 (16)	0.87 (23)
Larger business	[a] (3)	0 (7)	0 (7)				

[a]Less than seven cases; averages meaningless

112

much more shaped by one's place in the administrative social system than intellectual style. Even the modernized part of the staff and intermediate line in industry is less central to the problem-solving communications structure than the high executives. The low-level industrial employees are almost out of it.

The general pattern of cognitive behavior in organization roles is very clear. The more a man has been exposed to written culture through schooling, and the more cosmopolitan his social attachments, the more intellectual, innovative, and meeting activity he engages in during his work. In general, modernism or cosmopolitanism of background is a more powerful influence on the cognitive behavior of industrial bureaucrats than is hierarchical position. The central source of the innovativeness of bureaucracy appears to be its tendency to recruit cosmopolitan types of people to positions of power.

Achievement Motives versus Thought

It appears then that the common imagery of the motivational accompaniments of "entrepreneurs" is mistaken. The dominant image is that men innovate by putting more energy into their work. The facts shown in our data seem to indicate that men innovate by putting more thought into their work. And the kinds of men who put more thought into their work appear to be those who have already seen and read about diverse social and technical systems and who continue to hear and read about them through their multiple, nonlocal, social attachments and through their inclination to use written media of communication. The image of each firm creating new technology de novo is mistaken. Innovations derive basically from a body of technical and organizational culture outside the immediate firm. The more exposed men are to that culture, the more they think, read, write, and calculate to improve the efficiency of the firm they are in. The pressures for great effort appear to derive from the tendency of subordinates to bring routine problems to their superiors. These pressures tend to drive out thought and reflection from the work life of executives. The combination of cosmopolitan background and staff status (with few levels of subordinates) produces the environment in which innovative thought goes forward most easily. This is exactly the opposite of the situation of the typical small entrepreneur, who is poorly educated, has local attachments, and has subordinates for whom he is ultimately reponsible.

Modernism and Other Occupational Behavior

For noncognitive behavior at work, a modern background is either of small importance or the results are trivial. For example, among the low-status groups, an intermediate level of modern background (i.e., education) characterizes clerks, a low level characterizes those manual workers who were in our sample.

There is some slight tendency for more modernized people to have more contacts during the previous day with people outside the organization. There is a moderate tendency for staff personnel, intermediate line industrial, and city bureaucrats to spend more time in visual supervision or inspection if they are less modern in background. Perhaps this indicates some feeling on their part that the papers are not real and that control cannot be exercised without visual inspection. Less modernized men have somewhat more of a tendency to spend working hours on personal affairs and recreation.

There may be some slight effect of modernism on hierarchical communications behavior. There is a suggestion of an "interaction effect" between status and modernism on hierarchical communication patterns. The more educated and cosmopolitan a low-status person, the more he communicates with his (mostly educated) bureaucratic superiors. The more educated and cosmopolitan a high-status executive or staff person, the less he communicates with his superior. This suggests a structure of apprenticeship, or a set of aides, whereby low-status people who can expect to become executives are closely supervised by their superiors to gain varied experience. But once arrived, the educated man responds more to the task and to impersonal (paper) controls, and less to oral hierarchically organized communication. See Table 4.7.

In general, when we look at the scale of modernism in attitudes and behavior, our results are in the same direction as those from the "modernism of background," but weaker. This is compatible with the notion that the causal force operating to change congitive styles is a deposit of men's educational and migration biographies, which then shapes both their general *Weltanschauung* and their style of cognitive behavior at work,

Conclusions

Our general purpose in Chapters 2 through 4 has been to analze the sociological and social psychological foundations of the distinctive patterns of cogntive behavior of industrial bureaucrats. Industrial administration of a modern technical system poses a different set of cognitive problems than the typical administrative system of more traditional parts of the economy. In particular, the gale of innovation in the internationally competitive industrial markets requires constant innovation on the local scene. Retail trade, schools, and professional practice compete locally, and they can "afford" to be less efficient than firms abroad. A stagnant school system can last indefinitely (as many have). But only a constantly rising tariff barrier can protect a stagnant industrial firm. What is required in industrial administration, then, is "routinization of innovation."

Throughout our discussion on the intellectual life of industrial bureaucracies, we have been contrasting two approaches to the explanation of innovation.

TABLE 4.7

Hours during Which Communication with a Superior Took Place, by Status and "Modernism Predictor"[a]

City nonindustrial

Status	Modernism predictor		
	Low	Med.	High
Employees	0.20 (25)	0.35 (34)	0.10 (10)
Bureaucrats	[a] (1)	0.16 (8)	0.73 (11)
Small business	n.a.[b]	n.a.[b]	n.a.[b]
Larger business	n.a.[b]	n.a.[b]	n.a.[b]

Industrial

Status	Modernism predictor		
	Low	Med.	High
Low	0.49 (38)	0.69 (43)	1.25 (11)
Intermediate line	[a] (6)	1.08 (29)	0.98 (26)
High executive	[a] (0)	[a] (6)	0.70 (56)
Staff	[a] (3)	1.16 (16)	0.52 (23)

[a] Less than seven cases; averages meaningless
[b] n.a. = not applicable—no superiors

115

One might be called the "Protestant ethic" explanation. It argues, essentially, that some kinds of people are more strongly motivated to do well in occupational roles. Being more strongly motivated, they work harder at introducing innovations.

The alternative explanation that we have argued for here rests on the sociology of cognition rather than on the sociology of motivation. It argues, essentially, that some kinds of people think better about the problems involved in innovation. It rests on the assumption that there is more variation in what people know how to do than there is in people's motivation to do well.

The process of thinking about a system of activities may be conceived of as having the following elements:

(1) The receipt of information about those activities, shaped by the structure of the channel of information and by the structure of the person's mind which determines what he pays attention to

(2) The "apperceptive mass," the preexisting set of categories, sensitivities, and theories in a person's mind, that determines what future courses of action he sees as possible, and in particular what innovations in the system of activities he conceives.

(3) His style of analysis of the information received and other information or theoretical structures he can bring to bear

A crucial dimension of each of these elements is the degree of (relevant) abstraction. For innovativeness, a crucial dimension is the degree of psychological "reality" that different future courses of action have; in particular, the relative "reality" of a continuation of the present pattern of action and the "reality" of its various alternatives. For the cognitive adequacy of problem solutions, and hence the likely success of innovations, there seem to be three crucial dimensions of the whole process. First is the adequacy of the causal schema with which a man analyzes the data and the alternatives. Second is the adequacy of his information about the present activities and about their alternatives. Third is the degree of reflectiveness, the degree of calculation and thinking, in the treatment of a problem.

Table 4.8 gives a summary of the relation between the cognitive elements (information received, apperceptive mass, and style of analysis) and the dimensions of cognition related to innovation. Each entry in the chart is a description of that state of the element which best fulfills the requirements for successful innovation. For example, in the third row, corresponding to the "adequacy of causal schemata," the element "information received" is most favorable to innovation if the information is organized in categories or variables that correspond to the causal forces at work. The element "apperceptive mass" is in its most favorable state when the man has learned the appropriate causal schemata in his previous training and experience. The element "style of

TABLE 4.8

Dimensions of Cognitive Elements Encouraging Solution of Problems of Innovation

Dimensions of cognition	Information received	Apperceptive mass	Style of analysis
Degree of abstraction	Information free of irrelevance	Facility in dealing with symbolized abstractions	Calculation paradigms for abstract information
"Reality" of alternatives	Information relevant to alternatives	Alternatives seen elsewhere, or written descriptions seem real	Divorce from thought about current operating problems
Adequacy of causal schemata	Information organized in terms of adequate causal schemata	Experience and training in relevant causal schemata	Deal with one causal system at a time—cognitive specialization
Adequacy of infromation	Adequacy of administrative information, access to outside sources	Information stored from education. Inclination to use outside sources	Information permanently recorded so as to be available at right time
Reflectiveness of treatment	Temporal organization of information to allow thorough analysis	Positive orientation to long-range plans	Divorce from urgent problems interfering with reflection

analysis" is in its most favorable state when the problems presented to a man are those treating one system of interdependent causes at a time.

If we move from the individual to the intellectual social system, we can ask what general conditions of that system will tend to bring these cognitive dimensions to a high level. The analysis of this part of the book has revolved around three main causes of adequate intellectual functioning. The first is the degree to which the information on the system is written, and the structure of abstraction in the information flow system. The second is the orientation of the members of the system to outside sources of ideas, information, and alternatives—especially the cosmopolitanism of men's backgrounds. The third is the structure of demands on their attention in the performance of their roles.

The concrete social structure which best exemplifies the high development of these three forces is the staff structure of industrial bureaucracies. Embedded in a bureaucracy which routinely provides data in written form, the staff deal with abstracted written forms of information. Recruited from among those with backgrounds that produce a cosmopolitan orientation and a facility with abstractions, their apperceptive mass is appropriate for the intelligent solution of problems. Divorced from responsibility for operative subordinates, their time horizons tend to be longer range and their attention is not so distracted by the jumble of problems brought to them by subordinates.

Thus, from a cognitive point of view, the most likely kind of social structure for producing innovation is the staff of a bureaucracy.

But the place where we expect to find most intense effort (and where we do find it in our data) is among high executives and enterpreneurs. Thus, it is significant for the argument advocated here that the industrial staff men spend much more time working on innovations than either of the more "effortful" roles. Unless businessmen and executives achieve much more innovation per hour worked on innovation, our finding decidedly undermines the Protestant ethic explanation of innovation.

But if the superior innovativeness of bureaucracy is because of its structural arrangements for thinking and planning, how do these arrangements themselves come about? They are, after all, both quite subtle and quite powerful. The recruitment process sorts out men to be high executives, of whom 90% have a highly cosmopolitan and educated background, and 81% have highly modern attitudes and behavior. Of the lower ranking industrial bureaucrats, only 12% have such backgrounds and 16% such attitudes.

One clue comes from the comparison between larger and smaller businessmen. The larger businessmen (i.e., those with two or more levels of subordinates) are much more likely to be cosmopolitan and modern. They also spend much more time thinking and innovating. This naturally suggests that they got to be larger businessmen by thinking and innovating. The larger enterprises, created by the influence of cosmopolitan leaders, are likely to be those that give form to the administrative and technical traditions of bureaucracies. That is, the contrast between larger and smaller businessmen suggests that a Darwinian process has selected out structures and traditions that maximize the intellectual capacities of the enterprises.

This is reinforced if we examine, even casually, the patterns of behavior of a business elite. A typical pattern of entrepreneurial biography in the higher echelons includes participation in organizing a wide variety of enterprises, often with a wide variety of different coalitions. The great entrepreneur is often not a man who devotes himself to his "local" enterprise, but instead a business cosmopolitan who has organized other things before.

But it seems unlikely that this is the full explanation; it does not account, for example, for the innovating role of governmental bureaucracies. The steel plants might be innovative because the government adapted an intellectually effective form from American and Italian private firms. But other government bureaucrats are not imitating such firms—the recruitment of educated prople to the civil service, with its cosmopolitanizing influence, goes back deep into the historical development of Western and Oriental governments. In the United States, public administration is one of the industries with the highest proportion of professional workers, and of course most of its "officials" are of cosmopolitan background as well. The affinity of governments for intellectually effective structures and for people with a cosmopolitan cognitive style is not easily explained by Darwinism.

Appendix

A NOTE ON ACQUIESCENCE

Many of the items in the modernism attitude scale we have discussed are so keyed that an acquiescent response is also a traditional response. Even though the scale contains one item (the number of books) that would be affected in the opposite way by acquiescence, we need to explore the question of what it would mean if all that the attitude items measures were acquiescence. To prefigure the conclusion, I would maintain that the argument still holds in full, even if all the attitude items measure an acquiescent response set. I do not believe they do, because many items keyed the same way were eliminated in the scale analysis.

Let us consider what the data mean if the attitude items measure an acquiescent response set. Then we have shown that acquiescence is: (1) negatively related to reading books, (2) negatively related to education, (3) negatively related to having friends in other places, (4) negatively related to migration and travel, and (5) negatively related to innovative and intellectual behavior at work.

Evidently, then, the degree of acquiescence measures very well a variety of background experiences which should produce, we would expect, a distinctive cognitive orientation. Furthermore, it in turn predicts quite well what sort of cognitive behavior a man carries out at work. But, if an acquiescent response set is so closely related to the characteristics of a man's biography, and if it predicts part of his behavior very well, it must be a measure of something rather fundamental about his orientation to the world. Let us consider, then, what might be measured by an inclination to agree with everything, regardless of semantic content, in an interview.

It is clear that what is involved in an acquiescent response set is a failure to abstract the semantic content of a question from the grammatical form or from the interviewer's presentation. Imagine a man in industrial administration who keys his response to the grammatical form of the material presented to him. All the salesmen will talk in such a way that the acquiescent response will be to buy. All the cost accountants will frame their requests the opposite way. The foreman of the affected operation, who will generally be a local and hence acquiescent himself, will be trying to figure out what the man's position is, so he can acquiesce himself. The man will generate such noise and random behavior that his contribution to intellectual analysis will be gladly foregone.

If our scale is measuring the failure to conduct even the elementary abstraction of differentiating the semantic content of a statement from the interview situation, then it is doing what we want it to. We expect that an acquiescent response set will be a feature of those with the *least* inclination to abstract.

For our purposes, then, whatever acquiescent response set the attitude items pick up is all to the good. We certainly do not want to put people whose response depends greatly on grammatical form into the group of the most rational men. Of course, if we are trying to measure some aspects of the personality, then an acquiescent response set should be controlled. But here it would be as foolish as if we were to control for occupation in a study of the effects of social class.

PART III

The Motivation of
Economic Activity

CHAPTER **5**

The Bureaucratic Model
and Career Organization

The Inspector of Traffic in San Felix not only was deficient in figuring out how to do his job well; he was also deficient in motivation to do it well, because the obvious things, like working a full day, had not been done. We need to explain why industrial administrators were reasonably responsive to the requirements of their jobs, but the Inspector was not.

The Petty Capitalism Model of Economic Motivation

A theory of the motivation of some concrete set of activities must answer two rather distinct questions: (1) How does the reward system attach rewards to activities? and (2) Why do people want the rewards? If the Inspector's rewards came from mending fences in Caracas rather than from issuing licenses, then he would be motivated to spend his time in Caracas. If the rewards offered by the system for issuing licenses were not sufficient to motivate hard work in reorganizing the office in San Felix, the Inspector still might go to Caracas.

As a model for a complete or closed theory of motivation, we can analyze classical economics. There are three basic elements of the classical economic theory of motivation:

(1) Whatever motives men have, *if* they can be satisfied through marketed goods and services, *then* men's degree of motivation will be an increasing function of net money return.

(2) Men's motivations and decisions in the market place are efficient and complete causes of what economic activities they carry out.

(3) Net money return to an activity is determined through competitive market mechanisms.

The great achievement of classical economics was to show that if individuals' motives and capacities had the proper form, then they would be motivated in such a way as to produce market equilibriums with certain well defined properties. In particular, the marginal products of a given number of dollars worth of all factors of production would be equated, and the marginal utilities of all commodities of a given cost would be equated, and this equilibrium would have certain optimal properties. Let us examine these elements of the classical synthesis to see in more detail how to build such models of motivational systems.

The first assertion is that people want the rewards of the system, and that their motives for doing one or another activity *within the system* are increasing functions of the reward. That is, a man may want to be rich for the sake of pride, for family continuity, for the sensual pleasure of mink coats, for pure achievement motive because money means to him that he has achieved a standard of excellence, for its anal-erotic significance, or for any other reason. As long as *more* money gives him more pride, continuity, pleasure, achievement, or anal satisfaction than does *less* money, the reward system of the market will have hold of him where he lives. If, however, for irrational reasons, he prefers making toilets to making frilly underwear, even when frills pay better, then the motivational theory is incomplete.[1]

The key simplification, then, is to reduce the variety of things men want to a single measure of the level of reward distributed by the system. If the reward is not controlled by the market system (as for instance, most sexual reward is not), it is assumed to affect behavior in the system randomly and with small effect. If we can express total rewards in the system as a monotonic function of money, then the systemic part of men's behavior can be well understood by studying the distribution of money.

The second major assertion of classical economics is that men *can* control their economic activities. If the number of workers in goldsmithing is set by law, and there is nothing an entrepreneur can do to change that number when

---

1. As long as the unresponsiveness to money takes idiosyncratic forms for different people, most of the aggregate results of classical economics hold. The dispersion around those results will be higher.

demand goes down (or up), then the level of reward (profits) can go up and down without effect on the activity. The key simplification here is to regard all activities of a "firm" to have been decided by the man who collects the net profits. This simplification is approximately true for petty capitalism of the eighteenth and early nineteenth centuries, when the theory was being elaborated. This does not mean that the market equilibriums may not be the same for corporate capitalism. It means, rather, that modern market equilibriums are achieved in spite of the fact that the decisions are made by salaried officials rather than by profit takers. That is, the classical theory is no longer a theory of motivation of decisions. (In fact, we will attempt here indirectly to answer the question: How can one get classical market equilibriums from salaried officials?) An increasing level of reward for an increasing amount of an activity can only motivate that activity if the man who gets the reward *can* increase the activity. One of the crucial questions of the origin of capitalism is how men in new businesses—nonaristocratic men—ever got the authority to tell workers what to do, and the freedom to lay them off when demand fell off. Feudal lords could not lay off their tenants, nor feudal artisans lay off their apprentices.

The final element of the theory describes how rewards are distributed among activities. I do not intend to discuss how the competitive mechanism works. What is important is that the reward for an increased amount of a given activity varies with the state of the system as a whole in such a way as to motivate men to reach an equilibrium. From the point of view of economics as a discipline, these mechanisms of adjustment of rewards are the most interesting part of the theory. From our point of view, we need only know that they are there.

Capitalistic and Bureaucratic Reward Systems

The bureaucrat generally occupies an official position with fixed or slowly growing rewards, rather than taking profits. His rewards come in the form of future promotions, rather than present profits. His discretion is generally limited by regulations and by his superiors' authority, and promotions come by the judgment of his superiors and perhaps his test scores or education, rather than from an equilibrating competitive system. Offhand, the bureaucratic motivational system seems an unlikely substitute for petty capitalism. Yet in the advanced capitalist countries, capitalists themselves are substituting large bureaucratic corporations for petty capitalist enterprises—evidently because they are, in some sense, more efficient systems.

With the model of classical economics to show us what a motivational theory of a system of economic action should look like, let us try to construct a theory of bureaucratic motivation. We are, of course, aided in this by the fact that Max Weber has been here before us. What we will be doing, then, is asking about the motivational significance of various structural features of bureaucracies which have been analyzed by Weber.[2] Our theory would look like this:

(1) The rewards that the system distributes are *promotions to higher office*. Hence men will be best motivated by these rewards:
  a. If they have a vivid vision of future rewards.
  b. If they have a firm conviction that excellence of present activity is a cause of future rewards.
  c. If they have a long future in which to be rewarded.

(2) The rewards are distributed according to various measures of the *performance capacity* of people. These will motivate good performance:
  a. If measures of performance are based on variables whose effective cause is the action of the man. (We usually say "authority commensurate with responsibility.")
  b. If performance measures reflect the performance that is in fact good for the system—promotions should not be based on poker playing ability, for instance.
  c. If performance capacity in higher offices is well predicted by good performance in lower offices.

(3) As for the reward system itself, it must consist of such a system as will in fact distribute rewards as specified in (1) and (2). More specifically.
  a. There must be higher offices to distribute, under the control of the organization.
  b. Criteria other than performance capacity must be excluded from the promotion system.
  c. There must be pressure on those who set up the reward system to change measures of performance capacity as the requirements of the organizational mission change.
  d. A man's future rewards, and the criteria used to get them, must be communicated to him in sufficient detail ahead of time, so that the future rewards will motivate the present behavior. Such symbolic reward systems as grades, evaluations by superiors, cost accounting measures of efficiency, and so forth, must be infused with rewarding meaning by their connection with future advancement.

In combination these several statements about a bureaucratic motivational system answer all the questions that the classical economist answered about the

---

2. See H. H. Gerth and C. Wright Mills (Eds.), *From Max Weber: Essays in Sociology*, New York: Oxford University Press, 1946, pp. 196–204. Anthony Downs also presents bureaucratic structures as motivational systems after the model of economics in *Inside Bureaucracy*, (Boston: Little, Brown, 1967). Many of the ideas in this chapter were stimulated by discussions with Raymond Breton on the simulation of such a motivational system on computers.

market motivational system. We could say about classical economics then that the more closely a concrete social system approximates the model we have set out, the more closely its behavior will approximate that of a competitive market. Likewise we can say about a bureaucratic motivational system that the more closely a concrete system approximates the model of bureaucratic motivation, the more closely its behavior will approximate that of an efficient bureaucracy.

The Ideal Competitive Market and the Ideal Type Bureaucracy

The classical economist could describe concretely some social structures which ought to approximate the competitive market. These structures had many firms, all buyers and sellers in communication, goods of known quality, and so on. In the same way, Weber has provided us with a set of structural features of organizations which ought to produce a motivational system of the bureaucratic kind. Let us take a few examples from his analysis, to see how he proceeds.

Weber says that the organization of offices into a career, which should normally occupy a man's full time for all of his life and provide for his retirement, is a feature of bureaucratic administration. This structural feature has several consequences. It makes the future status of a man—including that after retirement—nearly entirely dependent on the organization. Hence it increases the power of the reward of promotion. It also tends to exclude from a man's own decisions his interests deriving from a part-time job, or a future job outside the organization. These other interests might affect, in particular, his decisions on whom to hire or promote, and hence disturb the bureaucratic reward system. For instance, he might not promote people who refused to buy insurance from him, if his part-time job were selling insurance.

Weber further says that in bureaucracies, the office is sharply separated from the household, office money from household money, office status from status in royal or other lineage, etc. This feature again has several functions. If high office goes to family members of the boss, there are few promotions to distribute. If kinship considerations permeate office decisions, then the measures of performance which are applied are likely to be kinship loyalty measures rather than technical effectiveness measures.

Weber says that offices in a bureaucracy have clear jurisdictions, with the superior's jurisdiction including the inferior's. This again serves several functions. It gives the superior control over the reward system of those people for whose activities he is responsible. This allows for clarity in performance measurement. Clear, nested jurisdictions provide a basis for allocating appropriate authority to those who have jurisdiction, so that their decisions are, in fact, the cause of variations in performance in that jurisdiction.

The same analysis can be applied to virtually all Weber's criteria of bureaucracy. That is, in outlining the ideal type of a bureaucracy as one with organized careers, separation of office from household, clear jurisdictions organized in a nested fashion, etc., he was describing a structure within which the bureaucratic motivational system would be the most effective. The causal law that Weber was arguing can be summed up as follows: The closer a social structure approximates the ideal type of bureaucracy, the more closely the motivational system of that structure approximates the model of bureaucratic motivation, as described before.

The Functions of Bureaucratic Motivation

But why was Weber interested in this particular motivational structure? Because it produced *effective hierarchies, or "discipline."* What Weber wanted to know was: Under what conditions will criteria of decision set down at the top of an organization actually govern the behavior of people who make the day-to-day decisions, when decisions are made by people who are paid a salary? He was interested in this problem for two reasons. First, since capitalists do not in fact stay small enough to make all their own decisions, how does it come about that large firms, as well as small, behave according to the profitability to the entrepreneur or the stockholders? That is, how is a capitalistic market possible with large factories and corporations as units? Second, how is it possible that legislation worked out in the kings' courts or in parliaments actually governs local areas? How is the modern state possible, when local officials have so much more knowledge and power in a local area that the central government can have? These two questions are both questions of how hierarchy is possible.

Weber's answer to how hierarchy can be effective, then, has two components. First, he asks: How must a man be motivated so that he will be guided by the decision criteria of his superior? Second, what are the social structures in which this motivational system will apply to all levels of a hierarchy?

Bureaucratic Motivation from a Subjective Point of View

The most important fact influencing the subjective construction of career motivation in a bureaucracy is that the rewards are in the distant future, constituting an expectation by the bureaucrat of what his whole job life will be like. The means that the *reward system itself is a set of convictions about the future.* Both the future rewards, and the causal connection between present activity and future rewards, must be subjectively real before the system can work. Weber's description of the objective structural features of a bureaucracy implies that, in general, a subjective construction of a future reality comes about if objectively that reality is highly probable, given the objective structure. People will be motivated to do good work by promotions if promotions in fact depend on good work.

Much of our sample is, in some sense, confronted with the same objective reality: the steel plant bureaucracy. We can check Weber's implict hypothesis that perceptions of career chances are determined by the objective structure of organizations. If the career motivations of bureaucrats are not in fact different from those of commercial and professional people, then the theory is undermined. But there are also variations in individual openness to structural influences. For instance, older men are less open to the reward of future promotion than younger men. Because we want to explore the motivational consequences of bureaucratic structures, and because individuals vary in their openness to structurally organized motivation, we need a measure of bureaucratic motivation from a subjective point of view.

We suggest that, for practical purposes, the degree to which a man is engaged by a bureaucratic motivational system can be measured by the degree to which he perceives his career as organized. *By career organization we mean the degree to which a man perceives that he has arrived at his present position as a result of his past occupational activities, that he will continue to advance, and that his future advances will depend on how well he does in his present position.* That is, a man with high career organization conceives of himself as being at a certain point in a coherent life plan. He got where he is by part of that plan, and thinks he is going somewhere by completing that plan. The degree of career organization is pretty much equivalent to the degree of coherence of a life plan. The proposition involved here is that the more coherent a man's life plan, the more responsive he is, and will be, to a bureaucratic motivational structure.

A Scale of Career Organization

With this general notion in mind, we can suggest the features of men's perceptions and biographies that will make them open to the influence of bureaucratic motivational systems. Consider how a man will view his past occupational biography if his present status is seen as the result of following a life plan.

He will be likely to have had previous jobs in the same organization, and to conceive of himself as having been promoted to his present position. He will be likely to think of the qualifications he got in his previous jobs as useful in this one. And he is likely to be fairly well satisfied with where he is, though naturally his life plan will have better jobs in it for the future. The key notion in following a life plan is that one can be satisfied with the *trajectory* one is on, though one hopes to get to a higher level in the long run.

Satisfaction with one's status and perceiving that one is on a career trajectory seem in fact to be highly related. Men probably experience the constraints of a status more intensely than the rewards, because the constraints create problems to be solved. These problems occupy the mind, and make the constraints more salient. We can assume, then, that almost everyone finds his status unsatisfactory in some respects. But if an unsatisfactory status is thought of as a point on a satisfactory trajectory, the constraints have a purpose and larger meaning which justifies them. At any rate, in our survey the item measuring satisfaction with one's position correlated highly with the scale of career organization.

We measured this trajectory aspect of career organization with the answers to four questions. A man received one point each on a scale of career organization (1) if he had a previous job within the organization, (2) if he found that job "very useful" for doing his present job, and (3) if he had been promoted or had his job expanded during the previous two years. Thus one's immediately previous job could furnish three points of career organization if it were in the same organization, if it were useful, and if it were of lower status and one had left it less than two years ago. It happened that characteristics of men's previous jobs *outside* their present organization had no relation to other items of career organization. What may be going on is that people perceive the relevance of their past lives to their present and future lives in terms of an organizational framework. They may section their lives into segments which are hardly connected in their minds, but are strongly connected internally. Thus, a person who is a professor but was a private during his 2 years of military service, probably does not conceive of himself as upwardly mobile unless he has been promoted *within* the university. Movements between sectors of the economy may then be thought of as good luck or bad luck in a career, but not as part of a systematically planned and socially organized career structure. Career organization is preeminently an effect of being promoted within a given organization. (4) A man received two points if he said he had achieved more than he hoped to achieve as a youth, one point if he said he had achieved about what he hoped, and none if he had achieved less or did not answer. Thus perception of the organization of one's career in the past could give a man five points.

Of many questions dealing with orientations toward the future, only two turned out to be very closely related to the complex of items of past career experience. Both of these had to do with men's perceptions of the *organization* they worked for rather than of their own careers. Men with highly organized *pasts* thought that the organization they worked for had been successful in the last few years, and would grow in the future. We gave two points if they thought the organization would grow "a great deal," one point if they thought it would grow "somewhat," and one point if they thought it had been successful. Their perception of the organization could contribute three points to their score on career organization.

Organizational Growth and Career Prospects

We are now faced with the problem of why perceptions of organizational growth should form an important component of career organization. I think that there is a combination of spurious and valid reasons. In Latin America, steel is a new industry. Its initial rate of growth has been very high because it has been expanding according to the elasticity of substitution of domestic steel for imported steel. Hence, steel employees have experienced a high rate of growth. But steel plants are bureaucratized, and we have greatly oversampled them. Thus, by oversampling a group in a highly bureaucratic growth industry, we have spuriously elevated the correlation between career organization and perceived growth. But many other attitudes about future prospects that we probed are not as highly related to past career organization, though they should be spuriously elevated by the same oversampling of extreme groups. Let us then consider what elements of validity there might be in the correlation.

If a bureaucracy (1) recruits at the bottom and promotes from within, (2) maintains a fixed span of control, and (3) has a constant set of seniority-specific death and retirement rates, then the *rate* of promotion depends on the rate of growth of the organization.

It should be noted here that a given *rate* of promotion may give rise to different *average distance* promoted during a lifetime. If the bottom positions are occupied for longer periods and the top positions for shorter periods, more people can reach the top positions. Conversely, if men are hired directly into the top positions at the beginning of their careers, there would be no promotion. To relate the span of mobility to the demography of a status system, one must take account of the temporal aspect of status occupancy.

If we suppose that rates of pay for salaried officials are determined by their hierarchical rank, rather than by the profitability of the enterprise,[3] then the amount of reward (i.e., the rate of promotion) for bureaucrats depends on the rate of growth.

If we suppose that people make fairly accurate analyses of their career prospects, then it follows that most bureaucratic structures will be better motivational systems when they are thought to be growing. The average man in stable organizations should see his chances as equal to the distributed retirement and death rates. In growing organizations, men should see their chances as equal to these *plus* the expansion of positions because of organizational growth.

As Bernard Levenson has pointed out,[4] the number of promotions caused by a retirement depends on the rank of the man retiring, if all replacements are from one level down. A retirement at rank 2 will cause a promotion from rank 1 to rank 2, and another promotion to replace the man just promoted from rank

3. Evidence that this is approximately the case is presented by D. R. Roberts, A General Theory of Executive Compensation Based on Statistically Tested Propositions. *Quarterly Journal of Economics*, **20**, 1956, 270–294. The same data is reanalyzed by Herbert Simon, The Compensation of Executives. *Sociometry*, **20**, (1), 1957, 32–35.

4. Bernard Levenson, unpublished manuscript. See also a more extended development in Harrison White, *Chains of Opportunity* (Cambridge, Massachusetts: Harvard, 1970), Chapter 7, pp. 147–192, especially pp. 166–179. White starts with the promotions to predict growth, but finds the same sort of dependence between the two that we argue here.

0 to rank 1. Let each rank, i be defined as the number of levels of subordinates below a man, $i = 0, 1, 2, \ldots, k$. Then if we have a rank-specific retirement rate per year r_i, a rank i will create a number of promotions ir_in_i. Summing across ranks we would have, for an organization with $k + 1$ ranks (the bottom rank being $i = 0$)

$$P = \sum_{i=1}^{k} ir_i n$$

If we suppose that the span of control is a constant s all the way up the hierarchy, then the number in rank i will be

$$n_i = (1/s^i)n_0$$

Then k, the number of ranks above the 0 rank, will be determined by n_0 and s, and by whatever correction for continuity C is appropriate (one cannot have $10\frac{1}{2}$ ranks)

$$k(n_0, s) = (\log n_0/\log s) + C$$

Substituting

$$P = \sum_{i=1}^{k(n_0,s)} ir_i(n_0/s^i)$$

The promotion rate R_0 for fixed n_0 (no growth) will be, then,

$$R_0 = \frac{P}{N} = \frac{P}{\sum_0^{k(n_0,s)} n_i} = \frac{\sum_{i=1}^{k(n_0,s)} ir_i(n_0/s^i)}{\sum_{i=0}^{k(n_0,s)} (1/s^i)n_0} = \frac{\sum_{i=1}^{k(n_0,s)} (i/s^i)r_i}{\sum_{i=0}^{k(n_0,s)} (1/s^i)}$$

Now suppose that all promotions during a given year go to the people already in the organization. Then increases in size of the organization *for that year* will increase the n_0 in the numerator but not increase the denominator. The promotion rate with growth, R_1, would be

$$R_1 = \frac{\sum_{i=1}^{k(n_{0_t},s)} ir_i(n_{0_t}/s^i) + \sum_{i=1}^{k(n_{0_t}+\Delta n_0,s)} i(\Delta n_0/s^i)}{\sum_{i=0}^{k(n_0,s)} (1/s^i)n_{0_t}}$$

$$= \frac{\sum_{i=1}^{k(n_{0_t}+\Delta n_0,s)} (i/s^i) \left[r_i + (\Delta n_0/n_{0_t})\right]}{\sum_{i=0}^{k(n_0,s)} (1/s^i)}$$

The denominator is the same as before. The numerator is increased by an amount equivalent to the effect of increasing each retirement rate by the percentage rate of growth.

This computation assumes that the retirement rate at various ranks would be the same in stable and growing organizations. Faster promotion will result in younger men occupying higher positions in the growing organization, which will usually decrease the retirement rate. Ignoring this effect for the present (and probably people psychologically ignore it in calculating career plans), the promotion rate of an organization with a fixed span of control depends on the rates of retirement for different ranks and on the percentage growth of the size of the bottom rank. If the retirement rates were such that their average effect was that of 3% per year (a career of about 30 years), then a growth rate of 3% per year would about double the promotion rate, a growth rate of 6% would triple the promotion rate, etc.

What this means, then, is that the amount of reward a bureaucratic system has for securing hierarchical discipline can easily be doubled or tripled by growth rates that are quite within the possibilities. In most bureaucratic systems, the primary determinant of a man's career chances will be the rate of growth of his organization. The primary determinant of his past promotion experiences is likely to have been the past rate of growth.

Relative Deprivation and Career Organization

The most famous analysis of the psychological effects of different promotion rates is that in the *American Soldier*. The analysts showed that in the (rapidly growing) Army Air Force, there was faster promotion than in the (slowly growing) Military Police; yet they found that the Military Police, *not* the Air Force, were more satisfied with their promotions. They interpreted this to mean that since Air Force men saw most people being promoted, their promotions seemed less rewarding, and their failure to be promoted more punishing.[5]

We might think that this lower level of satisfaction would result in the lesser effectiveness of the reward system. Perhaps if a promotion gives less satisfaction, there is less motivation to work for it. I do not believe this is so because I do not believe that people are generally motivated by something as evanescent as "satisfaction." I think what most people want is more money, rank, privilege, and honor, not more "satisfaction" with their position. If they have frequent opportunities to get these good things by working hard and well, they will do so. If they are also frequently rewarded, in fact, with money, rank, privilege, and honor for having worked well, they will continue

5. Samuel A. Stouffer *et al.*, *The American Soldier*, Vol. 1, Princeton University Press, 1949, pp. 250–258. See also, R. K. Merton and Alice Rossi, "Contributions to the Theory of Reference Group Behavior." In R. K. Merton and P. F. Lazarsfeld (Eds.), *Continuities in Social Research*, Glencoe, Illinois: Free Press, 1950, reprinted in Merton's *Social Theory and Social Structure*, New York: The Free Press, 3rd ed. 1968, pp. 279–334.

to do so. They will work even if they believe that their position is still unsatisfactory.

It should be pointed out that even without this crass motivational theory, our own results hold up. For we find that, in fact, men in growing organizations who have been promoted are more likely to say they have achieved their youthful ambitions. This may not be quite the same as "satisfaction," but it definitely does not indicate a greater alienation in more rapid systems of promotion.

It is quite possible that only status systems that are detached from men's biographies can strongly affect what men expect. In the wartime army, one's civilian aspirations were defined as irrelevant. But it seems unlikely that civilian men trained in the same school systems, paying taxes to the same governments, attending the same churches, belonging to the same clubs, would form radically different conceptions of "success." The promotion system of a civilian bureaucracy is part of the occupational stratification system. The effect of that system in defining success for the bureaucracy is probably greater than the effect of the bureaucracy on defining the stratification system.[6]

Furthermore, we must distinguish the saliency of the hope of promotion from the satisfaction gained from a past promotion. If no one gets promoted, all may be satisfied with their present condition, but their hopes for the future will not be strong motives. They may be satisfied and also not think about it. When there is a high rate of promotion, men may be dissatisfied and also think a lot about how to get promoted. For humans, hopes are probably more powerful motivations than past rewards (though hopes are partly determined by past rewards). Humans can learn under the influence of rewards that are yet to come.

Recapitulation

The motivational aspect of a system consists of the attachment of rewards to activities. But rewards, to become motives, have to be wanted. The theory of a motivational system for a social structure has to include a theory of what people want and a theory of what they have to do to get it. In the classical economie theory of petty capitalism, they want profits, and to achieve such profits, they have to make entrepreneurial decisions that equate marginal product to marginal revenue. Our purpose here has been to develop a comparable theory of bureaucratic motivation systems. Our notion is that what people

6. This is the import of the equality of evaluations of occupations by differently situated men. See Albert J. Reiss, O. D. Duncan, Paul K. Hatt, and Cecil C. North *Occupations and Social Status*, New York: The Free Press of Glencoe, 1961, pp. 162–238. I have argued at various places in my *Rebellion in a High School* (Chicago: Quadrangle, 1964), that schools are not free to shape the meanings of their own rewards because the meanings are determined by the occupational system.

want in a bureaucratic system are promotions. What they must do to get promotions is determined by their superiors. The superiors, in their turn, do what their superiors want. The basic theory says, then, that hierarchical discipline is motivated by promotions.

But we need to find out how such a motivational system would be looked at subjectively so that we can see the variations in its degree of effectiveness. When the effectiveness of the system is at its maximum, we will expect men to see their lives as a succession of promotions. These promotions will be to jobs whose content is related to the previous job. Thus, the overall effect will be to organize a person's life into a career, so that he conceives of his present status as part of a life plan. Career organization is made up of the perception of a tight causal connection between what a person has done in the past, what he is doing now, and what he will be doing in the future.

We would expect that people would have to recieve rewards fairly regularly if they are to organize their lives in terms of them. But it is easy to show that, if an organization retains a stable structure and tends to recruit at the lower ranks, then its rate of promotion is intimately dependent on its rate of growth. We would, therefore, expect that people's own perceptions of the rate of growth of the organization would be a constituent part of their career organization.

CHAPTER **6**

Career Organization and the Supply of Effort

We suggested in Chapter 5 that the organization of a person's life into a career is a requirement of bureaucratic motivational systems, and also a product of them. A promotion means more if it is an index that one's whole life is going to work out all right. But a promotion can only be such an index in a bureaucratic structure that provides promotions as rewards in a regular and predictable fashion.

In this chapter we want to do two things. First we want to show that, in fact, the steel plant bureaucracies produce career organization, a sense of being on a life trajectory, in their employees. Second, we want to show that this organization of people's careers produces work motivation and industrial discipline. Unfortunately, this second task turns out to be empirically very difficult, because bureaucracies affect the supply of effort by other devices, as well as by offering careers. In particular, the importance of schedules of work is much greater in bureaucratic organizations.

This creates an empirical tangle that mars the easy logical flow of the argument. After some wandering in the branches of this tangle, we will conclude that the argument that growing bureaucracies create subjective career organization is strongly supported by our data, that the argument that career organiza- creates motivation to work is weakly supported, and therefore worth pursuing in further studies specifically designed to minimize the empirical confusion between bureaucracy's motivational and scheduling effects.

The Social Sources of Life Plans

Panel A of Table 6.1 gives the mean level of career organization for the structural groups outlined in Table 3.1. The career organization scale was developed in Chapter 5, and consists of items measuring whether a man had a different previous job in his present organization, whether this previous job was useful in his present job, whether he had been promoted or his job expanded in the previous two years, whether he had achieved as much or more than he had hoped to achieve as a youth, whether he saw the organization he worked in as successful, and whether he thought it would grow in the future.

In this top panel, we see that all bureaucratic positions have a higher level of career organization than both smaller and larger businessmen, and also a

TABLE 6.1

Panel A: **Mean Career Organization, by Industrial Involvment and Structural Position, for the Three City Samples Combined, and for Each Steel Plant**

City nonindustrial			Industrial bureaucrats		
			Chile	Argentina	Venezuela
Employees	3.20	Low	5.50	4.79	4.54
Bureaucrats	4.60	Intermediate	6.24	5.69	4.89
		High	5.85	5.83	5.58
		Staff	5.40	5.27	3.88
Small business	2.89				
Larger business	3.47				

Panel B: **Standard Deviation of Career Organization, for Each Group for which the Mean is Given in Panel A. Base Numbers May Be Obtained from Table 1 in Chapter 3** [a]

City nonindustrial			Industrial bureaucrats		
	SD		Chile	Argentina	Venezuela
Employees	1.82	Low	1.41	1.70	1.52
Bureaucrats	1.27	Intermediate	1.13	1.70	2.03
		High	1.57	1.61	1.35
		Staff	1.71	1.53	1.73
Small business	1.29				
Larger business	1.66				

[a]The standard deviation of career organization for the whole sample of 402 is 1.91.

higher level than city employees. Except for the staff and lower line in Venezuela, all groups in the growing industrial bureaucracies have higher levels of subjective career organization than the nonindustrial bureaucrats of the cities.

The bottom panel of Table 6.1 gives the standard deviation of subjective career organization for each of the structural groups. The median standard deviation is about 1.6, which is roughly the distance between the industrial bureaucrats and the urban middle classes. This means that there is relatively little overlap in subjective career organization between the steel bureaucracies and the nonindustrial urban middle-class sample, and that most of that overlap is created by the bureaucrats in the city sample. The degree of overlap is set out in Table 6.2.

This strong relation supports very strongly the idea that growing industrial bureaucracies produce high career organization. But it creates great difficulties for multivariate analysis. We have very few steel plant bureaucrats to compare with the "lows" in career organization from the city, and very few city employees to compare with the "highs" from the steel plants. Further, many of the comparisons cases are presumably measurement errors rather than truly comparables cases. The lows in a high group or the highs in a low group for a short scale with considerable measurement error are disproportionately measurement mistakes.

This creates substantial difficulties because, as we will show shortly, distinctive features of bureaucratic schedules obscure the relation between career organization and the supply of effort. Thus, what we will be able to show is that people with high career organization have regular bureaucratic schedules, which is not at all what we set out to do.

The locus of one's job in the industrial sector or in other bureaucracies has a powerful effect on subjective career organization. Other biographical variables, such as education and cosmopolitanism, which are related (in our sample) to bureaucratic employment are, therefore, related to career organization. But

TABLE 6.2

Bureaucratic Employment Produces Career Organization

Career organization[a]	Small and large business	City employees and bureaucrats	Industrial bureaucrats
Low	66%	47%	16%
Medium	32%	40%	39%
High	2%	12%	45%
Totals	100% (56)	99% (89)	100% (257)

[a]"Low" means scale scores of 0, 1, 2, 3; "Medium" 4, 5, "High" 6, 7, 8.

when we examine separately the relation of education or cosmopolitanism to career organization within the steel plants or within the nonindustrial middle classes, the relation disappears (tabulations omitted). That is, for our sample the relation of education or cosmopolitanism to career organization is spurious, and due to the fact that educated and cosmopolitan people are disproportionately employed in bureaucracies. A dentist or lawyer or physician in the traditional educated middle-class occupations is no more likely than a city employee to experience a succession of connected jobs with increasing reward. A less educated clerk or foreman in the steel plant is as likely as an engineer in that plant to have experienced promotion to a job connected to his previous job, to be satisfied with his accomplishments, and to look on the future of his organization with hope.

Neither previous work experience outside the present organization nor a person's education or cosmopolitanism affect his perception of career organization. But his position within his present organization influences his perceptions strongly. In Table 6.3 we summarize in a different format a conclusion which can also be inferred from Table 6.1, that higher ranking people perceive their career trajectories as more organized, once the structural involvement in industrial bureaucracies is controlled. Within the steel plants, intermediate line and high executives answer in a way showing a higher degree of career organization than do low line and staff. Among the city employed, those with few subordinates (employees) have a lower level of career organization than those with two or more levels of subordinates (bureaucrats). And although Table 6.3 does not show it clearly, Table 6.1 shows that large businessmen have significantly more subjective career organization (by a t test for the difference between smaller and larger businessmen, $p < .01$). It is of course hardly surprisingly that higher ranking men should have got where they are by promotions and be more satisfied with their achievements.

TABLE 6.3

Higher Ranking People[a] Have More Organized Careers (Percentage "High" in Career Organization)

City nonindustrial			Industrial bureaucrats		
Employees	9%	(69)	Low line	36%	(92)
Bureaucrats	25%	(20)	Intermediate line	57%	(61)
			High executive	57%	(62)
			Staff	31%	(42)
Small business	0%	(39)			
Larger business	6%	(17)			

[a]For definitions, see Table 3.1, (Chapter 3).

TABLE 6.4

Percentage "High" in Career Organization, by Occupation and
Industrial Involvement

Occupation	City nonindustrial		Industrial bureaucrats	
Entrepreneurs	2%	(56)		
Manual and Foremen	3%	(31)	40%	(53)
Clerical and sales	12%	(16)	33%	(33)
Professional, except technical administrators	10%	(20)	26%	(19)
Administrative and technical	27%	(22)	52%	(152)

Different activities within the same structures also are located differently with respect to the structures that organize people's careers. In Table 6.4 respondents are classified by occupation. There is a substantial difference in the degree of career organization between the industrial bureaucrats and the city nonindustrial middle class, even when we take people who have approximately the same occupations.[1] Clerks and administrators seem generally to have a somewhat higher level of career organization wherever they work; but they have a much higher level of career organization if they work in a growing industrial bureaucracy. A strong sense of being on a career trajectory is especially prevalent among administrators in heavy industry. The difference between manual workers and foremen in industry and manual workers and foremen who turned up in our middle-class random sample is striking.[2]

The overall result is that a high level of career organization is associated with industrial bureaucracy in three different steel towns. This strong association of life plans and bureaucracy carries in its train an association of life plans with everything else associated with industrial bureaucracy. Educated and cosmopolitan people are more likely to have organized careers because they are more likely to be hired by growing industrial bureaucracies. The association between

1. An occupation is a description of a man's activities, and an industry is a description of an organization's activities. It is quite hard to match very precisely people's activities when the overall system they work in has a different set of activities. Thus, a clerical person working in a factory actually does different things during a day than a clerical person working in a bank. An occupational classification tries to match them according to some relatively abstract characteristics of their main activities, but the match is certain to be a loose one.
2. Unfortunately for the argument, this difference could be because of differential measurement errors in the sampling process. The stratification of the city by housing style is probably less accurate than the stratification of the steel plant by salary category. Hence, the steel manual and foremen are likely to be truly successful occupationally, while many of the city manual and foremen are likely to be less successful people, included either because of our poor eye for architecture or their own overinvestment in housing. See the Appendix on Method.

biography and the degree of career organization disappears when we control for men's present occupational situation.

Furthermore, it is in the distinctively industrial—bureaucratic occupations of administrative and technical workers that the degree of career organization is highest. It appears that the more bureaucratic the organization, or the more bureaucratic the occupation in a given organization, the more organized a man's life is likely to seem to him.

In the middle class, then, organization of a man's life into a career is not a product of his biography. Instead, life plans are attached to structural positions in the economy. If he is in a bureaucratically organized administrative structure that is growing, he will have perceptions and experiences that tend to orient him toward regular promotion, however he got into that position. His past biography, except for the fact that it led him into a position in which he sees himself as having opportunities, has no appreciable further effect on his perception of his future. If a man's education and luck have put him into a high position in a part of the economy which is not organized bureaucratically and not expanding rapidly, he will not see himself as having an organized career. If the same education and luck put him in a position in an expanding steel bureaucracy, he will see himself as having an organized career.

This finding is of profound significance for the theory of motivation of economic effort in poorer countries. It implies that the strength of motivations to work toward the modernization of the economy is not determined by the culture of a country, but rather by the structure of its economy. If the economy is so organized that it puts people into bureaucratic structures which are expanding, it will produce a system appropriate for motivating vigorous bureaucratic work, and this, to a considerable extent, will be regardless of their biographies and their cultural backgrounds (e.g., regardless of their exposure to modern Western culture through schooling). If the economy is so organized as to put modernized men into nonbureaucratic structures which are not expanding rapidly, then it will not motivate them adequately to perform modernizing roles well. The motivational level of the population, rather than being a cause of economic expansion and reorganization of the economy, is instead the result of the level of expansion and bureaucratic reorganization of the economy.

It might be useful to outline the comparable argument for nonbureaucratic entrepreneurship. We have no evidence for this argument, but it may be that the rate of profit determines the level of entrepreneurial motivation. That is, it may be that the reason fewer people in underdeveloped countries start businesses (if that is true) is that the rate of profit (including the payment for entrepreneurial labor) is lower than in more advanced countries. When the rate of profit is rasied (by technical innovations making new lines of business more profitable, by tariff protection increasing the price of a product, by expansion of the market, or by any other force), then more people begin to be motivated to go into business. The rate of profit in poorer countries might be lower because it is objectively impossible, with the lack of a supply of competent managerial labor and other resources in the economy, to compete with foreign firms. The rate of profit might be depressed by the political situation, especially by the way the taxation laws are administered. It might be depressed because the price of capital is higher, because of fiscal or political uncertainties, or because of discrimination by lending institutions and other sources of loan capital. These objective determinants of the rate of return on investments of entrepreneurial capital and entrepreneurial labor might cause a low level of motivation to enter businesses. If this were the case, then we should find that new lines of business which had been entered by natives would, if they give high rates of return to the first entrepreneurs, create a sudden development of entrepreneurial motivation in populations which had hitherto been culturally traditionalistic.

Hobsbawm,[3] for instance, has argued that the burst of entrepreneurial energy that produced what is generally called the "industrial revolution" (namely the reorganization of the English textile industry into factories) was created by the opening of the Indian and South American markets by the English Navy near the beginning of the nineteenth century. This drastically increased the market for textiles—Englishmen did not wear many more clothes after the industrial revolution than before—and consequently increased the rate of return from producing textiles in mass. This increased market, combined with some technical innovations, gave the English a large competitive advantage over artisan weavers in India and South America. And this competitive advantage in new markets created a high rate of profits in the textile business in the early nineteenth century. The Protestant ethic had already been around a long time without producing a reorganization of the textile industry. But the opening up of markets produced a reorganization in a hurry. Hobsbawm's argument implicitly asserts that the level of entrepreneurial motivation is determined by the level of profits, rather than by the values and personalities produced in different areas.

The Regulation of the Supply of Effort

If we eliminate small businessmen, for whom a classical economic motivational scheme applies, then the more organized a man's career, the more effort he should put forth. But there are substantial difficulties with this notion. Bureaucracy is not only a system for motivating effort; it is also a system for planning

3. E. J. Hobsbawm, *The Age of Revolution 1789–1848*, New York: Mentor, 1962, pp. 52–55. Incidentally, the evidence that the reorganization and expansion of the textile industry led, directly or indirectly, to the reorganization into factories of other lines of production, say of steel products or clothing or gin, is very unsatisfactory. Such a general impact on the economy would be required to justify calling the reorganization of textile production an "industrial revolution."

a coordinating cooperative effort in an interdependent productive system. One of the main devices for planning and coordinating effort is a schedule. Thus, exactly those people who are most subject to bureaucratic motivational structures are slso most subject to formal scheduling.

Table 6.5, taken from data in the 1960 U.S. Census on weekly hours worked, gives evidence that men in the same occupation have a *lower variance* of hours worked if they work in bureaucratic structures. Table 6.6 gives the standard deviation of reported hours generally worked per week, for industrial and nonindustrial employees and for small businessmen from our sample. Table 6.7 gives the standard deviation of hours actually worked on the last previous full working day before the interview. The overall result in Tables 6.5, 6.6, and 6.7 is that

TABLE 6.5

People Who Work inBureaucratic Organizations in the United States Are Less Likely to Work Either Very Long or Very Short Hours [a]

	Percentage who worked	
Occupation	More than 60 hourr	1 to 14 hours
(1) More bureaucratic		
Engineers	4.0	0.6
Less bureaucratic		
College professors and instructors (NEC) [b]	12.8	8.6
(2) Most bureaucratic		
Foremen (NEC), communications, utilities, and sanitary industries	2.8	0.2
Medium bureaucratic		
Foremen (NEC), manufacturing	4.6	0.4
Unbureaucratic		
Foremen (NEC), construction	6.6	1.1
(3) More bureaucratic		
Operatives, manufacturing, meat products	4.6	2.4
Less bureaucratic		
Operatives, meat cutters except packing house and slaughterhouse	16.8	2.4
(4) More bureaucratic		
Policemen and detectives, public	10.4	0.7
Less bureaucratic		
Sheriffs and bailiffs	24.0	1.6
Marshals and constables	30.6	6.2

[a]The data are for men only.

[b]The notation in parentheses (NEC) means "not elsewhere classified." Thus, a foreman classified in some other occupation would not be included among foremen. Source: These data are computed from U.S. Bureau of the Census, "Detailed Occupational Characteristics, 1960," pp. 184–203.

TABLE 6.6

Industrial Bureaucracy Regularizes Weekly Schedules. Standard Deviation of Hours Usually Worked per Week in Main Job, by Structural Position and Industrial Involvement, in Hours, the Three Countries Together

City nonindustrial[a]	SD		Heavy industry	SD	
Employees	15.0	(66)	Low line	6.8	(92)
Bureaucrats	12.9	(19)	Intermediate line	9.0	(61)
			High executives	8.6	(62)
			Staff	6.1	(42)
Small business	14.0	(37)			
Larger business	16.3	(17)			

[a]See Table 3.1 (Chapter 3) for definitions. Those who did not answer or did not work are eliminated. The numbers in parentheses are the number of people who answered in each group.

industrial bureaucracy produces a much lower variance in hours worked than do other economic structures.

That is, the rules about how long one *should* work have a stronger effect for bureaucrats on the supply of hours of work than do their own motivations. In any contrast between bureaucrats and other people, we would be contrasting people whose hours reflect the rules with people whose work hours reflect their motivation. This vitiates hours of work as a decisive measure of the supply of motivation in the economy.

Although we will mainly have to work with other indexes of the strength of motivation to work, the data on mean hours worked per week are given in Table 6.8. There is a tendency for the steel plant employees to work longer hours than city employees. There is a slight tendency for men with more organized careers

TABLE 6.7

Industrial Bureaucracy Regularizes Daily Schedules. Standard Deviation of Hours Worked on Last Previous Working Day, by Structural position and Industrial Involvement, in Hours

City nonindustrial[a]	SD		Heavy industry	SD	
Employees	2.39	(63)	Low line	2.20	(92)
Bureaucrats	2.74	(19)	Intermediate line	2.09	(62)
			High executives	1.44	(62)
			Staff	1.75	(42)
Small business	2.29	(36)			
Larger business	2.84	(17)			

[a]People who gave no account of last previous working day are eliminated.

TABLE 6.8

Mean Hours Reported Worked per Week in Main Job by Industrial Involvement, Employment Status, and Career Organization

Career organization[a]	City entrepreneurs (small and larger businesses)	City employed (employees and bureaucrats)	Industrial bureaucrats (line and staff)
Low	55.6 (35)	45.6 (38)	47.9 (42)
Intermediate	53.6 (18)	45.3 (36)	49.7 (99)
High	—[b] (1)	44.2 (11)	51.3 (116)
Total means	54.8 (54)	45.3 (85)	50.1 (257)

[a]"Low" means scale scores 0, 1, 2, 3; intermediate 4, 5; high 6, 7, 8. Those who gave no report are eliminated.

[b]Average meaningless; this man worked 50 hours.

to work longer hours in the steel plant, but this tendency is reversed in the city. Table 6.9 gives the average hours worked on the last full day before the interview. Men with more organized careers have, on the average, worked slightly longer. But these differences between men of higher and lower career organization are not statistically significant, except for the marginal statistical significance of the difference in weekly hours between high and low career organization among industrial bureaucrats. That is, the last column in Table 6.8 shows some evidence of a difference that is statistically reliable. This certainly cannot be taken as good evidence for our argument.

There are two ways to look at this confusing picture. The most obvious interpretation is that career organization does not provide the social psychological base of bureaucratic discipline and motivation to work. Career organ-

TABLE 6.9

Mean Hours Worked on Last Previous Working Day, by Industrial Involvement, Employment Status, and Career Organization[a]

Career organization	City entrepreneurs	City employed	Heavy industry
Low	9.54 (34)	8.18 (35)	8.70 (42)
Intermediate	9.44 (18)	8.12 (36)	8.91 (99)
High	—[b] (1)	9.66 (11)	8.75 (116)
Total means	9.52 (53)	8.35 (82)	8.80 (257)

[a]Those who did not report are eliminated.

[b]He worked 10 hours.

ization, then, would be an epiphenomenon of bureaucratic structures.[4] The true source of conformity would be the effectiveness of bureaucratic schedules, the straight economic trade of money for the regulated amount of time. No deep structural source of motivation is required to explain why a person paid to work 8 hours indeed works 8 hours.

But we recall the Traffic Inspector and his colleague who do not work their 8 hours; and we recall the responsiveness of executives in the steel plant to measures of downtime in the tube mill, and the extensive efforts to improve the system in many ways to reduce downtime. That is, we still have something to explain, even though the data we have used to test our proposed explanation has difficulties. The theory of 8 hours work for 8 hours pay is not logically sufficient to explain variations between bureaucracies in their degree of discipline.

An Indirect Measure of Discipline

Our problem now is to see whether there is any evidence in our data that a further exploration of this line of theorizing is likely to be useful. What we could like would be some measure of the adequacy with which people do their jobs that would not be too affected by the scheduling pecularities of bureaucratic organizations. This will then tell us whether it is likely to be useful for other investigators to develop really adequate measures of discipline in work to develop the theory further. Since the degree of certainty which we now want to urge is simply that there may be something there worth further investigation, it is not worthwhile to detail the failures of alternative measures from this study. For example, indirect measures of commitment to a present job derived from a series of questions about whether respondents are willing to leave the job for another are not consistently related to career organization.

The only measure in this study that supports the argument that career organization produces work discipline is the number of hours spent on personal affairs and recreation during working hours. In Table 6.10 subjective career organization is related to hours spent in nonwork activity during working hours.

The first notable thing about this table is the large difference between the Argentine plant and all the others. Argentine steel bureaucrats spend much more of their working hours in personal affairs, conversation, recreation, and

4. I have argued extensively on the connection between career organization (called "articulation" there) and motivation to conform in my *Rebellion in a High School* (Chicago; Quadrangle, 1964), Chapters 3 and 4. However, I gave reason to believe that the relation of conformity to articulation would be higher among adolescents in school than among adults (in Chapter 5 of that book), so the results there cannot be generalized to our problem here. That argument, if it is accepted, merely goes to show that there are environments in which career organization has motivational consequences. It does not show that the jobs of adults are such environments.

TABLE 6.10

Mean Hours Spent on Personal Affairs and Recreation during Working Hours, by Industrial Involvement and Country, and by Career Organization (Entrepreneurs Excluded)

	Industrial involvement and country			
	City nonindustrial (3 countries combined) eliminating business	Industrial bureaucrats		
Career organization		Chile	Argentina	Venezuela
Low	0.46 (38)	—[a] (4)	1.01 (18)	0.35 (20)
Intermediate	0.60 (36)	0.21 (32)	0.62 (32)	0.17 (35)
High	0.09 (11)	0.03 (39)	0.50 (43)	0.23 (34)

[a]Too few cases for meaningful mean.

resting. Inspection of the marginals (the numbers in parentheses) shows that this is *not* because of a lower level of career organization (see also Table 6.1). Thus *if* time spent out of the work role is an indication of lack of discipline, *then* there are clearly structural causes of lack of discipline which are not related to career organization.

I suspect, on the basis of impressionistic evidence, that the administrative controls in the Argentine plant are sufficiently inefficient so that much of the time people do not know what they are supposed to be doing. This state of role anomie would mean that increased motivation to succeed might produce more increased anxiety and demoralization than increased discipline. Argentine bureaucrats might be similar to those hard-working students who do not understand what a course is about well enough to guess what will be on the examination, who anxiously participate in the preexamination discussion but still cannot figure out what to study. But this is just a guess. What would be required to check it out would be a measure of the "moral density" of each man's role, in the sense of the degree to which he can tell what he will be accountable for in each segment of time.

Leaving aside this problem of the Argentine plant, within each column there is a general, but irregular, tendency for time spent out of the work role during working hours to decrease with increased career organization.

Conclusions

We can try to explain the supply of motivation and effort in economic activities by two different strategies. We can argue that populations differ in the motivations they bring to the economy, and that this explains differences in the rates at which they introduce structural change into the economy. Or, we can argue that motivations are created by situations, by the objects that present themselves to a man, so that men presented with desirable objects to pursue will be more strongly motivated than men presented with a barren future. We have been interested here to show how bureaucratic structures create objects (specifically, career trajectories) which produce motivation to work.

We may return to the three components of the model of bureaucratic motivation that we introduced in the last chapter: rewards of promotions to higher office, the distribution of these rewards according to measures of the performance capacities of people, and a system for administering these rewards so as to preserve their value and to distribute them according to appropriate performance standards. Our argument is that such a reward system is created by bureaucratic administrations. The effect of the reward system is supposed to be the organization of the sequences of jobs which a man has into a career, with a consequent willingness on his part to devote energy to adequate performance in the sytem. That is, the more a concrete structure approximates a bureaucratic administration (more precisely, a growing bureaucratic administration), the more it should produce in its employees the conviction that they are on a satisfactory career trajectory. The more they think they are on a satisfactory career trajectory, the more motivation they should have to put an adequate amount of administrative energy into their jobs, and the more they will be willing to stay at their jobs and to use the expertise they have developed there in the service of the organization.

The steel administrations that we studied are type-cases of bureaucratic structures. They are hierarchical; the men in them are hired with the expectation that they will spend their careers there; there is an extensively developed set of performance measurements, especially cost accounts and production statistics, by which they are supposed to be judged; the enterprises have been growing; the capital is governmental or corporate, not the property of the administrators; they are administered by written files; and so forth. We have shown that such structures do, in fact, produce a high degree of subjective career organization—much higher than the amount of career organization produced by the nonbureaucratic structures in which the majority of nonindustrial middle-class people of the nearby cities work. Further, the structures in the city that most closely approximate the bureaucratic structure of the steel plants also produce a high degree of career organization. Our "bureaucrats," defined as employed people with at least two levels below them and at least one level above them in the hierarchy, turn out to have more organized careers than other city employees. Thus, the proposition that growing bureaucratic structures produce the subjective phenomenon of highly organized careers is well established.

The evidence is much more tenuous on the connection between a highly organized career and the motivation to do well on the job. This has to do with the nature of our data. It would be ideal to have performance measures in the same kind of work, for people who believed they had a bright future and those who did not. But with the great diversity of occupations studied, and our failure to collect performance measures, we have only indirect indications of the effect we want to measure.

Furthermore, the most common-sense measure of the level of motivation, namely, the number of hours worked, cannot serve the purpose. The supply of hours is determined both by the level of motivation and by the rules of the work place. Both in the United States and in our sample, bureaucracy is associated with a decreased variance in the hours worked. We interpret this to mean that rules—which tend to produce uniformity in the supply of hours—are a more important determinant of hours supplied in bureaucracies. Since subjective career organization is so powerfully determined by bureaucratic structures, and since the determinants of hours worked are so different in bureaucratic structures than in nonbureaucratic ones, these two effects of bureaucracy confound each other and give no clear results.

When we use measures of the amount of time spent out of the work role, the main hypothesis is weakly supported. The more vivid a man's vision of his future, and its connection to his present and past jobs, the more of his time at work is spent on work. This argument is again confounded somewhat by the differences in the work roles of men at different levels of career organization. Men with well-organized careers are more likely to be in administrative roles because movement up a hierarchy puts them into administration and because the bureaucratic reward system reaches its fullest development in hierarchically organized status structures.

The failures of any given study are only useful to the discipline if they tell us something general about the way the world works, and how that way the world works affects the performance of the measures used in the study. It may, therefore, be useful to examine our methodological difficulties from a theoretical point of view.

The central distinction between the dependent variable in the theory of cognitive effectiveness and in the theory of discipline is that the first is a theory of the *content* of roles, while the second is a theory of the *performance of that content*. The measures used in Chapters 3 and 4, such as hours spent on innovations, are therefore measures of role content. We showed that such measures are strongly dependent on the structural position of the role (Chapter 3) and on biographical factors such as education which should influence how a man conceives of a role (Chapter 4). Thus, when the theory is about the content of roles, the substance of what a man feels obliged to do, measures of the substance of what he, in fact, does on the job work very well.

Our principal methodological problem in this chapter was that the main measure we proposed to use to indicate the quality of performance of that substance, namely hours worked per week, turned out instead to measure a *different* aspect of the substance of role obligation. In particular, it measured the presence and amount of obligation created by schedules that determine working hours. Previous studies which have successfully measured performance of role obligations have been mainly conducted among factory workers with identical substance of role obligations, so that variations in behavior (productivity) could be related to morale or other causes of discipline. If our guess about the causes of greater amounts of time spent out of the work role in the Argentine plant is true, if roles are indeed more anomically defined in that plant, then the same difficulty is true of our alternative measure of discipline.

What would be required for an adequate measure of disciplined performance of roles with varying substance would be indicators of how far *each* different substantive activity was conducted in accordance with the norms of efficiency. But that requires a theory of the exact nature of the fundamental contribution of each activity to the enterprise.

For an example of the difficulty involved, Ivan Vallier suggested in a conversation that maybe the explanation of the greater amount of innovative work in a bureaucracy was that innovation is harder. The more staff departments there are, the more different people have to be convinced that an innovation is worthwhile before it gets instituted. If people work hard at creating difficulties for each other, measures of hard work will be inflated both because there are more difficulties to be overcome, and also because decreasing the efficiency of a competitor for a promotion may take a lot of disciplined effort.

The conclusion, then, is that we need a better theory of the nature of disciplined behavior in economic roles before we can effectively study the career organization theory of the causes of that discipline. The obvious measures are too contaminated by the content of the obligations of roles to render the theory operational.

PART IV

The Politics of
Economic Development

CHAPTER 7

An Essay on
South American Politics

Economic development requires that the economic activities of a society be governed by standards of technical and economic efficiency. Imposing the discipline of efficiency requires a constant improvement in the theories of how to accomplish productive ends. It requires constant change in those activities to respond to new possibilities of technology, to new conditions of demand in the market, and to new conditions of costs of factors of production. The reorganization of knowledge and activities requires social reorganization of the economy. And such social reorganization involves the creation of new roles, the rearrangement of reward systems, the modification of men's career prospects, the movement of men into and out of employment, the reanalysis of the purposes of organizations (and consequently the reevaluation of the justifications for authority relations), the dispersal of families and primary groups, the change of educational requirements for jobs, the formation of new contacts with a cosmopolitan technical and organizational culture.

But men are not indifferent to changes in their status and prospects, to the grounds of legitimacy of authority over them, or to the importation of foreign ideas. Social reorganization of the economy generates political passions, passions about the distribution of rewards and of status prospects, passions about the organization of authority relations, passions about the direction of development of the society as a whole. Wage levels, employment security, grievance machinery, retirement insurance, health care, housing, union organizing rights, all have to be decided for new groups of industrial workers. How they are decided will determine how easy it is to reorganize social relations in the economy and what unresolved grievances workers will carry into the political system.

The Historical Context of South American Development

South American economic development has presented these general problems of economic development in a peculiar context. In all three of the societies studies, Chile, Argentina, and Venezuela, the original influx of wealth and of bureaucratic forms of social organization of the economy was in the export sector, under foreign influence. In Chile, the nitrate industry, and then copper mining, created the first modern proletariat whose work was supervised by bureaucratic administrations. In Argentina, English-induced investment in meat and grain production created the first impetus toward economic development, and massive European immigration peopled the new economic sectors in Buenos Aires. Something like half of the national income of Venezuela is produced by foreign corporations in Venezuelan oil fields. When foreigners come into a country to reorganize its social structure and to claim most of the benefits of that reorganization, special problems of legitimacy of profits and authority are created.

Modern development in South America has occurred in a distinct historical political context. The revolutions of the early nineteenth century that gained independence for the various countries were carried out under a combination of French and American democratic ideals, and constitutional forms of the political system were generally inspired by American models, modified in a French centralist direction. By the 1960s, Chile's constitution was quite similar to that introduced by de Gaulle in France, with a multiparty congressional system and a plurality presidency which tended toward a two-candidate presidential election. In Argentina and Venezuela, the liberal—democratic tradition has been strong enough to reestablish elected governments fairly regularly after periods of dictatorship. But both countries have seen this constitutional tradition undermined during the nineteenth and early twentieth centuries by a kind of a political gangsterism, *caudillismo*, in government. In Argentina, the political incorporation of the new immigrants and their children, who made up the proletariat and the urban middle classes, provided social fuel for the growth of the eminently political *caudillo*, Juan Perón. Despite the weakness of the liberal democratic constitutional tradition in the actual running of the state, the middle classes both in Argentina and Venezuela have a general commitment to liberal democratic ideals. But weak and shifting parties and coalitions create precarious governments during constitutional periods, and the tradition of forceful intervention by the military and police threatens their stability.

The economic ideology of the dominant political groups in all three societies is capitalist, modified by populist and anti-imperialist rhetoric. But the vigorously innovating parts of the economy are mostly foreign firms and the government. Foreign firms are in close contact with international and cosmopolitan technical culture and are oriented to foreign markets. The government in each country is the main native employer of technically trained people. But besides being the native institution most in contact with world technical culture, the government is also the only institution that can regulate and tap the large flows of national income generated in the foreign sector. The copper companies, oil companies, and food exporters are not oriented toward local capital markets; they take little bourgeois pride in orderly and just government among their South American hosts; and they regard their social welfare responsibilities, if they have any, as limited to "their own" country's citizens. Only the government can divert the flow of export income into domestic investment, into domestic social welfare programs, into guaranteeing the status of the domestic proletariat, and into securing career prospects for the domestic white collar workers and professionals. Politically this creates a tension between the dominant governmental capitalist ideology, which tends to favor the interests of foreigners, and a lukewarm socialist policy, which tends to divert foreigners' income into domestic investment and social welfare.

The Problems of Socialism in South America: Government Income

The income of governments in South America varies roughly with the proportion of foreign trade and of production for export in the national income. The greater the dominance of production for foreign export, the greater the domination of the government over the domestic part of the economy because government income comes from taxing the foreign sector. The greater the domination of foreign capital, the greater the push toward socialist development. By "socialism" I mean three principles:

(1) Public ownership of the means of production, or substantial public participation in the profits of enterprises

(2) Organization of the proletariat into strong organizations, which gain substantial powers in the enterprise for the defense of the rights of workers and which enter into politics on behalf of workers, particularly securing social services for the poor and

(3) Limitation of the political power of capitalists and large landowners, especially limitation of the power of foreign capital

Since "socialism" is overloaded with ideological meaning, and since that meaning changes with the generations, I should point out the following features of this delineation:

(1) The socialism of a political system is a matter of degree; not a matter of yes or no.

(2) The definition turns on the means used, not on their degree of success in bettering the lot of the poor or worsening the lot of the rich.

(3) The definition is compatible with large-scale bureaucratic collectivist organization of the economy, of trade unions, and so forth. The syndicalist ideas of self-government by the poor and of small group freedom, which have been associated with "socialism" in the New Left, are not included in this definition.

The domestication of foreign income flow creates macrocephaly in the domestic economy. The difference between the salaries the government can pay and the salaries and profits of private domestic enterprise tend to be larger in economies with rich foreign trade. Social welfare benefits, housing investment, urban development, growth of education, all can be financed with less political trouble when the taxpaying entities are foreign owned. The government can pay more and do more in countries with rich foreign trade.

But there is a rich man's and a poor man's form of socialism. The flow of income from foreign trade can be channeled into civil service salaries without social policies, into investments in monuments and monumental public buildings without productive purposes, into impressive military and police apparatuses, into civil service pensions, and into Swiss and American bank accounts of dictators with precarious political futures. Or it can be channeled into industrial and port development, highway investments, health programs, schools, proletarian housing developments, and sewerage systems. Government employees can transform society, or they can drill on parade grounds or hunt political favor. The more dominant the government, the more it matters whether its socialism is serious. The greater the foreign trade sector, the more domestic social welfare depends on socialist initiatives.

Modernism and Socialist Aspects of the Labor Contract

The regulation of the labor contract for both workers and middle-class people is far more a matter of public concern and bureaucratic institutions in the modern sectors of an economy. The labor contract in modern societies creates rights in the job and in career prospects of the job. It ordinarily includes seniority rights to employment security and to promotion chances. Holding a given job implies inclusion in a given income class, whose relative and absolute buying power need preservation. Such worker and middle-class rights are regulated, in bureaucratic enterprises, by a system of rules. These rules create vested interests, which are defended by some combination of public administrative intervention, union organization, and rights of legal action in the courts or in administrative tribunals. Public agencies for industrial relations, unions, and labor tribunals are all chartered by governments; their internal structure, power, and regulations are established to a greater or lesser degree by governments. Such government charters involve the government in the creation and administration of the stratification system of the modern sector of the economy. The government is also involved in creating that system because it is itself a large part of the modern sector. The formation of stratification systems informed by political standards and influenced by political pressures is part of the essence of socialism. The modern sectors of almost all economies are more socialistic in this sense.

But the creation of politically regulated stratification systems in South America also appears in a somewhat special light, for the first two sectors to be regulated extensively by the government are the foreign corporations and the civil and military services. Both these sectors tend to create specially privileged groups. The foreign corporations, especially in Chile and Venezuela, are capital intensive enterprises. Total costs do not depend very much on wage and salary rates. If foreign trade income is diverted by regulations and unions into wages, salaries, social services, and pensions for the small labor force of the industry, this has no appreciable impact on the profits. The civil service is constituted by men who are educated, and hence highly regarded in the developing modern sector. They are often from priviledged families or in favor with the ruling political groups. Thus, it is easy to divert foreign trade income into privileges of a small modern proletariat, the civil service, and the officer corps.

The normal result of large government income and politicalization of stratification in the modern sector is a socialism of and for the rich. Government regulation of the labor contract and the vesting of workers' interests, mainly protects those who have good jobs at high pay with many social services and good career prospects. The poor in the traditional sectors of the economy are left to Ricardian economic principles, and fare about as well as the English poor did in Ricardo's time.

Socialism and Efficiency

Whatever the vigor of social policy and the direction of stratification intervention by a government, its activities may or may not be governed effectively by principles of technical and economic efficiency. When government services do not go to the same people who pay taxes, and when the social and political status of civil servants is much higher than that of the people they govern, the capacity of the population to demand efficiency and effectiveness is reduced. Governments are not ordinarily subject to the controls of market competition. The bases for competition in the political arena are not exclusively criteria of efficiency, especially when the civil servants are better organized than the people served. A crucial problem of socialist administration, therefore, is to institute measures of performance of publicly administered services and to make civil servants responsive to them.

Thus, the main dangers to socialism in South America are that the government may decide to do nothing with the flow of income created by foreign trade, that what it does do will favor small groups of privileged workers in the export sector and the civil service, or that what it does do will be done ineffectively. All these dangers are magnified when the proportion of national income created by foreign exporting firms is larger. All are magnified when the ideology of capitalism and government inactivity inspires a government that is the main channel through which export income can contribute to the general welfare. All are magnified when shifting coalitions form precarious governments without the courage or the legitimacy to follow a vigorous social policy and to put civil servants to work. Under such conditions, the macrocephaly of government, induced by heavy foreign trade income flows, creates a massive, mushy growth of ineffectual administration, of which the Traffic Inspector of San Felix is a local tumor.

The Problems of Liberty and Democracy in South America

South American governments have a historic charter of liberal republican government from the auspices and ideology of their independence movements. The only really ambivalent case is Brazil, whose independent government was at first a monarchy. In recent times most elections have been carried out with universal or nearly universal suffrage. The twentieth-century history of most South American countries has been one of alternation between democratic republican government under a constitution, and dictatorial or junta government, not responsible to a formal constitution. Roughly speaking, then, there are two main alternative forms of government: constitutional republican democracy or unconstitutional military elitism.

In some countries, there is more or less continuous constitutional republican democracy: Chile, Uruguay, Costa Rica, Mexico. In some there is more or less continuous unconstitutional military elitism: Haiti, Nicaragua, Guatemala, Paraguay. In most of the countries, there is more or less regular alternation: Argentina, Brazil, Venezuela, Peru, Ecuador, Colombia, Panama, the Dominican Republic.

Political democracy implies that the poor and the proletariat will vote, and in a poor country there are a lot of poor people. If the attachments of the poor to political organizations are strong, those organizations will work out a systematic left-wing policy. If party and union attachments are weak, the poor will be attracted to populist rhetoric, a rhetoric that promises to do something for them and to give them historical dignity. Generally, party and union attachments are strongest in the modern bureaucratic part of the economy which is subject to a governmentally administered stratification system.

Class divisions in politics are generally stronger in the cities, and strongest in industrial or mining cities. But when the city is merely the seat of a macro-cephalic government, whose private sector provides services to an elitist civil service, encouragement of class conflict is reduced. Many of the great capital cities of South America vote more heavily rightist than the country as a whole, as do provincial commercial and governmental centers. The poorest parts of the population are usually on the social periphery of the society, where class divi-sions are not so well organized. For instance, in Chile the strength of the center-right-wing Presidential coalition (e.g., in 1964 the vote for Frei) is greatest in the governmental and commercial centers of Santiago and Valparaíso, in the *hacienda* (or *fundo*) area of the central valley, and in the small farming area of the south. The centers of leftist strength are in the mining areas of the northern desert and in the industrial and coal-mining area of Concepción (where our Chilean data were taken). That is, the richest and the poorest areas of the country give dominant support to the center right, while the intermediate industrial and mining areas support the left.

The greater the dominance of foreign trade in the national income, and con-sequently the larger the proportion of civil servants in the urban population, the more the weight of the relatively conservative civil service and commercial current. Yet to win an election, the right-wing must gain many votes from the service and agricultural poor. Winning these votes generally requires demagogic parliamentary populism.

Thus, in countries (and areas within countries) with a low proportion of industrial and mining workers, the typical politician's role is to make vigorously left-wing speeches at election time and "practical" coalitions when parliament is in session. The lack of firm organization among the agricultural and service poor means that these people do not have full-time class leaders who might watch over and discipline parliamentary representatives while they are in power. Under such circumstances, the idea gains hold that political promises are meaningless, that all politicians are corrupt, and that politics is the art of saying one thing and doing the opposite. The population is therefore not willing to turn out in time of coups d'etat to defend "their" representatives because they never thought the representatives were really theirs. They may even take a mean satisfaction in politicians getting their comeuppance.

When the poor are badly organized, there is a tension between the political rhetoric appropriate to a democratic polity in which the poor rule and an actual polity in which foreigners and civil servants get most of the benefits. There is always a danger that the populism will turn serious. The South in the United States turns out demagogues by the score, but every once in a while produces a Huey Long, or a serious Populist Party, that actually tries to use the power of the government to redistribute income. South American political systems produce a lot of radical speeches, but also occasionally produce Juan Perón, or Lazaro Cárdenas, or Fidel Castro. Perón actually encouraged the growth of the power of unions and the multiplication of social services in Argentina. Cárdenas actually redistributed land to the peasants of Mexico. Castro actually socialized the economy of Cuba.

When populist speeches and democratic political forms start to turn serious, the casual complacency of middle-class democratic liberal beliefs is challenged by the prospect of taxation or expropriation to pay for the reality promised in the speeches. It is easy to love democracy so long as it has few costs. But when it comes to mean paying taxes for the benefit of the poor, or losing property, it is more threatening. The withdrawal of middle-class support from constitutional regimes when they try to act out their populist rhetoric weakens the regime, since the poor already have a general distrust of politicians and a weakness of political commitment.

Most of the military regimes of South America have not stamped out the tradition of liberal democracy. Very few of them have had an ideology that completely denies the legitimacy of political representation of opposing interests; few have attempted to extirpate the social base of opposing tendencies in the way the Soviet Union did during the 1920s and 1930s, or the Nazis did in Germany in the 1930s and 1940s. The idea that there are people who should lose all citizenship because of the obnoxiousness of their interests and ideologies is not very widely held.

Instead, the dictatorships generally incapacitate the opposition by imprisoning its leaders or forcing them into exile. Gangster governments like that of Haiti may be quite terrorist in their policy toward opposition, yet not permanently destroy it. There are, of course, some exceptions, such as the relatively long deprivation of political rights of the Catholic clergy in Mexico (now much modified), the long refusal of the Argentine military to tolerate any representation of Peronist currents, and the systematic exclusion of bourgeois interests from the politics of Cuba. By and large, though, the political complexion of the society after a dictatorship is quite similar to that before the dictatorship. The recurrent reelection of President Velasco Ibarra of Ecuador, after his recurrent ousting by the military, has been an example of this.

Thus, there are three primary variants of South American political systems at any given time. The first is a democratic republican polity with strongly organized lower-class interests, in which the middle classes tolerate the power of the lower classes and the leftist direction of policy. Chile has been an example of such a system. The second major variety is a populist government in societies with poorly organized lower classes. It is usually characterized by low political involvement of the general population, a middle class that is intolerant of making the populism into serious government activity, and a recent history of military intervention in the political system. Venezuela is a good example of such a system at the present time. The third major variety is the military dictatorship or junta government ruling under suspension of normal constitutional processes (or occasionally without there being any constitution to suspend), usually with a nontotalitarian ideology that keeps opposition political forces in abeyance. Governmental inactivity (except, of course, activities of political repression) in military regimes usually tends to favor the preservation of the status of the middle and upper classes. Argentina has recently been, and was at the time of the study, an example of such a government.

New social developments in South America, such as the growth of an employed industrial middle class, become politically significant as they affect these variant forms of political organization. Our three countries are at roughly the same level of economic development—with Argentina slightly ahead and Venezuela (despite considerable modernization because of the foreign oil industry) slightly behind. Yet, they showed the three main varieties of South American political organization. Thus, we will expect that the social influences of industrialization—such as the growth of an employed industrial middle class—will have a different impact in the different historical circumstances of the three societies. The growth of the new middle class does not seem to me a very important determinant of political dynamics. It is only one among many changes in social structure that influence the politics of modernization. This is the fundamental reason that our study of the new middle class tells us little about the political dynamics of modernization.

Government Activity in the Political Context

The primary question of the relation between politics and economic development in South America, then, is the question of what kind of socialism the political system will produce. Our theoretical problem at this point is to relate the problems of whether the government will do anything useful with its income, who it will do it for, and whether it will be done with some efficiency, to the varieties of political dynamics we have identified. That is, we want to relate the problems of South American socialism to the problems of South American liberty and democracy. The impact on economic development of political attitudes and political activities will depend on the links we can trace between the political order of these societies and the direction and efficiency of government activity.

The central theoretical problem is the one posed, for a different society under different political ideas, by Alexis de Tocqueville in his *Old Regime and the Revolution*. Tocqueville thought that the cause of the illegitimacy of the royal government of France in the eighteenth century was that privileges defended by the government (especially tax exemptions of the nobility) had lost their connection to public functions and public purposes which might have justified them. When privileges that might have motivated the adequate performance of public duties became detached from them, the government became increasingly incompetent to manage the resources of the country for winning wars and other political purposes. Governmental powers were mainly used to fill the purses of the rich, purses that were only supposed to be full because the men attached to the purses rendered public services. The society lost several wars; the nobility had their privileges because they were supposed to help win wars; the mass of the nobility contributed little to military activities. This complex of organized nonperformance and privilege Tocqueville thought robbed the regime of its legitimacy.

In legally administered and defended status systems, then, privilege may come to dominate the purposes to which the system is devoted. Policy may be shaped by the privileges and positions of power it preserves, rather than by the results it offers. *We have to ask, then, what are the conditions under which public purposes will dominate in the working out of the reward systems of public agencies, so that rewards will be tied to results, rather than to the occupancy of a vested position in the structure?* Under what political conditions will the career prospects of the Traffic Inspector of San Felix be made to depend on whether he issues drivers licenses?

Every administrative structure creates positions of privilege and career opportunities for men in the structure. The natural tendency of such structures of vested interests is for the people who hold them to make them more secure. Under what conditions, then, will men make their status and prospects secure by serving, as best they can, the purposes of the administrative apparatus as a whole, and under what conditions will they make them secure by attaching the rights to their persons, regardless of any public functions? When will men seek power over their own fate by rendering service and when by individual and collective self-defense? In the eighteenth century in France, according to Tocqueville, they had been led in the latter direction, while in England, the privileged orders were defending their positions by public service. (I do not have to take a position here on whether Tocqueville was right about eighteenth-century France as compared to England.)

We may call a government "strong" if it can change and modify the privileges of vested interest groups in the light of public policy. A "weak" government is one that allows the vesting of interests to be detached from the performance of public functions, so that publicly defended statuses and careers become the private property of those who occupy them. We would say that Louis XVI of France was a "weak" king because he allowed the vesting of interests, defended by the royal government, to be detached from public purposes and to become the inheritable property of families, or of oligarchies of privileged corporations, regardless of the effectiveness with which they discharged the functions of their positions. Peter the Great of Russia, on the other hand, was a "strong" king because he managed to make the privileges attached to public functions noninheritable and dependent on service to the Czar. The postulate is that the strength of the government determines the degree to which civil servants will be constrained to achieve public purposes in order to protect their careers and to advance themselves or, conversely, to play the bureaucratic game in a system of irrational jockeying for position and for royal or political favor. The strength of the government in a monarchy determines whether the men surrounding the king are courtiers or civil servants. The strength of the government in South American countries determines essentially the same thing.

There seem to be two good measures of the strength of South American governments. One is the size of the army. The army in South America is not, in modern times, an effective instrument for the achievement of public purposes. Its growth beyond some minimal level, and the specially privileged position of the officer corps in the stratification system as a whole, indicate that well-organized groups of people with vested interests are predominant over the public purposes of the polity. A second indicator is the capacity of the government to collect taxes for public purposes from privileged sectors of the population, especially the middle classes. The unwillingness of the kings of France to call the estates general to approve taxes (and consequently to approve the purposes of the royal government) indicated the weak condition of the monarchy in eighteenth century France. The incapacity of many South American governments to collect taxes (except on foreign corporations) reflects much the same weakness relative to the privileges of the middle and upper classes. For our purposes, the expropriation of property (e.g., in land reform programs) has much the same significance as the collection of taxes. If a government can expropriate the property of natives, it is a strong government.

Applying these two criteria (size of army and capacity to levy taxes) to Latin American governments, it is fairly clear that the stable constitutional governments are stronger. Uruguay and Costa Rica have relatively small armies (and small paramilitary police forces). Chile and Mexico have larger armies than would be demanded by this analysis. However, in both countries the relative size, power, income, and prestige of the military have been declining. The Chilean army had a public function around the turn of the century, conquering and defending the mines of the North. The Mexican army was swollen after the Revolution by the incorporation of many irregular troops. Thus, a more exact statement is that strong governments lead to a relative decline of armies that no longer serve a public function. Argentina and Venezuela, and most of the other precarious populist democracies and military regimes, have large and highly privileged armies. The Mexican government has expropriated land on a large scale in its land-reform program, and has a moderately efficient internal taxation system. The Chilean government even before Allende collected large social-security taxes on wage bills, and has recently been improving drastically its income tax system and expropriating land owned by native Chileans. The Venezuelan government, on the other hand, collects its meager income tax mainly when people apply for permission to leave the country. In Argentina, tax evasion is routine.

Thus, we find a broad correlation between the types of governments we have just outlined and the strength of public purposes as compared with the defense of middle-class privilege. Unstable populist republican governments (recently established after a military government has been overthrown) and military regimes are generally weak governments. The assertion here is that strong governments tend to be characteristic of democratic regimes with a well-organized lower class. Therefore the government growth stimulated by the flow of foreign trade in such countries tends to be actively devoted to the welfare of the public and to putting civil servants to work for the achievement of public purposes. In countries with weak governments, civil servants are put to work shuffling papers.

The Social Bases of Democratic Government

The argument just stated implies that it is not sufficient to examine the constitutional forms of a government at a particular time to tell whether it is democratic or not. The constitutions of unstable populist regimes are generally very similar to those of the stable democracies. We want to locate features of the social structure of politics which constitute a nation's predisposition toward unstable government.

We have located two such factors in the given argument. First, if the population is well organized politically, into functioning interest groups and solid political parties, then it can hold a government responsible for actually carrying out a large part of the promises made about public policy. Political groups form a countervailing power to the interests and intrigues of the civil service, of the military, and of those parts of the private economy with government protected status rights. Second, if the middle classes accept the consequences of democracy—the increase of the power of the organized poor and the vigor of government social service programs—then the normal functioning of democracy will not alienate them as much. The latent legitimacy of military intervention created by an alienated middle class, offended by populist policies, will not tend to grow.

The brunt of my argument is that *democratic political life tends to create these social bases for democracy.* That is, democracy causes democracy. Each year that democracy lasts, it increases the strength of attachment of the population to the trade unions and political parties that try to influence public policy through democratic channels. Each success of such organizations adds members to them, and confirms present members in their attachments. Successes come during democratic periods. Democracy teaches the middle classes that the interests of the poor are legitimate objects of public policy. The longer democratic structures last, then, the tougher they are to eliminate.[1]

There are a number of mechanisms by which this self-sustaining character of democracy can be explained.

(1) We would expect, for instance, that the strength of attachment to a political party would be greater for people if they are the second generation in which their family or peer group has been attached to the party. But is the parties are shifting and unstable, or are periodically destroyed by military regimes, then there will be fewer second-generation primary groups with continuous political attachments.

(2) We would expect that those people who have actively campaigned for a candidate will be more likely to accept those compromises with other interests in the society which are necessary to build a winning coalition. But the greater the number of elections, the more people will have had electioneering experiences. Since in poor countries there are many poor, some of those coalitions will have been directed at winning the votes of the poor.

(3) People will be more likely to invest their time and substance in an interest group organization if they think it will be around, and still effective, in the future. But the expectation of the future effectiveness of an organization will tend to be greater, the less frequently such organizations have been destroyed or incapacitated by dictatorial governments in the past.

(4) In democratic countries, the lag between the formation of a new social group (e.g., industrial bureaucrats) and the representation of their distinctive world view in separate organizations will tend to be shorter. Because the rich environment of rapidly adapting organizations will attract more of the interests of the population, the people will be likely to be better organized.

(5) On their first introduction, new organizations of the poor and bureaucratic intervention in the administration of the stratification system are surrounded by cataclysmic myths about the destruction of all the virtues of the old regime. The longer the experiences with the introduction of new structures by the poor and by the government, the less believable do such visions of cataclysm become.

(6) The greater the power of political parties in a government, the more governmental privileges will be distributed by political parties, and the fewer will be determined by interpersonal pull and office intrigue. Since powerful political parties have more power to reward followers— especially the crucially important lowest level of active popular leaders—

---

1. The self-causing nature of democracy is one of the main arguments in S. M. Lipset, M. Trow, and J. S. Coleman, *Union Democracy* (Glencoe, Illinois: The Free Press, 1956), especially pp. 393–400.

they can build more solid structures among the public and devote more efforts to perfecting their organization and strategy. Powerful political parties in one generation cause powerful parties in the next generation.

The Egalitarianism of the Chilean Middle Classes

The first strategic factor for an understanding of the stability of Chilean democracy and specifically, the capacity of the Chilean government to modify systems of privilege, is the high degree of egalitarianism of the middle classes. The dilemma for a poor country becoming a political democracy is that there are a great many more of the poor than there are of the rich or well-to-do. If the poor have access to the political system, they will urge policies of equalization, of taxation of the rich, public services to the poor, the right to organize unions and to strike, land reform, subsidized bread and taxed caviar, and so forth. In poor countries, if a movement institutes political democracy, it will have a heavy push to the left, because in poor countries, there are more of the poor and they are poorer.

Then the question is whether the middle and upper classes will accept the left policies that are implied in workers' and peasants' right to vote and organize. The vacillating stance of many South American liberal currents is due, I think, to the middle class wanting a constitutional democracy, but a conservative policy. After a period of dictatorship, their constitutional preferences hold sway, and a revolution against dictatorship has their support. A democratic structure is set up, but then its pristine constitutional purity is sullied in the eyes of the middle class by democratic, left-wing policies. In such situations, a constitutionally unfortunate coup d'etat may be the only way to "save the constitution" from corruption, dictatorship, and Communist infiltration.

Thus, unless the middle class is inclined to accept the power of the poor, which is implied by their own democratic constitutional preferences, democracy in the long run alienates them. Such an alienated middle class, in Polanyi's brilliant phrase diagnosing the Weimar Republic in Germany, "takes the risk out of revolution" for the right wing and military.

There are two sorts of evidence to be offered on the greater egalitarianism of the Chilean middle class. The first is their heavy vote for a left Christian Democrat, Frei, as President in 1964, and for the Christian Democrats in 1970 election. Frei's vote was heaviest, about 60%, in the Santiago—Valparaíso metropolitan area where the commercial and governmental middle-class workers are concentrated, in the South in the German influenced small farming areas, and in the rich central valley which was organized in latifundia. His main opponent, Allende, a left social democrat somewhat similar to Nenni in Italy, received his heaviest vote in the mining areas on the North and the heavy industrial area around Concepción in the South.

Frei, the *middle class and latifundist* candidate advocated land reform of a serious character, government participation in the mining and copper processing export industries, more governmental services such as education and medical care, opposition to the U.S. Caribbean policy, a secular state and freedom of religion, etc. That's what the right wing was like.[2]

A second type of evidence comes from the survey. We asked a series of questions about whether social classes (workers, peasants, businessmen, and landlords) should have more, the same, or less power. The most egalitarian response would be that the lower classes (workers and peasants) should have more power, and the higher classes (businessmen and landlords) should have less. We scored respondents by degrees of egalitarianism by scoring 0, 1, 2 for less, same, or more power for workers or peasants, respectively, and reversed the scoring for businessmen and landlords. Thus, the most egalitarian pattern would produce a score of 8. The percentage with scores of 7 or 8 (i.e., leaving at most one class in the *same* power position, the other three moved in an egalitarian direction) are given in Table 7.1. We see that Chilean middle class respondents in 1964 were much more accepting of increased power of the lower classes then were comparable respondents in Argentina and Venezuela. The peaceful acceptance of socialist electoral victories since then, in Chile, as compared, for example, to the long continuation of repression of left Peronism in Argentina, may be explained by these attitudes. What then explains the attitudes?

Let me suggest first that plurality electoral systems socialize the middle-class electorate in an egalitarian direction. Chile has a very peculiar electoral system, in which parliament is selected by a system favoring multiparity candidacies, while the presidency is, in effect, a plurality electron. I will not go into details on exactly how it works, because we are here interested in the effects. What happens, then, is that the presidential campaigns are fought out by a few significant candidates, ranging from two to about four. These significant candidates are put forward by coalitions of parliamentary parties, and have to cam-

TABLE 7.1

**Chileans Are Much More
Egalitarian (Total Samples)**

	Percentage highly egalitarian[a]
Chile	57 (136)
Argentina	37 (142)
Venezuela	31 (124)

[a]Scores of 7 or 8; see text for explanation.

2. The following explanation of Peron's failure in Argentina and Allende's success in Chile looks sort of silly now. (September, 1973)

paign on a platform sufficiently appealing to win a plurality. There are no seats as minority president as there are minority seats in parliament. The 1970 Allende vote, for example, was just barely over a third in a three candidate election. But neither candidate with almost a third is in the presidency.

What we get in a presidential campaign, then, is at least one middle-class candidate (in 1970, two) from the relatively more conservative parties. But, as in the U.S., he has to win a plurality. In a poor country that means he must get a large vote from the poor. There are enough rich and their followers to keep a small party in parliament, but not enough to elect a president. This candidate must, then, appeal to some of the poor. He tends to be chosen either from the nonpolitical types, as Alessandri was (just as the most popular recent Republican President of the U.S., Eisenhower, was nonpolitical before his election), or from the left-most party of the conservative coalition, as was Frei, the president elected in 1964. The left parties tend to form a coalition around the right-most large member of the coalition, the Radicals in the Popular Front government of the 1930s and early 1940s, and the Social Democrats in the 1964 and 1970 elections.

Election campaigns in such a system have (as they have in two-party systems) a strong socializing effect. The middle-class voter hears *his* candidate, supported by *his* party, endorsing benefits for the poor, supporting union organization, using a rhetoric that portrays workers as full members of the society, and so forth. Being attached to his own candidate, as against the candidates of the left, the middle-class voter becomes attached to the candidate's policies, including his policies in favor of the poor. The poor, conversely, hear their candidate, Allende for example, urging support of formal democracy in which middle-class parties have a right to exist and to try to take power.

Both Venezuela and Argentina had had short electoral histories when the data was collected—and it begins to look as if Argentina would never have a long electoral history. The Perón dictatorship in Argentina and the Pérez dictatorship in Venezuela, were things of the recent past. Moreover, the new electoral systems deprived parts of the left of political rights. Hence, the middle class has not yet had a chance to become socialized to egalitarian ideals.

The argument, to this point, is that a strong government that can manage public enterprises, and that can discipline the rich and the privileged workers in a way to make public enterprises a source of social advance, rather than pockets of privilege and corruption, can be created by strong democracy. But a precondition of strong democracy in a country with many poor people is an acceptance of egalitarian principles. We have suggested that the Chilean middle class shows much more acceptance of the power of the poor than do the middle classes of Argentina or Venezuela. And we have suggested that this is because they are socialized to such acceptance by their own presidential candidates, who must appeal to a well-organized poor electorate.

Briefly, the argument, then, is that democracy makes socialism possible without the massive emigration of the middle classes that attended the institution of socialism in Russia, Eastern Europe, Cuba, and perhaps China. By democracy we mean specifically that the representatives of middle- and upper-class interests must justify themselves to the poor.

Social Sources of Political Responsibility

By "political responsibility" I mean the degree of correspondence between what politicans advocate and what governments do when those politicians come to power. A democratic polity is subject to the dangers of demagogy. Demagogues criticize governments from utopian and impractical standpoints, and their incapacity in power to institute utopias tends to create cynicism as politicians in power forget what they have said. A rough correspondence between what the electorate has been told and the policy of the government once elected is at the root of democratic consensus. High promise combined with low performance is a breeding ground for revolution and for cynical bickering over the division of the spoils.

How, then, might we recognize a high versus a low degree of demagogy? First, a lower degree of demagogy will be indicated by campaigns organized around issues—especially moderately concrete governmental programs that might actually be carried out. We would expect such campaigns to result in people in the electorate giving programmatic or ideological reasons for preferring their candidate. Among Chilean voters in the middle-class sample, only 7% gave personality, "don't know," or other nonideological reasons for their vote; in Argentina the figure was 30%; in Venezuela it was 21% ($N = 136, 142,$ and 124, respectively).

We would also expect some consensus on the major problems confronting the society. In answer to a question asking which problem they would deal with first if they were president, 30% of the Chileans gave the modal response— education; the modal category in Argentina was finance and inflation, mentioned by 30%; in Venezuela it was poverty and unemployment, again given by 30%. Here, then, the evidence contradicts the argument.

Second, we would expect that such organization of political campaigns around issues would result in an organization of the electorate by ideology. This is, *if* an individual can tell what a party or candidate will do, *then* he will vote for or against that candidate according to what he himself believes. This will result in voters for parties having a distinct ideology on social questions. If, on the other hand, a campaign is conducted around personalities, or if shifting demagogic parties try to appeal on all sorts of issues that could never be government policy, then we would expect idiosyncratic voting, and little relation of party choice to ideology. That is, we should expect that in Chile the constituencies of the different parties and candidates would differ in ideology, that leftists would support left candidates and parties, while the rightists would support rightists candidates and parties. In more unstable electoral systems with shorter histories and weaker governments, we should expect little relation between electoral choice and ideology.

If we relate political party preference to ideology in Chile, the Socialist party loyals were 92% "high" (7 or 8) on egalitarianism, the Christian Democrats 63%, and the Radicals 41% (12, 41, and 27 cases, respectively). The overall span, then, was a 51% difference. In Argentina, of the 16 Peronists, 19% were "highly" egalitarian; of the 36 Radicals, 8% were "highly" egalitarian, for an overall span of only 12%. In Venezuela, the supporters of the Christian Democrats (COPEI) were 28% "high," while the supporters of Acción Democrática were 41% "high," for a span of 18%. That is, the Chilean parties were much more differentiated ideologically along the dimension of egalitarianism. It is worthy of note, however, in the light of this discussion, that the most right wing of the Chilean parties with a substantial following in our sample had at least as egalitarian a following (41% "high") as the most left wing of the major parties in either of the other societies (19% for Argentina 41% for Venezuela).

Demagogy and the Relation of Center to Periphery

Perhaps what I am arguing will become clearer if it is formulated in terms of the structural distinction, elaborated by Eisenstadt, between center and periphery.[3] The notion is that in developing polities, especially, alternative policies of government are worked out in the center. Concretely, they are formulated by a political elite working in the capital city.

A crucial problem in modernizing a polity is to organize the general population, the periphery, in terms of the policy alternatives worked out at the center. This organization is usually carried out by parties and interest groups. The question to ask is whether the dimensions along which the population at the periphery is politically organized correspond to the dimensions of policy alternatives worked out at the center. For instance, suppose that we scale the various notes of congressmen. We also scale the attitudes of the electorate toward public policy. The first question is: Do the scales which differentiate the congressmen correspond in content to those which differentiate the population? The second question is: Does support for a congressman with, say, a high score on liberalism in foreign policy, vary with the liberalism of the voter in the same area, as measured by his attitude scale score? Are liberals much

3. S. N. Eisentadt, *Modernization, Protest and Change*, Englewood Cliffs, New Jersey: Prentice-Hall, 1966, e.g., pp. 11–15.

more likely to support liberal congressmen, or is the relation between one's own ideas and one's vote more or less random?

In general, such a correspondence will not be achieved by the average voter watching the votes of individual congressmen. If it is achieved at all, it will be by party and interest group links between the voter and the congressman. The voter will support parties and interest groups that favor his kind of foreign policy, and they in turn will support (or pressure) congressmen to support that policy.

In this light, we can ask what the relative degree of party organization of the electorate is in our three societies. Asked what political party they favored at the time of the interview, only 38% (of 136) of the Chileans did not give a party (this is, of course, a middle-class sample overweighted with educated people). Of the Argentines, 54% (of 142) did not, and 65% (of 124) Venezuelans did not. Venezuelan nonparticipation is elevated by a relatively large number of foreigners not eligible to vote, especially among steel plant and mining employees. The Chileans are much more linked to the center through enduring party loyalties, know something of the ideological differences among parties and candidates and respond to them, and generally can be considered more organized at the periphery according to the dimensions of policy alternatives being fought over in the center.

The argument here is similar to that of C. Wright Mills's *Power Elite*.[4] Mills argued, essentially, that at the center in the United States, the really important policy alternatives were war and peace—that was (and is) where most of the money was going and where decisions of life and death were being made. But the periphery was organized according to ethnicity, region, class, and economic interest. Hence, he argued, the policies on war and peace, which were the main policies in terms of money and men, were made "irresponsibly," and the class interest politics of Congress and the electorate was essentially "demagogy," vote getting on irrelevant and inconsequential policy issues.

What I have argued about Chile, then, is that the electorate is more or less organized along the same dimensions that distinguish policies in the center—issues of more government services and more equality by socialist policies. Such an organization of the electorate along lines of policy alternatives was not nearly as prevalent in Venezuela or Argentina. Hence, in the latter two countries, electoral campaigns were on irrelevant and inconsequential issues, not on the policy choices facing the government. When the policy choices were made, they were made far more independently of the organized will of the people. This, in turn, meant that they did not have behind them a popular

4. C. Wright Mills, *The Power Elite*, New York: Oxford, 1956, 1969, especially Chapters 11 and 12, pp. 242–297.

consensus, and a large part of the population thought them merely the machinations of corrupt men.

Conclusions

Economic development involves the redistribution of privileges. The conviction on which this chapter is based has two parts: (1) privileges will be legitimate if distributed on socialist principles in underdeveloped countries, and (2) privileges will be effective for economic development if the middle and upper classes are required to earn privileges by public service. These two convictions lead, with a few loose joints in the logic, to the idea that some kind of socialism will be more effective for economic development of poorer countries than will capitalism. Except when a country is willing to pay the Cuban price of a one party government and emigration of the middle class, this means for Latin America that democratic socialism is the most effective way out of the political problems of economic development.[5] South America is similar to Western Europe in that regard, and as in Europe, the most legitimate of the democratic governments have large admixtures of socialism, and have had or have socialist parties in power.

Schumpeter argued that only socialist governments could discipline workers' inclination to strike; my argument here is that only socialist governments can put the middle and upper classes to work for economic development of the native sector and for other public purposes in Latin America.

If this argument is true, then two further political conditions of steady economic development of the native sector probably follow. The first is middle-class acceptance of working-class power. The bureaucratic reorganization of the stratification system of the modern sector, with unions and social security and pensions, invades property rights and recognizes new kinds of worker rights. Taxation of the middle classes and the rich for public purposes and for redistribution invades middle- and upper-class privileges. If economic development goes on under a democratic political system, and in South America there are strong forces for democracy, the legitimacy of the regime depends on tolerance by the middle classes of the power, property, and taxation consequences of a democratically governed reorganization of the stratification system.

This egalitarianism of the middle classes is probably produced by the political system itself, if it is a stable democratic system. The appeals to the poor required to get a majority in a system with widespread suffrage can teach the middle

---

5. I reached a preference for democratic socialism about a decade before constructing this argument for it.

classes that government policy is (at least, is also) about the legitimate rights of the poor.

The second requirement is a system of links, by parties and interest groups, between the policy-making centers of the society and the periphery. The disciplined pursuit of public purposes by a political elite, elite responsibility, is rarely effectively achieved by an ethic internal to the elite alone. Ethical systems without power behind them tend to become ethical rhetoric for the defense of privilege. Responsibility of the political elite to constituencies inside the country is the only long-run alternative to responsibility to a constituency of copper companies, *frigoríficos*, or oil companies. And that responsibility to national constituencies has stable structural supports only if the poor are organized into leftist parties and strong trade unions.

The conclusion of this chapter on South American politics is, therefore, quite simple. Probably, the development of effective industrializing bureaucracies in South American countries depends on the degree of socialism in their political systems: the more socialist, the more effective.

CHAPTER 8

Policies of Economic Development

In the Introduction, we described the variation between an effective modernizing bureaucracy in Venezuela and a new, but ineffective and traditional bureaucracy. The rest of this book can be thought of as arguing that effective economic bureaucracies are created by economic development. Part II, essentially shows that men think, plan, and innovate when they are paid to think, plan, and innovate. Part III essentially shows that people are motivated to do the bureaucratic jobs required for rapid growth if they are in rapidly growing bureaucracies. Part IV essentially argues that the institution of the socialist and other political prerequisites of the stability of bureaucratic stratification systems tends to be produced by the modernization of the economy.

That is, in several ways *we have argued that economic growth causes the changes in the social structure that favor economic growth*. The traditional social structure of these countries does not seem to have much toughness in stopping the development of modern structures. This suggests that people of almost all kinds, whatever their traditional culture and social structure, will respond to economic opportunity.

If opportunity does, in fact, create an appropriate social structure, then we must analyze why the opportunities are worse in poorer countries. First, consider again the English industrial revolution in textiles. During the early period of the industrial revolution in England, the amount of English textiles that was sold increased greatly. Of course Englishmen did not start wearing several times as much cloth. The opening of the Indian and South American markets, mainly by the British Navy, was mainly responsible for market expansion.[1] We might try to produce a Protestant ethic, a rational, disciplined devotion to work in a career and an ascetic tendency to save and invest, by increasing fivefold the foreign market for South American industrial goods.

We have been studying here a smaller version of the stimulation of modern social structure by economic opportunities. By erecting tariff barriers, the market for steel from plants within the barrier has been expanded rapidly. As we have seen, this has successfully produced pockets of rational disciplined pursuit of higher productivity in South America. What stops such pockets from expanding further?

The main factor seems to me to be economic nationalism in the world political system—the *same* economic nationalism that created the pockets of Protestant ethic. The big rich markets for industrial goods—the industrialized countries—have generally protected their domestic industries. They have especially protected the relatively labor intensive industries, such as textiles and apparel, processed agriculture products, steel. This creates two types of difficulties for the industries of poor countries. First, it increases poor countries' prices when they sell in the rich countries, in relation to the prices of producers in those countries. Second, it increases the complexity and the uncertainty of any attempt to invade that market. Successful invasion of the rich country's market usually involves a heavy merchandising investment, a heavy investment in finding out what the market will take, which commodities can stand the tariff and which cannot compete, and so forth. But successful invasion also generally increases pressure within the rich country to put up further barriers.

The same difficulties arise when an industry invades the market of another poor country, but with the additional disadvantage that once the industry gets the market of another poor country, it does not get much. It is nearly as hard, in effective shipping and merchandising costs, to sell Argentine shoes in Santiago, Chile, as it is in New York. But there are only 7 million poor Chilieans to be shod, 200 million rich Americans. The market for shoes in New York City alone is larger than the whole Chilean market. The policy of encouraging regional economic integration among poor countries amounts to the palming off of a destitute relative to the next poorest member of the family, since he would not fit in if he lived in the house of the rich relatives. The opening of rich countries to the industrial products of poor countries (without requiring reciprocal tariff reductions) would probably help. But such an opening seems to me considerably less likely than a sudden spurt of Protestant ethic among the South American aristocracy.

1. Eric J. Hobsbawm, *The Age of Revolution* 789–1848, New York: Mentor, 1962, pp. 52–55.

A second major factor explaining low profit rates in poor countries is a temporal one. The real cost of production of a good within a firm—the amount of capital and labor it takes to make a given quantity of goods—declines relatively rapidly at first as the bugs are worked out of the technical and administrative system; it then usually declines more slowly, but steadily, with time. Even if a firm in a poor country starts within the same advanced capital equipment as is used in rich countries, it is usually younger. This means that the firm's productivity will be lower even if, over time, it has the same performance curve as the rich country's. This means, in particular, that the product per dollar's worth of capital is generally lower. Since capital is, if anything, more expensive in poorer countries than in rich ones—both because of higher interest rates and because of special shipping and installation costs—the effective capital–output ratio in a given industry is likely to be lower in a poor country. Thus the more capital intensive an industry is, the more the competitive disadvantage of a new installation in a poor country would probably be.

If capital (and other internationally mobile factors such as technical experts) get the same return, while workers' wages make up for the inefficiency of capital, there is likely to be more inequality in the modern sector of poorer countries. This is further encouraged by the lower competitive wage rates in the labor markets of poor countries. Thus the cost of production of poorer countries tends to be higher than that of rich countries, especially in capital intensive and technically sophisticated industries. This tends to restrict the market of poorer countries' industries to protected areas. But workers resist paying the costs of inefficiency of capital, especially when the capitalists are very wealthy compared to themselves. The higher capital costs of production in poor countries tend to create explosive class tensions in the most modern sectors.

This leads us to the belief that if the industries of poorer countries are to enter the international market, they must probably show a substantially *higher* rate of technical progress than the industries of rich countries. They must catch up, even if they continue to pay lower wages.

Whether or not these economic arguments are valid, I hope they suggest that the profitability of rapid industrial expansion in poorer countries is by no means guaranteed. If the profits are low, then the rate of expansion is low, fewer people will be paid salaries to make innovations, fewer men will have the lure of an industrial career to keep them at work, and fewer organized interests will grow up to make politicians keep their promises. High profits produce profit-seekers; low profits in new pursuits confirm men in their traditional round of life. The key problem of policy, then, is the production of opportunities for profitable expansion of industries in poorer countries, rather than the production of men to seize opportunities already there.

Organization of Thought and Development

But if the basic energy for development comes from opportunities for profit, it can come either in the destructive flood of a gold rush or in the constructive impulse toward industrialization. The profits may go to the lucky, or to the privileged, rather than to those who create activities. As Weber pointed out long ago, the "adventure capitalism" of a gold rush does not produce viable factories. And Robert Heilbroner recently said: "The social universe that [modern economists] are attempting to reproduce in a set of [production and consumption] equations is not and cannot be described by functional relationships alone, but must also and simultaneously be described as a system of privilege."[2] We have to study how the energy derived from opportunities for profit can be canalized so as to produce a self-transforming system of economic organizations.

Thought is the central device for canalizing energy. But it is ineffective in transforming a practical system unless the criteria of excellence of the operating system are applied to the results of the thought. The criteria of excellence of operating systems are not the same as the criteria of excellence of thought itself. We have to ask, then, how thought can go on in an enterprise that is, for example, primarily devoted to making steel.

The first problem is to permeate the organization with standards that can be applied to new as well as old procedures. Such standards have to be sufficiently abstract, and sufficiently subject to calculation, that an operating system can be discarded for the sake of a drawing. Cost accounting data provide these abstract standards by providing estimates of the costs of the operating system that can be compared with the estimated cost of a drawing. The other main source of such standards is an operating system somewhere else—in a rich country—which is represented by the drawing.

Money savings and imitation of industry leaders are the two main criteria that guide technical thought. The permeation of a technical system with these two sources of standards depends on the intellectual quality and political position within the firm of cost accountants and of people sensitive to the news of the industry. If cost accountants are intelligent and powerful, staff departments are likely to produce valuable innovations. If executives or their consultants have traveled abroad, engineers who have not are nonetheless likely to be effective. The Argentine plant had poor cost accounting, few foreign trained men, and staff people who did not effectively introduce innovations— and it was in a bad way.

But if the government of thought by practical standards were all that were necessary, foremen and line executives and small businessmen would be great

2. *New York Review*, Dec. 5, 1968, p. 10.

innovators. They do, of course, do a lot of minor, day-to-day innovation. But detachment from operating responsibility is usually required before people can think; so most large-scale innovative thinking is done by a staff. Where we find a major component of innovative thought among hierarchical superiors, as in the Chilean plant, we also find indirect indications that the press of hierarchical operative responsibility has been cut down. The basic source of this press is that if each subordinate has ten urgent problems a week, and each executive has five subordinates, an executive has fifty urgent problems. Only by training the subordinate to solve most of his problems for himself, by education, by experience, by collective attack on classes of problems in committee meetings, can this press be relieved. If the subordinate can handle nine of the ten problems, the superior can do what he ought to do, that is, to consider long-run strategies.

People think more if they are educated. Furthermore, thinking seems to be a consequence of engineering education, among other things, for that is the kind our respondents mostly had. If we wish to canalize the energy of profit through thought, we can therefore give the following advice: Hire educated men; place at least some of them in staff structures without too many subordinates; cut the hierarchical pressure on high executives that keeps them from listening to the staff; permeate the whole system with criteria of cost accounting, or other performance measures, and with comparisons with industry leaders so that innovations are evaluated by the same standards as currently operating systems.

Systems of Privilege and Development

But thought alone will not canalize the energies created by profitable opportunities. Most of the energies set in motion by such opportunities are efforts to appropriate the opportunities as privileges. The first thing men ordinarily do is to see that the opportunity goes to themselves and only second that the opportunity is used best. Thus, a crucial aspect of an organization is its reward system, conceived of as *a system of privilege*. Performance in an organizational role also, in all stable organizations, provides tenure in an organizational system of privilege. How the energies of profitable opportunities are canalized depends on the system of tenures and privileges that the opportunities get controlled by. The destructiveness of a gold rush is caused by the instability of tenures. The destructiveness of a traditional dictatorship is caused by the stability of tenures. The trick is to make tenures depend on performance.

There are two parts to this trick. The first is to make virtually every *tenure of privilege a result of promotion.* By promoting people to higher privilege, the organization can reduce the gold rush anarchy by making the position worth achieving (because it is secure) and at the same time keep a firm organizational grip on the marginal reward. This combination of security with dependence is sufficiently valuable that universities create hierarchies where no technical requirement for them exists, just so every position of solid privilege can be a step in a career of promotions. Most industrial bureaucracies do not have to resort to such fictional hierarchies since there is some natural division of the problems of the enterprise by levels of abstraction, and this division makes a hierarchy technically appropriate.

The second trick of managing privilege is deeper, more difficult. This is the problem of creating and destroying roles in response to changing profitabilities, without at the same time destroying faith in the system of privilege as a reward system. In general, the problem is most severe in the creation and destruction of sub-units of an organization, especially if the sub-units include men's complete career cycles. If the sociology department of a university is given up as a bad job, there is nowhere to promote any of the people. Only a powerful central administration, administering generally recognized standards, using respected measuring devices, can change such blocks of privilege. That is why there are probably still more scholars studying any 100 million ancient Romans or Greeks than the 600 million contemporary Chinese. The positions of privilege of classics departments cannot be reallocated easily to Chinese studies.

This problem becomes particularly important in creating new modern industries in poorer countries. In many poor countries, to be employed is a privilege enjoyed by only about 80% of the labor force. Not only departments in firms, but whole firms, even whole industries, may be preserved because they are structures of privilege. South American armies have often been such superfluous structures of privilege. Even a strong government like the Chilean which handed the job of cutting its losses in the nitrate industry to one of its most respected agencies (CORFO), cannot shut the industry down when it operates at a loss.

Apart from the need for strong governments, the primary organizational requirement is for clear measures of the efficiency of agencies and units of governments. In steel plants there are performance measurements provided by the international market. These can be more or less concealed from the political system, depending on how the subsidy is paid to the industry. If it is paid by consumers, by means of a tariff wall, then the plant is protected fairly well from governmental evaluation. If it is paid by the government, with little tariff protection, it will be evaluated.

In general, our measures of the efficiency of units of government are bad. For instance, they rarely count time lost by the client as a cost, which food markets are forced to do by competition. As a result, we all wait longer for government services than we do for food, or for any other services except medical (the combination of governmental and medical arrogance in public clinics is about the worst). Further, the measures of performance there are do not really have solid support in administrative centers. In undemocratic countries with illiterate and uncomplaining citizens, in particular, there is very little way to prevent governments from becoming merely boondoggles. Some technical innovations in performance measures of government agencies would be a great help to us all.

Social patternings of promotions, and of role creation and destruction, determine whether the energy created by opportunities for profit are canalized into productive and self-transforming enterprises. But for most poor countries, many main elements of the environment of enterprise are international. This study tells us very little about the dynamics of such international systems and how forces from them affect enterprises.

Organization Theory and Economic Development

How can a government and society that produces the Traffic Inspector of San Felix produce an administrative system that can reduce delays in a pipe mill? This is "The Problem of This Book," as we set it out in the first chapter. If the solution to the problem of economic development is some kind of organizational theory, what should that organizational theory look like?

Organizational theory deals with strong causes and small causes intertwined. The strong causes are the connection between one activity and another. If a steel billet has been elongated so that it will not go back in the furnace, yet it has gotten too cold to work on, it has to go into scrap. That is a strong cause. This cause of not being able to make pipe out of a given piece of steel is a problem for somebody—or more likely different parts of it are problems for different people. This problem may be well or poorly solved. Various social, psychological, and administrative conditions help determine how well it is solved. But the causes of good and bad solutions—at least as far as we have found them in this book—are small causes.

To find the cause for throwing away a great cold spaghetti of steel, no one needs a stratified sample or a reliability coefficient. But to find the effect of career structure on the amount of energy put into problem solving requires considerable finesse, because career structure does not have a very big effect on energy. Any small sampling or measurement difficulty makes the relation disappear into the random turbulence of social life.

At any particular time, as we look at a system of organized activity, the strong causes are more prominent. The difficulty is that the strong causes are nearly the same in different societies. Cold spaghettis of steel are scrap in advanced and in poor countries. Thus, the strong causes cannot explain why some societies can produce steel pipe to compete on the world market and some cannot. Small causes can cumulate over time in such a way that they explain gross differences among economies. This is particularly true of such small causes as technical and organizational innovation. For example, a minor change in energy devoted by the executive and technical elite might raise the rate of technical change from, say, 3% per year to 7% per year. It would require a fairly sensitive measurement to detect that 4% difference within a year, and even more delicacy to find signs of it in a cross-sectional survey study. Yet such an evanescent difference, a little under 4%, cumulated for 20 years, makes a difference of almost two times in the efficiency of the plant.

The problem for organization theory is to connect the small cumulative causes to the analysis of the system of activities dominated at any particular time by the strong causes of the technical system. To do that, we need sufficiently cheap methods of getting data so that we can relate activities to weak causes—such weak connections require more data, yet the quantity of data required means that detailed observation of activities is too expensive. The time budget data used earlier are one strategy for obtaining a sufficiently cheap measurement of activities.

Furthermore, the activities analyzed have to be classified in general categories rather than concretely described. A general feature of an activity, such as whether it is "thinking" about a piece of paper or not, may be determined partly by staff status and education. Whether the piece of paper refers to schedules of repair on a reheating furnace depends on the strong causes of what the furnace was made of, how it has been used, and whether the plant rolls steel at all. The categories of "intellectual" activities in Chapter 3, or the category of time outside the work role in Chapter 6, are examples of such abstraction.

What this argument comes down to is the reintroduction of the concept of role into organizational analysis. By role we mean the activities a man does as an occupant of a certain position. The reasons for reintroducing roles is that the effects we are interested in, such as economic development, are the consequences of activities rather than of attitudes, or role conceptions, or what not. These activities are in turn partly determined by attitudes and role conceptions, but they are also partly determined by whether the steel is all curled up. A solution to the scientific problem of studying entrepreneurship in poorer countries depends on developing ways of studying entrepreneurial activities, rather than entrepreneurial character and biography.

Appendix on Method

This study falls between an exploratory study and a hypothesis-testing study. In balancing the objectives of productivity of new interpretations (and consequent flexibility in data collection) and certainty of conclusions (and consequent fixed procedures), a large number of strategic and tactical decisions were made. These range from rephrasing, or not rephrasing, a question in an interview, to including, or not including, a result in the written report.

I am a very poor interviewer when it comes to providing a fixed stimulus for each respondent because I am constantly tempted to find out what is going on in his mind. A fixed stimulus does that for some respondents, and not for others. But the same type of arbitrary choice enters into the writing of a report. For instance, consider the question: "When you think you have been insulted, do you get angry more easily than the majority of people, about the same, or don't you get angry as easily?" The answer to this question are quite strongly related to many of the variables we have analyzed here. I have left that out of the report because I cannot figure out what is going on. Most of the hypotheses that occur to me would require personality measures to explore. It got into the study because Weber mentioned that bureaucracies functioned "*sine ira*," and because impulsive aggressiveness has been attributed to various traditional and lower-class cultures.

An Appendix on Method should outline the principles of strategy behind all these decisions, and also report on decisions and facts that may affect the evidential value of the observations as they were used in the report. There are two broad strategic considerations that dominated the whole research process.

The first has to do with my own belief that many of our principles of study design are derived from purposes of estimating means and proportions—problems now rarely of sociological importance. Studies of causes should have quite different basic designs. The second major strategic consideration has to do with the use of time budget techniques to study the structure of activities. I will discuss each of these strategic considerations in turn, describing, where appropriate, the decisions that I took. Then I will turn to some miscellaneous facts and decisions of sample design, interviewing, and so on, which affect the value of the observations as evidence for the arguments presented.

Causal Studies: Design and Analysis

When we use analysis of covariation to study the causal structure of the relations between variables, rather than to estimate the characteristics of populations, different parts of statistical theory are relevant. In this section, I will suggest some of these differences in relevance and some of their main implications for survey design and analysis. The most efficient design for a survey of causes is very different from the most efficient design to estimate population parameters.

To analyze the causal structure of a set of variables, we need to know only whether the covariation between two variables (or partial association with some other variables controlled) is positive, negative, or "not importantly different from zero." *Any function of population measures of association that preserves the sign of the covariation or partial relation serves equally well.* As long as the sign of the association is preserved, the statistic used can have any bias whatever as an estimate of any population parameter.

The following kinds of bias have no unfavorable effect on causal studies provided they do not damage the power of tests for the sign of the association.

(1) The bias of the correlation coefficient (overestimation) by selecting extreme cases on the independent variable. In this case, the regression coefficient is not affected.

(2) The bias in estimation of the correlation coefficient and the regression coefficient by selecting extreme cases on the dependent variable, because the sign is not affected.

(3) The bias in the correlation coefficient (overestimation) by correlating the averages of groups (or proportions or any other such measure). Usually, the ecological correlation is efficient in locating the causal structure, for reasons to be explained later.

(4) Undersampling of some hard-to-reach groups in the population, provided that those who are sampled have the same pattern of differences among

groups as the population as a whole. Most of the objections to quota sampling thus fall down for causal studies.[1]

(5) Biases derived from using statistics that assume stronger levels of measurement than that actually available, provided the sign of the association is not affected. With exceptions that seem to me to be very minor, the decisions about signs of associations that one makes with "too strong" statistics are the same as those one would make by using the correct ones. *But the same is not true of many statistics that are "too weak"* because they do not preserve the sign of the true partial associations.

However, there is one very important aspect of an analysis of covariation to find causal structures that imposes very stringent requirements. This aspect is suggested by the phrase, "not importantly different from zero." In order to establish, for instance, that the correlation between x and y is "spurious," and a result of their common causation by z, one must establish that *in the population*, the covariation of x and y, with z controlled, is not large enough to be scientifically important. This means that we must *estimate* the association in the population as zero (or not importantly different). It is not satisfactory to say that it is not "significantly" different from zero, because that is a report on our study rather than a report on the population. A result can be "not significantly" different from zero, yet truly "importantly" different from zero, for any of the following reasons.

(1) Use of inefficient statistics
(2) Measurement error in one or both variables
(3) Too few cases
(4) Not enough variation in the variables

For a statistical procedure to be efficient for studying causal structures, it needs to satisfy two criteria. First, the measure of association (or partial association) must have an expected value near zero when there is no association (or no partial association). In particular, this is not true of partial associations obtained by "controlling" by a cross classification, when the cross classification is a dichotomy or trichotomy simplified from a continuous variable. Most survey analysis done after the Lazarsfeld—Columbia fashion is thus using inappropriate statistics, where the expected value of a zero partial relation has the same sign as the original spurious relation, rather than the sign of the population partial association.

---

1. More formally, the signs and relative sizes of measures of association are invariant under many more data collection procedures than are the absolute sizes of these measures. Most discussions of biases in surveys are irrelevant to causal analysis because they treat absolute sizes of parameters.

Second, the procedure must have enough power so that if the association or partial association is "important" by scientific criteria, it is highly likely to show up as "significantly different from zero." As a rough criterion, I would propose that a population correlation coefficient of 0.20 between measures of two variables (i.e., a somewhat larger true relation, since in the figure of 0.20, normal measurement error is allowed for) should have a probability of 0.95 of showing up as "significantly different from zero." This means that random samples need to contain about 325 cases as a minimum, if parametric statistics are used, with high levels of measurement efficiency, using a two-tailed test at the 0.05 level.

There seem to me to be five important ways to increase the power of a statistical procedure in survey analysis of causes.

(1) Use more efficient statistics. This is thoroughly treated in standard statistical texts under the concept of "power-efficiency" of tests, and need not detain us. However, it should be noted that the fashion of using cross classifications in sociological survey analysis is very wasteful of data, especially when the dichotomies are simplifications of well-measured variables. It has not been sufficiently realized that often "too strong" statistics do preserve the signs of partial associations, while "too weak" ones do not. Also, much power is thrown away by using two-tailed tests when one-tailed tests are appropriate.

(2) Increase the number of cases. This is also fully analyzed in traditional statistical sources. However, as sociologists become more interested in analysis of causal structures, they have not seen that the number of cases needed to assert that a partial relation is near zero is much greater than the number of cases needed to find a truly strong relation.

(3) Increase the variability of the observations. For example, the variance of the estimate of the regression coefficient of y on x is given by

$$\frac{\sigma_{y|x}^2}{(N-1)s_x^2}$$

where $\sigma_{y|x}^2$ is the true variance of y around the regression line, N is the number of cases, and s_x^2 is the variance of the sample observations of x, the independent variable. The increase in power obtained by selecting extreme cases is very great. If we can double the standard deviation of our independent variable by over-sampling extreme cases, we increase the power of the test as much as we would by quadrupling the number of cases.

Since most of the objections to quota samples do not apply to causal studies, there is room in sociology for much more powerful studies with the same resources. Quota samples are much cheaper to adapt to disproportionate sampling than are random designs. Random designs have some advantages, however, for at least part of the sample. But we can say generally that causal studies based on random samples with no oversampling are almost always wasting research money. Note that efficiency can be improved by disproportionate sampling on the dependent variables for most purposes, even though this biases all measures of association. The signs remain invariant in most situations.

(4) Decrease measurement error. Measures of association are decreased by measurement error. Therefore an increase in measurement error decreases the probability of finding a relation that is really there. This is the kind of error that we want to avoid in asserting that a partial association is near zero. There are two main devices for decreasing measurement error. One is obviously to develop better measuring instruments, and to use all the measurement efficiency we have instead of dichotomizing or trichotomizing. The other is to use, where they are cheap, measurements taken on groups, for group measures eliminate a lot of measurement error.[2]

(5) Decrease the amount of information used up in making controls of spurious or interpretive variables. In particular, controls of other variables made by ordinary partial correlation use up only one degree of freedom for each variable controlled. Thus, a sample of 300 still has 290 degrees of freedom to test a partial relation after controlling 8 variables. With controls by cross classification, one "runs out of cases" after about the third variable (except in the census), and there is very little power left to study these partial relations.

On the basis of these considerations, the following recommendations on the strategy of surveys for causal studies seem to me justified.

(1) Extreme cases at both ends should nearly always be oversampled, center cases undersampled. If convenient, increased dispersion should be on the independent variable, but increases on the dependent variable also greatly increase efficiency.

(2) Much more use can be made of quota sampling, or combinations of random sampling with quota sampling of extremes, or stratified random sampling with unequal sampling ratios, higher in the extreme strata.

(3) The samples should be larger than those used to try to confirm a hypothesis. A reasonable criterion seems to be that a true population correlation of 0.20 should be found about 95% of the time. This leads to minimum sizes for simple random samples of over 300 when parametric statistics are used, more for less efficient procedures and less when disproportionate sampling is used to increase the variation.

(4) Parametric statistics or other statistics having truly zero partial relations

---

2. I believe that much of the fun of "contextual analysis" is because our measures of group characteristics have much less measurement error than we are used to working with. This, and not the overwhelming power of society, makes it possible for us to find effects with samples of ten or fifteen groups, while studies of ten or fifteen people never come out. I think that the size of most contextual effects so far studied is rather small.

with expected values near zero, and using up little information when making controls, should be substituted for cross classification. The sampling distribution of measures of partial association must be known for the measure to be of any use.

(5) All possible reduction of measurement error should be sought. In particular, the practice of collapsing scales into dichotomies is a criminal waste of much needed information. Ecological or group data can often be used to advantage because group characteristics nearly always have less measurement error.

(6) Measures of association used in causal studies need not be estimates of the parameters of any concrete population, as long as they preserve the sign of the true association, and as long as their sampling distribution is known.

(7) Whenever the logic of analysis requires a positive statement that an association is near zero, the appropriate statistic is a confidence interval rather than a significance test; "not significantly different from zero" means "not importantly different from zero" only when the confidence interval is narrow. This implies that measures of partial association whose sampling distribution is not known are useless for causal analysis. In particular, most of the ordinal partial association measures have been useless for causal analysis, though they may have the function of counting the proportions of concordant and discordant pairs in cases where one is not interested in causal analysis.

I have not followed all of this advice here. I did substantially increase the variance of observations on most of the variables by oversampling the steel plants and oversampling still more the higher ranks. I did also spend some considerable effort in increasing levels of measurement efficiency by scale construction. The increased variance itself decreased measurement error variance. With this increased efficiency, I found that in almost all important cases, there was either a strong relationship in the data or else almost nothing. Consequently, I only occasionally computed correlation or partial correlation measures.

The Statistical Treatment of Time-Budgets

The analysis of time-budgets in Chapters 3 and 4 was carried on by looking at the mean time spent by different groups. This is not adequate for finer statistical treatment because of some peculiarities in the distribution of activities. There are two justification for the simplification in the text. First, the aggregate amount of work done of a given kind is measured by the mean time spent. Thus, when we are interested in a description of the effects on organizational economic performance, means are appropriate. Second, the proper statistical treatment is complex, and would confuse the main line of argument if presented in the text.

Further development of this methodology will depend, however, on more refined treatment of these statistical problems. In this section, we shall treat our experiences in handling this sort of data from a statistical point of view.

The Mixed Distribution of Time Spent

The basic problem presented by such data is that they are clearly combinations of two types of distributions. Many of the people in a given group do not do any of a given type of activity. The proportions not doing any of the activity vary radically among groups. We can conceive of the decision to do any of a given activity as an "event" that has a probability per day in a given group. This event has a higher probability in some groups than others.

On the other hand, once a person starts a given activity, we can measure how much of it he does as a continuous variable—the amount of time spent in the activity. We cannot, in the usual case, conceive of each new hour (or quarter hour) spent as another independent "event" governed by the same probability as the decision to do any of the activity.

The image suggested by the events (of engaging or not engaging in an activity) is that of a Poisson process, or one of its relatives. What we would need for such an image would be a count of the number of times that that event happened to a given individual during a day. But once people enter upon, for instance, the activity of making a given drawing for a new machine, they continue to draw until the task is done. Thus, there are no identifiable further "events" of the same kind which we can identify and count. The drawer does not "restart" the activity every hour. Instead, once the event of entering on a given activity starts, there is a process operating on the continuous variable of amount of time spent. The average time spent on a given type of activity also varies among social groups.

Table A.1 presents in Column 1 the mean hours of intellectual activity for the various city and industrial status groups. Columns 2 and 3 divide this up into two components: that corresponding to the proportions of the different groups that did any of the activity (2); and that corresponding to the mean time spent in the activity by those who were active (3). We see that the proportion who did any of the activity ranges from about one-sixteenth among the city employees, to over half among the high executives and staff. We also see that among those who were active, there is much less variation in the mean time spent in intellectual activity than in the overall means in the groups.

But (concentrating on the industrial administrators where there are sufficient cases), we also find that the forces determining the mean time spent among those who are active are of a different pattern. For instance, the high executives have the *highest* proportion of those who did some intellectual activity during the previous day, but they have the *lowest* mean time spent, among those who were active. Comparing the high executives with the low-level industrial employees,

TABLE A.1

Distributions of Intellectual Activities[a]

Subgroup	(1) Mean hours		(2) Proportion active		(3) Mean for those active	
City nonindustrial						
Employees	0.11	(69)	0.06	(69)	1.88	(4)
Bureaucrats	1.52	(20)	0.50	(20)	3.05	(10)
Small businessmen	0.42	(39)	0.10	(39)	3.12	(4)
Larger businessmen	0.75	(17)	0.18	(17)	4.25	(3)
Heavy industrial						
Low	1.01	(92)	0.27	(92)	3.73	(25)
Intermediate line	0.94	(61)	0.38	(61)	2.49	(23)
High executive	1.08	(62)	0.53	(62)	2.02	(33)
Staff	2.21	(42)	0.52	(42)	4.22	(22)

[a]People who did not work included as not doing any of activity.

for instance, there is a statistically significantly higher proportion of executives who engage in the activity, and a significantly lower mean time spent among those active. Obviously, no definition of "events" of entering into this kind of activity in a Poisson fashion will produce this pattern.

The Shape of the Distribution of Time Spent among Those Who Are Active

We have to ask next about the shape of the continuous component of the distribution. Inspection of the data for many activities indicates that the distribution is generally highly skewed. That is, many people do a little bit of the activity, while a few do a great deal. The median is often less than the mean. Further, the higher the mean time spent, the larger the variance of time spent on an activity in a group tends to be.

These considerations suggest the lognormal distribution as an approximation to the time spent distribution. On graphical inspection of several cumulative distributions, on lognormal probability paper, it appeared that there was generally a good approximation at the lower end of the distribution. However, when the mean of time spent on an activity in a group was above about 3 hours, there was a notable truncation of the upper tail, in the region of 8 hours.

This means that the normal distribution is a fairly good approximation for a subgroup's activities if the mean, among those who do the activity at all, is more than about 3 hours. The log-normal distribution is better for subgroups whose mean is less than 3 hours.

The Homogenization of Variance of Time Spent

Since fairly often, as shown in Table A.1, one or more of the groups has a mean high enough to run into the truncation problem (the staff and the low industrial group), while others are below that region (the high executives and the intermediate line), we can consider another criterion. We can ask whether the dispersion within subgroups on the amount of a given activity is more homogeneous when the distribution is treated as lognormal.

TABLE A.2

Standard Deviations, and Standard Deviations of the Logarithms (Base e) of Hours Spent in Intellectual Activities, for Industrial Subgroups Who Are Active

Subgroup	SD data	SD ln data
Low	2.52	.9404
Intermediate	3.08	.9112
High executive	1.32	.7047
Staff	2.39	.8696

In Table A.2 we present the standard deviations of the time spent on intellectual activities for various subgroups of the industrial administrators. Clearly, in this case the standard deviations of the logarithms[3] are much more nearly equal than the standard deviations of the original data. The smallest standard deviation of the logarithms is about 75% of the largest. The smallest standard deviation of the original data is about 43% of the largest.

Inspection of a number of tables of this kind, for various activities, indicates that in a majority of cases, the standard deviation of the logarithms is more homogeneous across groups than the standard deviation of the original data. In about half of the remaining cases, there is no appreciable difference between the original and the logarithmic dispersions. In only about a quarter of the cases do the normal distributions have more homogeneous standard deviations. These are usually cases where members of the sub-group typically either work full time in a given activity, or not at all.

3. Throughout this section, all logarithms are to the base e (natural logarithms).

Estimates of the Median

Another check can be carried out if we compare different estimates of the median, as in Table A.3. If a population is normally distributed, the mean should be a good estimate of the median. If it is log normally distributed, then the antilog of the mean log should be a good estimate of the median. If we compare the computed estimates of the median with the interpolated values from the cumulative distribution,[4] we get some idea which is the better distribution to describe the data. In Table A.3, the mean is a better estimate in those two cases where the median is above 3 hours; the antilog of the mean log is a better estimate in the two cases where the median is below 3 hours.

TABLE A.3

Comparison of Estimates of the Median, for Intellectual Activity among Industrial Groups

Sub-group	Graphical interpolation	Mean of data	Antilog of mean log
Low	3.3	3.73	2.43
Intermediate	0.6	2.49	1.46
High executive	1.3	2.02	1.45
Staff	4.0	4.22	2.79

General Conclusions on the Distribution of Time Spent

Overall, it seems that the log-normal distribution is generally somewhat preferable to the normal for the continuous variable of time spent on an activity. It has the advantage of homogenizing the variance in subgroups, of not having negative or zero values, and of recognizing the general skewness of these distributions. Occasionally for specific problems, where an activity is typically done either full time or not at all, a normal distribution might be preferable.[5]

Thus, we would advocate a description of the distribution of time spent in a given activity in terms of three parameters: the proportion of the group not doing the activity at all, the mean logarithms of time spent on that activity, and the standard deviation of the logarithms of time spent. We can then construct tests

4. I have used interpolated values between points on the cumulative distribution by whole hours since the nature of the interview tended to force respondents into giving information in whole hour units.

5. One could, of course, try to fit a log-normal distribution to such data with a point of truncation at eight hours. This makes the resulting comparisons between groups mathematically very messy.

of hypotheses about the distribution by considering the proportion that does none of the activity during a given day as a binomial variable, and by considering the logarithms of time spent in the activity as being normally distributed. Thus, the statistical description of time spent in intellectual activity would be as given in Table A.4. We have added a calculation to two places of the standard deviation within groups, which can be used for tests of various kinds, on the hypothesis that the variances of the logarithms are homogeneous.

TABLE A.4

Parameters of the Distribution of Time Spent in Intellectual Activity.

Sub-group	p = Proportion with no activity	N	Mean ln	Standard deviation ln	Na
City nonindustrial					
Employees	0.06	69	—[a]	—[a]	4
Bureaucrats	0.50	20	0.6080	0.8962	10
Small businessmen	0.10	39	—[a]	—[a]	4
Large businessmen	0.18	17	—[a]	—[a]	3
Heavy industrial					
Low	0.27	92	0.8868	0.9404	25
Intermediate	0.38	61	0.3756	0.9112	23
High executives	0.53	62	0.3694	0.7047	33
Staff	0.52	42	1.0263	0.8696	22
Estimated within Group *SD*				0.83	124

[a]Too few cases for meaningful statistics.

Testing Hypotheses on Time Spent

Given the hypothesis of homogeneity of variance of the logarithms of time spent, we can construct two tests of comparison of any two groups in the table. Suppose, for instance, that we thought that more high executive would engage in intellectual activity than low industrial salaried workers, but that the problems from subordinates would depress the amount of time spent on such activity.

Using the fact of normal approximation to the binomial, the variable

$$z_1 = \frac{p_1 - p_2}{[(p_1 q_1/N_1) + (p_2 q_2/N_2)]^{1/2}}$$

where p_i = proportion zero in group i, $q_i = 1 - p_i$, N_i = number of cases in group i, should have a normal distribution with a mean of zero and a standard deviation of one, under the null hypothesis. With the data as given, $z_1 = -3.31$, $p < .001$ (two-tailed). That is, the lower industrial employees clearly have a lower probability of engaging in any intellectual activity during the day.

We can consider the logarithms of time spent to be normally distributed with a common variance, and the within-group variance based on $124 - 8 = 116$ degrees of freedom to be very good estimate of the population variance. The variable

$$z_2 = \frac{M_1 - M_2}{[(S^2/Na_1) + (S^2/Na_2)]^{1/2}}$$

where M_i = mean ln group i, S^2 = estimated within-group variance of the ln, Na_i = number in group i who did any of the activity, can be considered essentially normally distributed with a mean of zero and a standard deviation of one. With the data as given, $z = 2.33$, $p < .03$ (two-tailed). That is, high executives spend less time thinking once they have started than low line employees.

For tests of more complicated hypotheses, the appropriate partitions of χ^2 computed from the tables can be worked out since it can be assumed that the different variables are normally distributed.[6]

Possible Generating Processes for Time Spent

As a practical matter, of course, we have arrived at the relevant conclusions of this test from the pattern of overall mean hours spent in intellectual activity. Perhaps more refined analyses of other activities would uncover patterns not noted in the tables of Chapters 3 and 4. But most of the information to be uncovered is in the original means. This material on distributions may, however, suggest the nature of the underlying processes that generate patterns of activity. There are a number of types of stochastic processes that generate a skewed distribution of a continuous variable.[7]

First, if time in an activity depends on another skewed variable in a close way, without too many other influences of substantial size, then time spent would be skewed. There seem to be three likely candidates for such a variable: rank, ability, and experience. Rank will be skewed because of the pyramidal structure of many formal organizations. More generally, for all types of communications nets were links established have a cost, while there are also economies in having as few links as possible between any two stations, there

---

6. See, A. Hald, *Statistical Theory with Engineering Applications*, (New York; John Wiley, 1952) for explanation and various examples of partitioning of chi-squares.

7. Most skew distributions of positive values with a long upper tail can be approximated fairly well by the log-normal distribution.

will be economies in having a few centers through which much communication passes. That is, the degree of centrality in a system of information flows tends to be skewed. Formal rank in an organization is generally a measure of centrality in the information flow system. Hence, the skewness of distributions of formal rank, and consequently, the pyramidal structure of formal organizations, is a particular case of the skewness of communications centrality because of the economies of nodalization. The same sort of skewness of centrality applies to transportation networks and the flow of commerce and commercial information. Hence, the skew distribution of some activities among individuals in an organization may have the same explanation as the skew distribution of commercial activities among cities, which is discussed in the ecological literature under the heading of metropolitan dominance. Any activity related to rank, or to communications centrality, will tend to be skewed.

Although ability is generally conceived of as normally distributed, this is based on the convention of adding up scores on items to get the total measure of intelligence. If one were to multiply the scores on items, or on subtests, one would get a skewed distribution of a log-normal type. We can hypothesize, for complex tasks such as analyzing a problem of production, that abilities and qualities of character multiply each others' effectiveness. For instance, if a man is bright and he works hard, his brightness makes his devotion more valuable, and his devotion makes his brightness more valuable. Men may be heavily involved in those activities which their combinations of abilities make them much more able to do well.

A third variable that tends to have a skew distribution, especially in a growing organization, is experience. Many people have suggested that organizations tend to grow by a certain percentage each year. We would expect, therefore, that normally a larger number of people would have been recruited last year than the year before that, and so on. In addition, people seem to have a constantly declining rate of leaving a particular organization with an increase in the number of years they have been there. But the steepness of decline in the probability of leaving is not great enough to prevent the proportion of all people hired the year before last who are still there, to be lower than the proportion of those hired this year who are still there. For both of these reasons, the distribution of seniority and experience will be skewed. If people are more able to do some kinds of activities when they have more experience, then the time spent in that activity will tend to be highly skewed.

A particular case of this seniority principle is "seniority in school." That is, a cohort of people have a certain probability of quitting school each year, or of passing on to the next year. If they pass on to the next year, they have a certain probability of going on to the following year. Within a wide range of patterns of dropping out, the resulting distribution of years of schooling achieved by adults of that cohort will be highly skewed. Thus, when the median education of a cohort is 12 years, there are ordinarily more people with 10 years than with 14, but more people with 20 years than with 4 years. Hence, any activity that depends directly on years of education will tend to be skewed.

Aside from dependence on skewed variables, a process in which activities of the same type make each other more efficient will also lead to skewed distributions. For instance, a man who has just come from a committee meeting on a related topic may participate more effectively in another committee. Or specialization in a certain kind of activity may enable a man to develop skills and arrange his working conditions so as to do the activity more effectively. Then when the organization has to select someone to do more activity of that kind, it would be more likely to add it to the specialist's responsibility than to other people's. Under general conditions, a stochastic process with this character generates approximately a log-normal distribution.

Another general type of process that generates skewed distributions is one in which a causal variable, as it increases, both increases the mean value of the dependent variable, and also increases the variance of the dependent variable. For instance, suppose that there is an independent causal influence of creativity in the solution of problems. By creativity, we mean the search for solutions in unconventional ways. Uncreative people will tend to have a low variance in the quality of their solutions since they will cluster around the conventional solution. Creative people may have a higher mean level in the quality of their solutions because they consider more alternatives. They may also have a higher variance in quality because solutions off the beaten track may be either very little better than the conventional solution, or very much better. Thus, variables influenced by creativity should tend to be skewed.

A final kind of process that can create skewed distributions of performance is one involving supervision of interdependent tasks in a productive system. Better supervision, which increases the productivity of each machine in a factory by a little bit, has a relatively small effect if those machines operate independently. But if the factory is so set up that all the machines must be operating simultaneously, then the effect of a small increase in the reliability of each component machine will generally increase productivity by a great deal. Thus, people with a rather slight advantage in any performance capacity that increases the productivity of each element of an interdependent system will tend to be encouraged to do that activity a good deal more than someone with slightly less ability, when the elements are interdependent. This will generate a skewed distribution of time spent in activities, which will be more skewed the more interdependent the system.

General Descriptive Comments on Distributions of Time Spent

Finally, we might make a few comments about some properties of the log-normal distribution, which may not be familiar to people used to working with normal distributions, and also some general descriptive comments about the distribution of time spent in relation to those properties.

A first general feature of the log-normal distribution is that the variance of logarithms is not affected by multiplying each observation by a constant. This can be seen easily by considering a given deviation score:

$$\ln(Kx_i) - \frac{\sum_l^n \ln(Kx_i)}{n} = \ln K - \frac{\sum_l^n \ln K}{n} + \ln x_i - \frac{\sum_l^n \ln x_i}{n} = \ln x_i - \frac{\sum_l^n \ln x_i}{n}$$

Another way of saying the same thing is that the contribution of any particular observation to the sum of squares of logarithms depends only on the ratio of the distance of that observation from zero and on the distance of the antilog of the mean log from zero (for a log-normal variable, the antilog of the mean log is an estimate of the median).

In general, it appears that the greater the amount of time spent by a group on an activity, the larger the variance. When natural logarithms are taken, the standard deviation of logarithms runs around 0.7 or 0.8. This indicates that, roughly, all distributions of time spent have the "same shape" with respect to the two points of 0 hours and median hours spent on an activity. The larger the variance of the logarithms of the observations, the more the log normal distribution is skewed. From this observation, we would guess that there is probably about the same amount of skewness of time spent in different activities. This degree of skewness would ordinarily be measured by a ratio of the mean to the median between about 1.3 and 1.4. Or if we take somewhat more liberal limits of the standard deviation of logarithms of time spent, between 0.6 and 0.9, the ratio of the mean to the median would range between 1.2 and 1.5.[8]

Another way of looking at this degree of skewness is that approximately 47.5% of the cases should fall in the interval $(1/4m < x < m)$ and another 47.5% should fall in the interval $(m < x < 4m)$, where m is the median. That is, the distance from the median to the 97.5 percentile is about four times as long as the distance from the median to the 2.5 percentile. For instance, for a median of 3 hours, the 2.5 percentile should be at about 3/4 hours, and the 97.5 percentile should be at

---

8. For a log-normal distribution, the natural logarithm of the ratio of the mean to the median is .5 times the variance of the natural logarithms of the data. Thus for a standard deviation of natural logarithms of .7,

$$\ln \left(\frac{M}{m} \right) = .5(.49) = .245,$$

and

$$\left(\frac{M}{m} \right) = 1.28$$

where M is the mean of data, and m is the median of data.

about 12 hours, if the distribution is log normal. This shows why truncation at 8 hours makes distributions with medians above about 3 hours depart rather substantially from a log-normal distribution.[9]

The Specific Structure of the Samples

The intention in the development of the sampling frame was to achieve a two-part sample:

(1) A sample of 75 of the salaried employees in each of the three steel plants, broken down by salary grades so that
   a. 25 (one-third) would come from the local male salaried personnel (i.e. excluding the central office in the capital, females, and wage workers) who were among the top 5% of the salary distribution among salaried employees
   b. 25 (one-third) who were in the next 20% of the income distribution among salaried employees

---

9. For computing percentages in an interval around the median of the log-normal distribution, the following relations may be used:

$$P(e^{z\sigma} m < x < m) = P(z < x < 0) \qquad \text{and} \qquad P(m < x < e^{z\sigma} m) = P(0 < x < z)$$

where $z =$ the unit normal variable, tabulated in the cumulative normal table, $\sigma =$ the standard deviation of natural logarithms of the observations, and $m =$ the median of the observations.

For example, if we want to compute for $\sigma = 0.7$, the interval below the median which would include 34% of the observations, then $z = -1$ (in the unit normal variable, 34% of the observations lie between -1 and 0, as read from a cumulative normal table). Substituting $z = -1$, and $\sigma = .7$, in the left-hand side of the first expression above, we obtain

$$P(e^{-0.7}m < x < m) = P(0.497m < x < m) = 0.34.$$

That is, the interval between one half of the median and the median should contain 34% of the cases if the variable has a log normal distribution and the standard deviations of the natural logarithms is 0.7. By applying the same reasoning with the second expression, 34% of the cases should fall between the median and two times the median.

For those who prefer to work with logarithms to the base 10, the following formulas apply to the logarithmic parameters σ and mean logarithms and to the median m and the mean M of the observations.

$$\sigma_{10} = 0.4343\sigma_e, \qquad \sigma_e = 2.3026\sigma_{10}$$

$$\sigma_{10}^2 = 0.1886\sigma_e^2$$

$$\log M/m = 1.1513\sigma_{10}^2$$

$$P(10^{z\sigma_{10}}m < x < m) = P(z < x < 0)$$

where mean $\log x_i$ is equal to 0.4343 mean $\ln x_i$ and mean $\ln x_i$ is equal to 2.3026 mean $\log x_i$.

   c. 25 (one-third) who were in the bottom 75% of the income distribution
     among salaried employees
(2) A random sample in the major city nearest each steel plant of the male
    heads of households living in houses which, by external inspection, we
    thought to be middle class. The projected sample size was also 75 in each
    country, though we ended up with a larger theoretical sample (from
    overestimating the number of households without a male head) and a
    smaller realized sample (because of a higher refusal rate and a failure to
    locate some men).

There are two sorts of difficulties in the samples. First, the universes sampled
were not exactly comparable. In Chile, several manual jobs were salaried (the
most important numerically was that of crane operator), while in the other two
plants, a relatively neat manual—nonmanual distinction was made. In Argentina, we were forced to use an organization chart rather than a payroll to
stratify the sample, so the top 5% are top in distance down the chart rather
than in salary. This might disturb the classification of the staff, who are defined
by a high income (in Argentina, high chart position) and a low number of
subordinates.

In the city sample, I was confused by tropical architecture in selecting the
first half of the Venezuelan city sample, and got too many manual workers. I
went back over the houses occupied by middle-class people and those occupied
by workers to do a sort of discriminant function analysis, and from that point
on selected only houses whose walls were connected to the roof without a gap.
This seemed to be the most reliable criterion of middle-class housing. In
Venezuela, the cities chosen for sampling were Puerto Ordaz and San Felix,
where most of the workers in the plant lived. But my car kept breaking down,
so the people in the newer Puerto Ordaz area where I lived were pursued more
vigorously than those in San Felix. This resulted in the Venezuelan city sample
ending up smaller, and probably more unrepresentative than in the other countries. At best, the heads of households living in middle-class housing are a poor
universe to equate with a group defined by salary category in a bureaucracy.
Probably with more expense and effort we could have come closer, but part of
the difficulty is inherent. The status system of a city is much fuzzier than the
status system of a bureaucracy.

The steel sample was constructed from a complete list of men in the appropriate salary universe, from which we took every nth name, where n depended
on the sampling fraction. The city sample was constructed by sampling city
blocks (since maps were bad in Venezuela, the "list" of city blocks was itself
difficult; in all three cities we eliminated some blocks which had no middle-
class housing, and in Chile we took all housing on the remaining blocks to be
middle class), listing all middle-class housing on those blocks on block maps,
and taking every nth house n depending on the sampling fraction that would

give a little over 100 houses (or living quarters attached to businesses, which are quite frequent). We thought that about a third of the houses would be either vacant or without a male head. This was a slight overestimate, but this mistake helped compensate for a higher refusal rate.

The refusal rate in the plants was very low, under 5% in all three countries. This was probably partly because we had the men's names and both their home and work locations. Refusals were least in the plant in Venezuela, where I interviewed on the premises. The refusal and other loss rate was higher in the city samples, ranging from just over 10% in Chile to just over 15% in Venezuela, as near as we could estimate. We are quite sure that some sample members "could not be located" because they or their family members lied to us about where they lived. The only systematic pattern that we noticed in the refusals were policemen, army people, and a customs officer in Venezuela who said "security officials" were not supposed to talk to anyone. (I did, however, interview an undercover policeman in Venezuela who told me in circumstantial detail about this work. He may have been putting me on.)

The Interviews

In Chile, the interviewing was carried out about half by Rene Marder and myself and half by students in the school of social work who had had previous interviewing experience. Marder or I edited these as they came in to clear up ambiguous points. In Argentina, Rene Marder did most of the interviewing; a few interviews were done by other trained sociologists visiting him there. In Venezuela, I did all the interviewing. Some national differences may be interviewer effects.

The interview structure was worked out as a result of borrowing from other studies, pretesting, and debating about what the questions meant. The time-budget section of the interview was very loosely structured because we found we had to do considerable probing to get people to reconstruct their previous working day. Different people required quite different amounts and kinds of probing.

The main distorting influences in the interviews themselves seemed to be two. First, there is apparently a considerable degree of randomness in the semantic content of the words of a question for different interviewees. The same string of words does not provide the same semantic stimulus to different people. This would quite often become obvious when a man would be stimulated (by the interviewer, or at random) to discuss what he had just agreed (or disagreed) with. Since the sample was middle class, or at least upper working class, it is unlikely that this variation in the meaning of questions is subcultural. I do not know where sociologists got the idea that a culture gives a single meaning to a given set of words. Our teaching experience in asking essay questions (where the response is rich enough to indicate what question the students thought they were answering) should have taught us that the relation between words and meanings is a statistical one. Inferring the modal meaning that people give to a question is a problem for scientific inference, in which its correlations with other items is evidence. Most of this analysis is buried rather than reported in this book (Chapter 4 discusses such questions, though not written that way).

The second source of distortion was that people had not always previously constructed for themselves the cognitive object about which we were asking. Thus, the question forced them to scan a gray unanalyzed mental haze and select out prominent features to talk about. This was most marked in our attempt to have people reconstruct the previous day. Some people do, and some do not, carry around a mental picture of how their time is divided into blocks devoted to different purposes. Thus, some men's answers to time questions are much less, and some much more, capable of influence by the form of the question. But some have their attention drawn to a prominence, in the haze that was yesterday, by a chance remark by the interviewer, or a chance outstanding event of the previous day, or some other random process. We might call this lack of temporal organization of memory the "Dylan Thomas syndrome." Thomas "can never remember whether it snowed for six days and six nights when [he] was twelve, or whether it snowed for twelve days and twelve nights when [he] was six."

Since in this case we were only trying to get information, the result of this kind of distortion for us was merely "ignorance and error," and therefore theoretically irrelevant. We have treated this distortion simply as unsystematic measurement error. On other questions, some people probably have a clear object to attach an attitude to: for example, they have some sort of concrete image of "planning," while for others "planning" is an inkblot. Such a difference is theoretically important because in the second case we will expect a man's attitude to change when his attention is drawn to the resemblance of the inkblot to something else.

Our usual procedures of item analysis would tend to select two types of items: (1) those where the main object referred to is clear for everyone, where the question taps an ego orientation, and (2) those where the object is very ambiguous and its presentation functions as a projective test of the simpler personality responses. We have difficulty simply with those items whose cognitive content is changing.

It seems to me that both of these difficulties are caused by our poor psychology of semantic content, as applied to the problem of what stimulus an interview presents. The semantic content of a given verbal stimulus probably depends on the psychology of attention and the psychology of mental abilities, as well as the social psychology of learning languages from subcultural milieus. A few of these problems are treated tangentially in the Appendix to Chapter 4 on acquiescence.

The effect of the analytical procedures followed here (which are the common ones in survey analysis) is to treat such variations in the semantic content of questions as not covariant with the independent and dependent variables being studied. Until they are shown to be nonrandom, we treat them as random. But probably some of the findings of this study will turn out to be relationships between, say, education and how people use words rather than between education and attitudes.

I did much of the interviewing and I am not a native speaker of Spanish. By the time I did most of it I had been among Spanish-speaking people continuously for six months, having started this period with just enough Spanish to lecture. I would judge that my Spanish, by the time I started the interviewing, was about at the median for educated native speakers. I think I probably missed about as much as would the average interviewer. People of course overestimate their own abilities in a foreign language. But then native speakers also exaggerate their command over their own language. A copy of the interview schedule may be obtained from the author.

Name Index

Subject Index